Apartheid and International Organizations

Westview Special Studies on Africa

Apartheid and International Organizations
Richard E. Bissell

The historical controversy over South Africa's policy of apartheid has not been without effect on that country's participation and status in the international system. The black African states have been particularly inclined to use the public forums of intergovernmental organizations such as the United Nations and the specialized agencies to press for domestic change in South Africa. Richard Bissell explores the impact of these efforts both on the racial policies of South Africa and on the international organizations where diplomatic battles to isolate South Africa occur. Dr. Bissell also examines the roles of the United States, the Western European countries, and the Communist nations, seeking to determine what influence their attitudes and actions have on one of the most salient human rights issues in recent decades.

Richard E. Bissell, research associate at the Foreign Policy Research Institute, Philadelphia, and managing editor of *ORBIS*, received his doctorate from the Fletcher School of Law and Diplomacy. Dr. Bissell worked extensively on the material for this book during a two-year postdoctoral appointment at the Center of International Studies, Princeton University.

Other Titles in This Series

Ethnicity in Modern Africa, edited by Brian M. du Toit

Written under the auspices of the Center of International Studies, Princeton University. A list of other Center books appears at the back of this book.

Apartheid and International Organizations

Richard E. Bissell

Westview Press
Boulder, Colorado

Westview Special Studies on Africa

Copyright © 1977 by Westview Press

Published in 1977 in the United States of America by
  Westview Press, Inc.
  1898 Flatiron Court
  Boulder, Colorado 80301
  Frederick A. Praeger, Publisher and Editorial Director

Library of Congress Cataloging in Publication Data

Bissell, R E
  Apartheid and international organizations.

  (Westview special studies on Africa)
  Includes bibliographical references.
  1. South Africa—Foreign relations. 2. South Africa
—Race question. 3. International agencies. I. Title.
JX1584.S7B6   327.68   76-57761
ISBN 0-89158-229-0

Printed and bound in the United States of America

Contents

Preface

Thirty years have passed since the founding of the United Nations (UN) in San Francisco, where, before the First Session had been adjourned, the General Assembly passed a resolution about South African racial policies. The output since 1945 of resolutions, debates, and publications, and the time expended on the subject of those policies known collectively as apartheid, has been enormous. Indeed, there seems to be an overall trend toward a progressively greater preoccupation with apartheid on the part of UN organs and related specialized agencies.

South Africa has certainly not been the only international pariah in this age of contending ideologies, but it has clearly been more isolated diplomatically, over a longer period of time, than any other state challenging the international majority. Major and minor examples of diplomatic isolation can be found in all parts of the world: Spain, Israel, Dominican Republic, Cuba, Yugoslavia, Greece, China, Portugal, and others. All have been subjected to social sanctions of varying intensity since 1945, and indeed, could profitably be compared with South Africa. None, however, has experienced isolation in universal and regional organizations in a comparably escalating fashion.

The widest possible significance of the apartheid dispute, therefore, must be found in South Africa's role as a nation-state, and its interface with international organizations. That interface involves the actions of a nation-state in the policymaking of an organization, as well as the implementation of resolutions. Likewise, the organizations need to be seen as targets of diplomatic efforts, by both South Africa and the other African states, and also as actors on the international stage attempting to influence South Africa. When one begins to explore the apartheid dispute fully, particularly over a long time, other states take on important roles, especially the United States and certain Western European states. At all times, however, the focus remains on South Africa and its interactions with the UN and the specialized agencies.

The unique qualities of the South African society and economy present equally formidable tasks of analysis. What, after all, causes the South African government to persist in returning to international organizations where the majority has denounced the very foundations of South African rule? One could possibly suggest a fundamental internationalism, possibly sheer masochism. Such a strong desire to participate in the international community seems strangely contradictory, in any case, given the record of South African intransigence over the recommendations of international organizations. The South African side of the interface between national policies and international action is thus of prime importance.

Aside from analyzing the course of pressures on South Africa from international organizations, this study includes an attempt to determine the consequences of this dispute for South Africa, for international organizations, and, briefly, for the world at large. Apartheid policies have been affected, even though the exact causal relationship between such changes and international action is hard to determine. For organizations, the lessons are more diffuse, related to the effectiveness of sanctions, the interests of organizations independently of particular blocs of members, and the roles of secretariats. For the world at large, the apartheid dispute has been a model for the recent efforts to apply sanctions against Israel.

Briefly, the study is constructed along the following lines. Chapter one describes the origins of South African racial policies, and how a domestic problem gradually escalated into an international conflict by 1959. The appearance of strong, persistent hostility to apartheid by the newly independent African states is the theme of chapter two. During that phase, roughly 1960–63, South Africa had little response to offer to attacks in international organizations. By the period 1963–64, covered in chapter three, the establishment of the Organization of African Unity conveyed remarkable continuity and momentum to the anti-apartheid movement. South Africa retreated from one organization after another.

The diplomatic counterattack by the South Africans during 1964–69 was thus a natural sequel to the devastating losses of international presence during the preceding period. While an objective measure of South Africa's strength during the late 1960s is somewhat difficult to obtain, it is clear that the momentum of the African drive had been checked. In the following years, 1970–76, as indicated in chapter five, the storm of protest against apartheid did not abate, but the South Africans learned to lean into the wind, and a diplomatic stalemate ensued. The conclusion, then, indicates how present patterns of interaction might be projected into the future, based on the course of the conflict to date.

The research for this book was undertaken at various intervals during the period 1970–75, and its completion would not have been possible without timely support and insights from numerous individuals, both official and academic. Those who deserve special thanks are Leon Gordenker and Cyril E. Black of the Center of International Studies at Princeton University, and W. Scott Thompson and Leo Gross of the Fletcher School of Law and Diplomacy at Tufts University. As is customary, only the credit is shared, not the blame for errors, which remain my own responsibility.

Abbreviations

CCTA	Commission for Technical Cooperation in Africa
CIAS	Conference of Independent African States
ECA	Economic Commission for Africa
ECOSOC	United Nations Economic and Social Council
FAO	Food and Agriculture Organization
IAEA	International Atomic Energy Agency
IBRD	International Bank for Reconstruction and Development (World Bank)
ICAO	International Civil Aviation Organization
ICJ	International Court of Justice
ILO	International Labor Organization
IMF	International Monetary Fund
IOC	International Olympic Committee
ITU	International Telecommunications Union
OAU	Organization of African Unity
SPC	Special Political Committee of the United Nations General Assembly
UAM	Union Africaine et Malgache
UN	United Nations
UNCTAD	United Nations Conference on Trade and Development

UNDP	United Nations Development Program
UNESCO	United Nations Educational, Scientific, and Cultural Organization
UNHCR	United Nations High Commission for Refugees
UPU	Universal Postal Union
WHA	World Health Assembly of the WHO
WHO	World Health Organization

1

Origins of the International
Dispute over Apartheid

South Africa has traditionally seemed an anomaly to Western civilization: hot in December, cold in July, and blooming with spring flowers in October. It is an outpost of industrialization in a largely underdeveloped part of the world. And it pursues a policy of racial segregation, at a time when the rest of the world is moving in the direction of color-blind societies. The result, as is well known, has been conflict and tension between South Africa and the rest of the world, particularly over its racial policies, collectively known as apartheid.

We need not linger long on the nature of apartheid. Webster's *New World Dictionary* defines it as "the policy of strict racial segregation and discrimination against the native Negroes and other coloured peoples as practiced in South Africa." More suggestive of the word's connotations, however, is the literal translation of the Afrikaans word *apartheid*, which means *apartness*. The racial policies that we call apartheid are in fact simply means to ensure the separation of the races, that separation being a moral or ethical value accepted by many South Africans. These racial policies touch upon all aspects of life in South Africa, and are recognized by most as not being ends in themselves.

The origins of South Africa's present racial policies antedate this century. The colonial traditions of Holland and Great Britain included varying forms of racial discrimination, and after formal slavery was banned in 1834, it was succeeded by other forms of white supremacy.

Many factors conditioned the settlers of southern Africa in the direction of apartheid. In the nineteenth century, much of the most "advanced" thought in all of the world was devoted to demonstrating the irreconcilability of different cultures. And in the resulting contest between cultures, it was natural that the social Darwinism of the latter part of the nineteenth century was used to justify the exploitation of the non-white peoples in southern Africa.

A second factor in the growth of apartheid as an accepted value was the chronology of the arrival of racial groups in southern Africa. When the Dutch settlement was established at the Cape in 1652, the only native peoples present were Hottentots and Bushmen in scattered, very small villages. The Hottentots gradually disappeared as a result of demographic pressures and diseases brought in by the Dutch, so that today the only group left with better claims on the Cape region than the Dutch is the Kalahari Bushman society of the northern Cape Province. The white settlers did not encounter organized groups of Bantu tribesmen until areas inland were occupied in the nineteenth century. In fact, Bantu groups were in a long-term process of migration southwards, and they could not have arrived in the territory of what is today South Africa much before the Dutch. Thus the Boer farmers of the nineteenth century felt little compunction about competing with the Bantu tribes, and, later, excluding them from the fertile lands of the Transvaal. It is somewhat ironic, therefore, that the South African government continues to describe the black population as "natives" in its legislation, as if to concede some form of right of prior presence to the black population.

A third factor was the value of self-reliance, built into early Boer society, and cultivated as a complement to apartheid. The Boer settlers did not use many slaves. They were fiercely independent, and relied to a large degree upon their families for farm labor. In that way, they avoided dependence upon black labor, and eschewed contact with the black tribes. The ethic of self-reliance was difficult to maintain after diamonds were discovered at Kimberley in 1866, for a great deal of human labor was required for their recovery. British entrepreneurs, with ample sources of capital and little reluctance about using native labor, naturally took the lead in exploiting the mineral riches of the Transvaal.

The fourth important factor that impelled South Africa toward an acceptance of apartheid was the demographic reality of four roughly identifiable racial groups (native, white, coloured,* Asian), of which the whites were only the second largest. Several events made the whites sensitive to that reality. The first Parliament in Cape Colony met in 1854, and self-government was granted to that colony in 1872. It was apparent that universal suffrage would result in a loss of power for the white political groupings. As they moved toward a modern industrialized society, too, the whites of South Africa found that they could avoid dealing with all non-whites as an aggregate unit. In other words, the "divide and rule" policy of British colonialism was particularly appropriate in South Africa. The coloured population was dependent upon the whites for its cultural identity, whereas the Asian and Bantu groups boasted many leaders intent on maintaining traditional cultures, kinship ties, and political structures. Thus a four-way division of the population was a logical policy for the ruling white groups to embrace, using the coloured population as allies in keeping the Bantus and Asians separate.

The description of these four factors from the colonial period is not meant to exclude others that influenced the development of apartheid. Indeed, traditional analyses of apartheid have dwelt upon the Calvinist religion that dominated the Africaners' lives, and Marxixt analyses have dwelt upon economic factors, with an emphasis on the exploitation of the black masses.[1] Both approaches have some validity but have generally been overstated because of a need for an ideological explanation of the development of South Africa's extraordinary racial policies.

The evolution of the structure of South African law to its present inclusion of apartheid legislation in all aspects has been gradual. It is true that the word *apartheid* has been used only by the National Party, in power since 1948, but the racial policies of apartheid have been in effect for centuries. What the National Party rule has been notable for is a

*Editor's Note: The term *coloured* is used here, not to mean black, as it has often been used in this country, but to refer specifically to those South Africans of mixed (e.g. black-white) racial backgrounds.

willingness to voice its commitment to white supremacy. Previous governments had described themselves as trustees for the black peoples, within one South African nation. The National Party has dropped all pretense of favoring eventual integration of racial groups. Of salience, then, are the means by which the successive governments of South Africa have maintained the separate and inferior status of non-white citizens.

Political rights of non-whites have traditionally been restricted. After 1854, non-whites had the right to vote only in the Cape Province, and even there they did not have the right to sit in Parliament after the South Africa Act of 1909. The franchise was limited for all races, however, for under the Parliamentary Registration Act of 1887 and the Franchise and Ballot Act of 1892, voting qualifications in the Cape had been raised, with the object of excluding both non-whites and poor white Afrikaaner farmers.[2] Under the so-called "entrenched clauses" of the South Africa Act of 1909, non-whites were assured the maintenance of their existing political rights unless unusual circumstances should arise. Until the crisis of 1951 arose over that issue, only symbolic damage was done to non-white political rights, as in the Representation of Natives Act of 1936 and the Indian Representation Act of 1946.

In 1951, the issue of non-white political rights precipitated a serious constitutional crisis.[3] The government forced through the Parliament a Separate Representation of Voters Act, which changed the method of black representation in Parliament. Such a move was in direct contravention of the South Africa Act of 1909, since the Voters Act carried by a simple majority and not by a two-thirds majority. The crisis eventually tested the role of the South Africa Appeals Court as a judicial review body independent of the Parliament, when the court judged the act to be unconstitutional. The constitutional question was not resolved for several years,[4] but in the process the non-white voters lost their representatives in the Union Parliament.

The thrust of South African legislation has thus been in the direction of ending all political rights for non-whites. The major black parties, the African National Congress and the Pan-African Congress, were banned in 1960, and even the Natives Representative Council, composed of government-appointed chiefs, has been abolished.

Related to political rights are various activities necessary to a free political system, and they have also been limited. Under the Suppression of Communism Act of 1950, the Minister of Justice was given the power to ban organizations, newspapers, periodicals, gatherings, or persons that threatened public order.[5] The government obtained even wider rights under the Public Safety Act of 1953 and the Criminal Laws Amendment Act of 1953, under which the maximum penalty for breaking a law to protest that law was increased to a £300 fine, three years' imprisonment, and ten lashes. In this way, the avenues of legitimate protest became severely restricted, for white and non-white alike.

Alterations in the system of justice and prison management were related to the perceived need for greater public order. The government has followed two lines in dealing with black South Africans. On the one hand, it has attempted to rejuvenate traditional tribal institutions of justice.[6] On the other hand, however, as many blacks have refused to accept judgments of the Native Courts, the burden has inevitably fallen on the regular court system of South Africa. Under white justice in South Africa, the black citizens have fared badly, and yet, in another sense, they have found their principal protector in the white society. In the latter sense, the judges at the lowest level often dismiss petty charges against blacks; after all, the prisons are overcrowded and fines are often uncollectable. For that reason the judiciary is sometimes considered the non-whites' best friend in South Africa.

In general, however, non-whites are not equal with whites before the law. Laws of detention have been used almost exclusively against blacks. The General Law Amendment Act of 1966 provides for interrogation and detention of up to fourteen days. The government, however, found that provision inadequate and obtained the Terrorism Act of 1967, which provides for indefinite detention. The latter act is supposed to be used only when the detainee is a suspected terrorist or has information about terrorists; it has clearly been overused, although its use is declining. In 1963, about 3,400 men and women were held under various detention laws,[7] and the annual figure is now in the hundreds.[8]

Prison sentences and the death penalty seem to be imposed

selectively on the blacks, judging from ample documentation on these issues.[9] One remarkable illustration of the non-whites' situation lies in the 1970 statistics on persons shot by police in the line of duty:[10]

	Killed	Wounded
White	2	5
Coloured	15	51
Black	37	93

The statistics for total numbers of sentenced prisoners admitted to prison during 1970 show a similar pattern:[11]

	Male	Female	Total
White	7,906	502	8,408
Asian & Coloured	55,344	11,385	66,729
Black	335,012	74,512	409,524

Rather than speculate upon the reasons for the seeming proclivity of the non-white population to run afoul of the law, suffice it to say that the penalties of the law fall more heavily on non-white than white citizens. The burden of the law is even clearer in the statutory limitations on the social and economic rights of non-whites.

Central to a person's social rights in South Africa is the provision of the Population Registration Act of 1950 that requires the classification of every individual as to race and, if applicable, tribe. It is on the basis of a person's classification as white, Asian, coloured, or native that the quality of his existence depends. This act has been the basis of continuing disputes in the courts, as the individual, not the state, is required to furnish the proof for a change in classification. Thus, a coloured person who believes himself to be white must provide an irrefutable genealogy for the courts. Successful appeals are rare, since sufficiently complete birth records are lacking in many parts of South Africa.

The effort to preserve the purity and separateness of the white race has included measures to prevent the birth of more children from unions of whites with non-whites. As early as 1927, the Immorality Act prohibited sexual contact between whites and Africans. Under National Party rule, the government went further and banned all racial intermarriage, as well as any sexual contact between whites and non-whites, in the Immorality Act of 1950 and the Mixed Marriages Act of 1949. These acts have been fully implemented, and now even apply to South African male citizens outside South Africa.[12] The limitations on behavior outside South Africa have been consistently ignored, however.

Race classifications were also basic to the reduction of contact between the races. Most obviously, segregation has been imposed in public places. The Railways and Harbours Amendment Act of 1949 divided the races on trains, and then the Reservation of Separate Amenities Act of 1953 ensured that the status of non-whites would be separate and unequal. The latter act was the result of a controversy in the courts, where it had been held that if separate facilities were provided in public places, they must be equal. The government overturned that decision by the 1953 act, providing that equal facilities were not required, and also that public establishments had the right to bar persons on the basis of race. Nearly all public places, particularly hotels and restaurants, quickly obtained clienteles of only one race.

In the minds of both supporters and opponents of apartheid, the most essential social right to be abridged has been the natives' freedom of movement. Three different types of laws have been used in the effort to prevent movement of non-whites: vagrancy laws, master and servant laws, and documents laws, all of which are sometimes referred to as "pass laws." The concept of regulating the movement of Africans originated with the Dutch in the 1650s, but has since become much more refined. Today the police have a legal basis for removing from white or urban areas any black considered undesirable.

The vagrancy laws were developed in the nineteenth century in stages, in 1834, 1867, and 1879, to deal with the problem of freed slaves who had no inclination to return to the Native Reserves. The 1867 and 1879 statutes remain valid and have been used infrequently in the last decade only because more sweeping statutes have been passed.

The Master and Servants Acts of 1834 and 1856 were merely the first in a long series of acts designed to regulate job contracts, with special emphasis on black labor.[13] The acts were concerned less with the state of the labor market, since there were always many unemployed black workers, than with the tendency of black workers to drift from job to job. This movement made it difficult to keep track of blacks, and so job contracts became a form of control on travel as well as on job transfer. The Master and Servants Acts were the basis for 22,517 arrests of blacks in 1970.[14] They have assumed importance in this century because of their usefulness in removing from urban areas any non-whites who are not gainfully employed. Thus the difference between the purposes and impact of these acts and those of the documents laws discussed below is only marginal.

The use of documents or "passes" to control movement of Africans is traditional. Over the last few centuries, non-white South Africans gradually became required to have a number of separate documents before entering white areas. The National Party found the separate documents unwieldy and consolidated them into one "passbook," in the Natives (Abolition of Passes and Coordination of Documents) Act of 1952. The provisions of the act were applied to African women in 1956. The passbooks have become symbols of an oppressive regime to most black South Africans, and this is in no small part due to the enormous number of arrests for violations of the pass laws: 621,380 in 1970, or 27 percent of all cases sent up for trial.[15] The burden on the courts has been enormous.

A separate mode of controlling African movement has been the withholding of a passport by the government. The first attempts by the South African government to refuse issuance of a passport, in 1949, were declared unconstitutional by the courts.[16] The response of the Ministry of Justice was to print new passports that included a statement to the effect that the passport could be withheld at any time. The statutory support for that administrative decision came in the Departure from the Union Act of 1956. In 1970, only 174 passport applications were refused, but they were, of course, submitted by people prominent at home and abroad for their opposition to the government's racial policies.

In economic realms, the question of land and housing has been part of the government's apartheid program since the inception of European settlement in South Africa. This century has been notable for successive efforts to delineate on a permanent basis the territories reserved for each race. The Natives Land Act of 1913 restricted native ownership of land to 8 percent of the South African land area. Further refinements of the principle of territorial separation came in the Native (Urban Areas) Act of 1923, the Asiatic Land Tenure and Indian Representation (Ghetto) Act of 1946, and, finally, the Group Areas Acts of 1950. The Group Areas Act, with several amending acts, provides for the separation of the races in housing and property ownership, and is the legal basis for the population shifts still occurring annually in South Africa.[17] By 1970, more than 111,000 families of white/coloured and Asian origin had been forced to move as a result of the Group Areas Acts[18] —blacks are not counted, since in theory they do not live in the urban areas on a permanent basis. The housing policies have been plagued by bad planning, especially regarding the total number of units needed, and so the separation of races has had to be a gradual process. Since the shortage of housing was due in part to the booming economy, attempts have been made recently to obligate employers to provide some housing for new workers.[19]

The labor legislation of South Africa is discriminatory in somewhat more complex ways, and has caused divisions among the white population as well as between white and non-white.[20] Blacks, for instance, are not allowed to organize labor unions. Strikes by blacks were abolished by the Native Labor (Settlement of Disputes) Act of 1953, which provides for severe penalties of up to three years in prison for participation in a strike. The legislation regarding black trade unions in South Africa, however, is not unusual; the government has shown general hostility to all trade unions, owing in part to their early infiltration by the Communist Party. Within the last few years, the government has shown signs of being willing to deal with black unions, even if only on a *de facto* basis. Legal recognition has not been granted, but the reality that illegal unions exist, particularly in the vital mining sector of the economy, has forced the pragmatists in the government to identify and, to a limited extent, work with the obvious leaders in black worker organizations.

A central paradox of discriminatory labor legislation appeared early in the twentieth century: the fact that if employers were allowed to discriminate against non-whites on the question of wages, the whites would suffer, since many jobs would go to the non-whites, who would be paid less. For that reason, many white trade unions have consistently opposed wage discrimination to the present day.[21] The government's answer to that problem has been the concept of "job reservation." As early as the 1922 Apprenticeship Act, jobs or training were reserved by law for whites only in certain trades, and today all occupations are classified according to race. In this way, it has been feasible generally to hold down non-white wages but avoid any non-white threat to the job tenure of whites. In the mining industry, for instance, the following average wages were paid in 1970:

White	341 rand monthly
Coloured	71 rand monthly
Asian	93 rand monthly
Native	19 rand monthly

The average native mineworker's wage was sixty-one cents per shift.[22]

The system of job reservation has encountered tremendous difficulties in a growing economy, and the government is under constant pressure from business to change classifications and thus enable labor-starved industries to hire non-white workers. In many mines in 1973, for instance, blacks drove the dump trucks and received 130 rand per month. Ten years previously, they had done only the digging in the mines. This situation was not unusual in other sectors of the economy.

The other major problem posed to the economy by apartheid measures stems from the legislation establishing the Bantu homelands and border industries. Those industries, designed to give the Bantustans some degree of economic viability, in fact undercut the comparable white-staffed industries in South Africa, and cause complaints from white industrialists that cheap low-wage labor is damaging South African industry. The government thus faces problems because of its desire to secure both apartheid and economic prosperity.

Education is a central element in the government's efforts to create several racial nations within South Africa. A series of Bantu Education Acts, the most important in 1953 and 1955, centralized control of Bantu education in the Union government, and redesigned the curricula along racial lines. Separation of educational systems, with ultimate content control by the Ministry of Education, characterized the South African educational reforms after the National Party came to power. The government, however, decided not to keep expenditures on African education at their traditional low levels. The expenditure rates per pupil still show tremendous disparities between the races, but the government has pumped increased funding into education in general: it now amounts to about 3.5 percent of the annual Gross National Product.[23]

Inherent in the decision to retain the expenditure discrimination against the Africans is the logic that it is better not to educate a person for a trade he can never practice. In other words, blacks have not been offered technical training in fields traditionally reserved for whites. However, as job classifications have changed rapidly, the educational structure has had trouble adjusting. Even more important, Africans are not given an education in European culture (history, literature, and social studies), from which the present government hopes permanently to exclude the non-white population. It has been feasible to offer an alternative cultural education to the Bantus and Indians, albeit at great expense, but the coloured population has no distinct culture of its own. The government is presently searching for a "coloured culture" to justify separation of that racial group's education.

Segregation of education has been most difficult at the university level. In 1954 Prime Minister Malan announced a plan to segregate all university education and to build separate universities for each major Bantu tribal group. The government soon realized the major commitment of resources that would be required for such a plan. As a result, the government announced that all university education was officially segregated by 1959, but that non-whites would be able to attend white universities by special permission of the Minister of Education. By 1971, even after the establishment of three universities for Africans, there were still 359 coloured, 857 Asian, and 224 African students attending white universities.[24] Many of these non-whites were attending the medical schools at the Universities of Capetown, Natal, and the Witwatersrand, since the expense of building a new medical school for non-whites would have been enormous. Even aside from the expense, however, segregation in the

universities has not been successful for other reasons, nota-
bly the opposition of many of the faculties and the student
unions. The National Union of South African Students
(NUSAS) has been a dogmatic opponent of the government's
racial policies,[25] and even today the universities' adoption of
nonracial sports codes has been a violation of the spirit, but
not the law of apartheid. In response to the limited effectiveness of the NUSAS, however, an all-black grouping of
students was formed: the South African Students Organization (SASO). SASO, alternately suppressed and tolerated by
the government, has an ambiguous role in the South African
political process. Its nominal orientation toward separation
of races, or so-called "Black Power," is attractive for the
government, but its demands for equality pose expensive
challenges.

The difficulty of reconciling apartheid ideology with the
ambiguous divisions of South African society has resulted in
constant turmoil over the future direction of government
policies. Within the National Party there exists a growing
faction, the reform-oriented *verligte* (enlightened), who
foresee greater contact among the races. Given this climate,
the government constantly strives to find a formula to satisfy
as many white factions as possible. The result is a form of
racial discrimination that varies a great deal from sector to
sector and from year to year.

On an internal plane, however, there are more than simply
impersonal logical contradictions that provoke criticism of
the apartheid policy. There are, as well, the personal problems and tragedies that are its natural result, and they are
causing the most spectacular breakdowns of the political
and social structure in South Africa. The difficult plight of
the non-white groups is obvious, and has been well docu-
mented.[26] There are also divisions within the white minority; some see a possibility that the English-speaking South
Africans, who control most of the finance and industry, will
use their influence to oppose apartheid.[27] Any such development, of course, depends upon whether the differences
between Afrikaaners and English-speaking whites are sufficiently fundamental. South African history has few examples of black gains at the expense of either white element.

Internationalization of the Apartheid Dispute

Apartheid is *prima facie* a domestic concern of South Africa. In practice, however, the controversial nature of such racial policies has resulted in international as well as domestic controversy over apartheid.

The implementation of apartheid has met with resistance, first domestically, and later externally. Domestic acts of resistance have brought only marginal changes, since the government prides itself on not being moved by violence.[28] The suppression of domestic unrest, however, has created tremendous sympathy abroad for South African non-whites, especially in the wake of particular incidents such as the treason trials, the Sharpeville shootings, passbook riots, or the 1976 Soweto disturbances, all the result of attempts to implement apartheid. Thus domestic unrest has been one contributor to the internationalization of the apartheid dispute.

Another source of international concern about apartheid has been South Africa's effort, actual or imagined, to export the policy to other parts of the African continent. The dispute over South West Africa (Namibia) has drawn attention to apartheid, which was implemented there at a time when, in the words of the League Covenant, South Africa governed it "as integral portions of its territory." Even more than in the past, now that a battle is in progress over the future government of that mandate, apartheid has become a useful vehicle for attacks on South Africa; the government would doubtless like to end the dispute over the mandate, if only to reduce the glare of publicity on its apartheid policy.[29]

The existence of the policy makes South Africa's foreign relations tremendously complex.[30] This is admitted to be true, by those sympathetic to the South African quandary,[31] as well as by those strongly opposed to any vestige of racial separation.[32] South Africa had traditionally relied upon only a few links abroad, London, Washington, Canberra, and the UN being the foci of its diplomatic efforts. With the growing foreign reaction to apartheid, however, South Africa naturally sought to widen its bilateral relations, especially with France, Israel, Germany, Brazil, and several states of central and southern Africa.

The expansion of South African interests within Africa

after 1964 is frequently described as an "outward-looking policy." Aside from a fear of the very real and practical effects of this new policy—commercial, financial, and political penetration of the weaker African states by South African interests—a recurrent fear of the black African states is of ideological imperialism. And apartheid is clearly a central element of South African ideology. This clash between the practitioners of apartheid and its opponents outside South Africa is the prime sustainer of the apartheid dispute which simmers constantly in the UN and other organizations.

The struggle between the black African states and South Africa, as played out over the question of apartheid, is an unequal contest. South Africa has the advantage of *de facto* diplomatic, financial, and trade links with the West. South Africa, too, controls the playing field on which the domestic contest over apartheid is fought. This means black Africans must forge external links in order to implement their policies in the face of South African power.[33] Many African leaders have avoided alliances, and so international organizations have become the foci of African diplomatic efforts.[34] Despite the existence of various African organizations for the formulation of policy, the black Africans, faced with an opponent of the stature of South Africa, have attempted to use more powerful groups such as the UN to achieve policy implementation.

An important question could arise as to the definition of the dispute in international organizations. Those who followed the apartheid question up to 1960 would maintain that the issue concerns human rights, and it is in terms of human rights that many resolutions have appeared in the UN.[35] One could, on the other hand, suggest that while the dispute was framed in terms of human rights from 1946 until the late 1950s, by 1960 it had become a "political dispute" and therefore warranted different handling by the UN. The behavior of the two parties to the dispute bears this out.

The anti-apartheid forces were manifestly concerned with human rights until the late 1950s. All resolutions were recommendatory in nature, originated principally in the UN Economic and Social Council (ECOSOC) and the General Assembly, and asked only for a negotiated end to apartheid. Force, at that time, did not appear to be the solution. As leadership of the anti-apartheid forces was taken over by the African states, however, the dispute was altered in tactics (by approaches to the Security Council)and goals (by protagonists' publicly and actively working for overthrow of the South African government). The dispute was thus highly politicized, in that it jeopardized the future of the South African polity, and involved the extraordinary powers of the Security Council. It is interesting to note that at the same time the Africans continued to invoke the human rights provisions of the UN Charter to justify the competence of jurisdiction of the UN. They also insisted that it was a serious political dispute, because they could then involve the Security Council with the problem: the UN Charter gives far greater powers to the Security Council than its human rights organs.

The South Africans have an equally interesting quirk in their logic, one which has done nothing to depoliticize the dispute. They have maintained from the beginning that it is a political question, but purely internal, and therefore of no concern to the UN. It is additionally clear from the internal legislation of South Africa that they regard the anti-apartheid forces as a political problem, and have used extraordinary powers to deal with the threat these forces pose to the existence of the regime. The South Africans, indeed, have refused to admit the jurisdiction of the UN organs concerned with human rights, thereby ensuring that the Africans would eventually seek aid from the Security Council and its powers under Chapter VII of the UN Charter.

The upshot of this gradual transformation into a political dispute has been a significant escalation of the stakes involved. Originally the ante in this particular game was simply the apartheid policy of South Africa, on one side, and the diplomatic prestige of the black Africans on the other. Through successive raises by each side, the very existence of the present South African governmental structure is imperiled, and the black African states have committed much of their political capital to a game with long-shot odds. Even more important, the members of the Organization of African Unity (OAU) have split in such a fashion that, no matter what the outcome, some governments will be embarrassed. In the investment, commercial, and strategic fields, there are also the interests of outsiders to be considered;[36] states such as France and Japan have a large vested interest in the present government despite their official opposition to its racial policies.

One cannot predict with precision, of course, the future direction of the dispute; that depends upon the contestants, who may realize that the stakes have become too high. For the period we are studying, however, it is clearly a political dispute, a contest for high political stakes, involving the use of many weapons, among which the most important are political.

Origins of the Dispute in the UN

Human rights themes dominated UN discussions of apartheid in the early years, especially the 1950s, when activity was centered almost entirely in the General Assembly. Action originated, and the focus remained, in that body.

The question of South African racial policies was first raised in the General Assembly in 1946, in connection with India's complaint concerning the discriminatory treatment of South African residents of Indo-Pakistani origin. Resolution 44(I) of December 8, 1946, recommended that South Africa treat Indo-Pakistanis in conformity with "international agreements" and the UN Charter.[37] At the Second Session of the General Assembly, no resolution obtained the necessary two-thirds majority, and at the Third Session Resolution 265(III) of May 14, 1949 included a provision for a round-table conference that never occurred.[38] Prodded by India, the General Assembly tried to fulfill a "good offices" function, urging the two parties each year to negotiate, and finally establishing a three-member Good Offices Commission in 1950.[39] The position that South Africa adamantly held, however, was that the question lay within South Africa's domestic jurisdiction, and that, in any case, India refused to negotiate in good faith. South Africa, in turn, refused to cooperate with the General Assembly. As a result, no progress was made in negotiations, and the question remained on the agenda of the General Assembly until 1962, when it was combined with the apartheid question.

The question of the Indians in South Africa did, however, represent one of the first disputes between Commonwealth members taken to the UN. This violation of the tacitly accepted *inter se* doctrine of the Commonwealth set the stage for later recourse to the UN over the apartheid issue itself.[40]

"The question of race conflict in South Africa resulting from the policies of *apartheid* of the government of the Union of South Africa"[41] could not be treated in the same delicately legal manner as the situation of the Indians. For one thing, legal agreements dating from the 1920s between the Indian and South African governments did exist. Many of the Indians also held British passports, rather than South African. As a result, there were international aspects to the problem that could be settled juridically. The case of apartheid and its effects on the black population of South Africa, however, was basically an issue between black and white citizens of South Africa. The black-white issue had not been in the international realm, and many members of the UN, therefore, were reluctant to become involved. The precedent that it might establish for UN handling of violations of human rights was also disturbing to nearly all members, since few could honestly say that they had removed the beams from their own eyes.

The year 1952 was a time of high tension in the Cold War, which complicated third parties' views of the situation even further. As a vociferous opponent of the Communist bloc and a contributor to the Allied forces in Korea, South Africa had a claim on the United States and the Western European members of the North Atlantic Treaty Organization (NATO). At one point, South Africa even proposed the expansion of NATO into a general Atlantic treaty organization, of which she would be proud to be a charter member: hence the reluctance of NATO members to press a dispute designed to undermine such a staunchly anti-Communist regime. The voting of the United States on the two questions concerning South Africa is most striking. From the Seventh Session through the Twelfth Session, the United States consistently voted with the majority on the Indian question and abstained on the question of apartheid in South Africa. Only with the votes of 1958 and later years did the United States abandon its English-speaking allies and vote with the majority attacking South Africa's race policies.[42] Thus the atmosphere into which India introduced the apartheid question in 1952 was not particularly friendly. It was, however, perhaps a typical situation for the UN, where one issue often carries implications for other far more political questions, and thus becomes a victim of larger superpower disputes. This fact of UN life caused many disputes, including apartheid, to be submitted to the General Assembly rather than the Security Council.[43]

The behavior of the Communist bloc is interesting in this regard, for at the time of the introduction of the apartheid issue it still felt itself to be a beleaguered minority in the United States–dominated General Assembly. The explanation of the USSR for its frequent abstentions was that the resolutions proposed in the General Assembly "did not go far enough" in the effort to eradicate apartheid.

In the Seventh Session (1952), the General Assembly dealt with the question of South Africa's race policies fairly lightly, and shunted the problem to a commission.[44] By the following autumn, the Commission on the Racial Situation in South Africa had completed its report,[45] and it was submitted to the Ad Hoc Political Committee of the General Assembly for consideration. The South Africans chose to adopt the same line toward this commission that they had maintained for some years toward UN treatment of the so-called Indian question; they said that they regarded "Resolution 616A (VII) as unconstitutional and that they could not therefore recognize the Commission established thereunder."[46] The report of the commission was not subjected to detailed scrutiny in the Ad Hoc Political Committee. The battle, as usual, centered on the question of domestic jurisdiction, and the largely conciliatory report of the commission was ignored in the argument. South Africa's draft resolution to reject jurisdiction of the UN was voted down (7 for, 47 against, 7 abstaining).[47] India then submitted its seventeen-power draft resolution describing apartheid as "contrary to the Charter and the Universal Declaration of Human Rights."[48] It passed by a solid majority of 37–10–9, and later passed in the General Assembly, with only slight opposition, to become Resolution 721 (VIII). The majority chose to maintain the commission in existence, asking it to continue its study of apartheid, and to suggest measures which would help to alleviate the situation and promote a peaceful settlement.[49]

The details of UN organs' dealings with the apartheid issue in the early years are interesting, in illustrating the ease with which these organs maintained a sense of harmony among themselves. The General Assembly and its subsidiaries had established procedures for dealing with grievances, such as that of India over apartheid. Decisions were made in committee, and the General Assembly acquiesced. These procedures were rather diplomatic and nonviolent compared to those of later years, and created no sense of conflict among the organs concerned.

Events surrounding the dispute settled into a pattern by the Ninth Session (1954), and seemed to be following an established routine in the Tenth Session. The commission would submit its report to the General Assembly to be considered by the Ad Hoc Political Committee.[50] Inscribed as agenda item 23 (IX and X), the issue would be discussed almost entirely in the committee, where India would introduce its draft resolution noting South Africa's noncooperation with the commission.[51] The resolution would then call for further investigation by the commission. In the Ninth Session, the draft resolution easily won approval by the General Assembly.[52] A major change in the routine occurred, however, following the approval on India's resolution in committee on November 9, 1955, by a margin of 37-7-13. The South African delegate took the floor to state that "his Government regarded in a most serious light the inquiry into the legislation of the Union which resulted from previous resolutions and from the draft resolution just adopted." Because this was "the most flagrant violation of Article 2, paragraph 7, of the Charter, a violation which no self-respecting sovereign state could tolerate," the South African delegation was withdrawn from the entire session of the General Assembly.[53] Perplexed by the South African action, the members of the Ad Hoc Political Committee could do little but report to the General Assembly, where some remedial action might be possible to repair the estrangement. The sacrificial lamb in this case was the Commission on the Racial Situation in South Africa, which was duly eliminated from the resolution on December 6, 1955.[54]

The issue of apartheid was thus subjected to the scrutiny of delegates with new strategies in mind. The commission, in the period 1952–55, had largely reflected the views of Hernan Santa Cruz of Chile (rapporteur), but had served the function of channeling discontent with South Africa's racial policies into an adjunct organ. The Ad Hoc Political Committee and especially the General Assembly were thereby saved from unduly prolonged perennial debate on the issue. With the abolition of the commission, tensions were dispersed throughout the organization once again, finally coming to rest, in large measure, on the shoulders of the members of the newly formed Special Political Committee (SPC). The debates of that committee became prolonged, and extremely time consuming.

Nature of Diplomatic Protagonists

The most striking common element among the nations pushing hardest for action against apartheid in the 1950s was their professed nonalignment. In the voting bloc that appeared each year for the debates on the apartheid issue could be seen the drawing power of what was in time to be called the Afro-Asian bloc, a misnomer for a group of nations that coalesced only on certain issues, especially apartheid. Indeed, throughout most of the decade, the correct terminology was the Asian-African bloc, an indicator of which geographical area provided both the leadership and the numerical preponderance; the former term came into use with the gradual shift of leadership to Africa (especially Cairo) and with the flood of newly independent African states in 1960.[55]

The Asian-African Conference at Bandung in April 1955 was the first international gathering outside the UN to deal with the apartheid issue in a substantive fashion. Its first decision, of course, was not to invite South Africa, "because it was believed certain that the Conference would single out the Union when it condemned racial discrimination."[56] Ironically enough, the reason given for inviting the People's Republic of China to the conference was to "socialize" her in the international scene.[57] But the political risks of inviting South Africa were obviously too great; the only certain areas of agreement for the participants were anti-colonialism and human rights,[58] and with South Africa present, even that bit of consensus would have been in jeopardy.

When it came to the question of action, however, it was obvious that the conference could not agree on the tenor of criticism that should be expressed concerning the policy of apartheid. The result, a harbinger of a future pattern, was to refocus attention on the UN as the possible arena for action, leaving the conference merely to express its solidarity with the non-whites of South Africa as stated in the final communiqué: "The conference extended its warm sympathy and support for the courageous stand taken by the victims of racial discrimination, especially by the peoples of African and Indian and Pakistani origin in South Africa."[59] The discussions in the conference emphasized coordination of the anti-apartheid movement at the UN.[60] Indeed, this coordination helped to provoke South Africa's subsequent walkout from the General Assembly, and the termination of the Commission on the Racial Situation in South Africa.

The eventual result, however, is of less importance than the demonstrated impact that outside coordination could have on the progress of an issue in the UN. The legitimacy and solidarity that this "concerted moral pressure" derived from the Bandung Conference was immeasurable— continuing to be drawn upon for another decade and a half. The gathering effectively involved governments in issues that had no immediate relevance to them. In a sense, it publicly committed the government leaders to a long-term program to eradicate colonialism, racialism, and violations of human rights (at least in South Africa). As the immediate *raison d'etre* of the Afro-Asian bloc, those issues were pursued more energetically in the UN than they had ever been elsewhere.

No sooner was the Afro-Asian grouping established and given some support outside the UN than the first division in its ranks appeared. It was clear that the Asian and African states did not have identical interests, and the Africans chose to make it official by establishing a separate identity for their "bloc." The scene was the first Conference of Independent African States (CIAS) in Accra, Ghana, in April 1958. While the apartheid question was far from the most important issue on the agenda of the conference, many aspects of it foreshadowed the trend of events in southern Africa.

A great deal of preparation went into the conference, with all participants, and especially the host, Ghana, concerned that African conference diplomacy, in its first solo flight, make a perfect three-point landing in front of the world

press. With all due civility, the organizers invited South
Africa to participate, but the South African government
counterproposed that all African colonial powers be included in the conference. One cannot be certain whether
South Africa made such a suggestion out of a feeling of racial
solidarity or from a perception of being a colonial power
itself. When that proposal was turned down by the other
participants, South Africa wired its regrets.[61]

In the debate on the question of apartheid, occasional
references were made to the Bandung and Cairo[65] conferences, but overwhelmingly the delegates referred to action in
the UN.[63] Ethiopia's delegate introduced a supplementary
proposal, in relation to the apartheid issue: "I think the
independent African States should obtain, as a matter of
right at the United Nations, a position in the Security
Council."[64] Overall, however, the debate was not particularly specific, as many delegates were more concerned with
racial discrimination in Rhodesia, Kenya, and other sensitive areas. Thus the final resolution sounded moderate in its
all-encompassing nature; besides offering "unswerving loy-
alty and support to the Charter of the United Nations" and
"adherence to the principles enunciated at Bandung," the
delegates created a platform with the wording:

1. Condemns the practice of racial discrimination. . . .
2. Appeals to the religious bodies and spiritual leaders of the
   world. . . .
3. Calls upon all Members of the United States and all peoples
   of the world to associate themselves with the Resolutions [of
   the United Nations and Bandung]. . . .
4. Calls upon all Members of the United Nations to intensify
   their efforts. . . .[65]

The resolution cited specifically South Africa on two occasions, following the basic form and content of General
Assembly resolutions on the subject.

Of greater importance to the future treatment of the
apartheid issue was the establishment of a permanent African group at the UN.[66] As New York was the only city where
all independent African states were represented, it was
logical that the permanent machinery be located there.[67]
What may have been unexpected was the impact the exist-

ence of the African consultation machinery might have on the UN. Given the general mandate of coordinating "all matters of common concern to the African states," the coordinators soon shaped the newly emerging African states into a force to be reckoned with on every vote in the General Assembly. Of greatest importance to South Africa, the African bloc took the leadership of the anti-apartheid campaign away from the Afro-Asian machinery by 1962, and carried it to a point unimagined by early advocates.

In the period between 1955 and 1959, however, the apartheid dispute became dormant in the UN. The attempts in the General Assembly to find a new focus of attack on South Africa following the demise in 1955 of the Commission on the Racial Situation in South Africa were both brief and desultory; within a short time, nearly all action was concentrated in that catchall organ of the General Assembly, the Special Political Committee (SPC).

In an attempt to involve the secretary-general in an active role, the General Assembly in early 1957 requested the secretary-general to "communicate with the Government of the Union of South Africa to carry forward the purposes of the present resolution."[68] The intention of the drafters was apparently to encourage Dag Hammarskjöld to take whatever private initiatives he considered potentially fruitful. In any case, the attempt failed, as there were no communications with South Africa to report.[69]

The treatment of the South African issue in the 1959 session was representative of the patterns of 1955–59. The issue was raised as a possible agenda item in a letter from thirteen powers proposing the "question of race conflict in South Africa. . .," dated July 15, 1959.[70] An attached memorandum succinctly summarized the arguments that had been put forth in the previous decade, citing South Africa's noncooperation, and urged action to secure the compliance of South Africa with the provisions of the UN Charter and the Universal Declaration of Human Rights.

When the question of including the issue on the agenda was considered at the plenary meeting of September 22, the General Assembly quickly adopted it by voice vote, and referred it to the SPC for detailed consideration. At this time, South Africa raised its ritual objection to consideration of the issue by the UN; its argument was based on two points.

The most obvious was the provision of Article 2(7), under which South Africa considered its racial policies to be a question of domestic policy, which had not yet come under the exceptional provisions of Chapter VII. South Africa then proceeded to buttress its arguments with evidence from the San Francisco Conference, where it had been accepted by Commission II (General Assembly), that "nothing contained in Chapter XI can be construed as giving authority to the Organization to intervene in the domestic affairs of Member States."[71] Needless to say, South Africa's objections were overridden, and the issue was passed to the SPC.[72]

The SPC spent a full nine sessions airing various views of South African racial policies.[73] As was customary, South Africa chose not to participate in these proceedings or when the report was sent to the General Assembly. Its viewpoint was that it had presented its objections at the time of consideration of the agenda, and if other members of the UN wished to engage in a procedure clearly *ultra vires*, that was their concern, but South Africa would not be present.[74]

The attack on South Africa was opened by the representative of Ghana, Alex Quaison-Sackey, an able, Oxford-educated diplomat later to be president of the General Assembly. He attempted to clear up, first of all, the question of domestic jurisdiction. Asserting that South African racial policies were obviously of international concern, he used as proof the speech of South African Minister of External Affairs Louw to the General Assembly on September 28, 1959, when Louw spent at least two-thirds of his speech explaining the policy of apartheid to his audience.[75] Quaison-Sackey went on to attack, in particular, the South African Bantu Acts, which provided for separate education and separate political development for blacks. He suggested specific improvements in South Africa's domestic policies: open elections, better and integrated education, and equal work opportunities.[76] This speech, hardly vituperative in tone, and certainly not militant in its suggested actions, was in fact the toughest during the nine sessions of the SPC.

Beginning with Philippine representative Guerrero, subsequent speakers rose to moderate the atmosphere of the committee meetings further. He was obviously concerned about possible transgressions of Article 2(7), and felt that "it was not for the Members of the United Nations to pass judgment on the moral and political issues of the country's domestic affairs"; at the same time, he felt that "it was their duty to make another appeal for conformity by all Members to the principles and purposes of the Charter."[77] In effect, he conceded the question of domestic jurisdiction to South Africa, and yet wanted some formula whereby the UN could express its contempt for South Africa's racial policy. When it came to a vote, however, the Philippines voted with the majority on all operative paragraphs.

Norwegian representative Lionaes offered a particular interpretation of Articles 55 and 56 for the committee's attention. Those two articles formed the basis of the UN's concern with apartheid during the late 1950s, since, in their generality, they encompass almost any problem in the world today. What Lionaes suggested, however, was the concept of "progress," for Article 55 states that the "United Nations shall promote," among other things, "universal respect for, and observance of, human rights and fundamental freedoms for all without distinction as to race, sex, language, or religion." In Article 56, "all members pledge themselves to take joint and separate action. . . . " Thus the key question, in the view of the Norwegian representative, was the *direction* of a country's policies, and not so much where they were at any particular time. Using this criterion, she found the Union of South Africa clearly in contempt of the UN Charter, for the principal aim of apartheid was racial separation, and therefore in the opposite direction of what was called for by the provisions of Articles 55 and 56.[78] In the end, however, she made no suggestion for UN action beyond the annual reminder to the South African government, but at least she did attempt to establish a new basis for UN consideration of the question.[79]

The SPC sessions closed with a "cold-war speech" by the delegate of the United States, whose main interest was in "hundreds of millions of people under totalitarian regimes [who] were still denied the exercise of those rights and freedoms."[80] It was clear that United States priorities allowed little scope for sustained interest in the apartheid issue. The United States, at that time, had virtually no stake in the dispute, a situation that would change drastically in the following ten years.

The position of the moderate Commonwealth members

on apartheid was expressed in the speech of New Zealand
representative Shanahan, according to whom "problems of
race relations could clearly not be solved by proclamation."[81]
His conciliatory message became clearer as he carried his
logic to a moderate solution:

> It [New Zealand] would deeply regret the erection of any
> barriers which might prevent the growth of greater coopera-
> tion between South Africa and the United Nations, and it
> could not contemplate sharing in any action which it did not
> regard as being directed towards encouraging South Africa to
> play its full part in the community of nations.[82]

The point, of course, is that there was talk beginning in the
corridors about sanctions or boycotts, at least among the
most radical states, and New Zealand made it clear that, at
least for many Commonwealth states, the accent must
remain on persuasion, not on coercive action. At the same
time, Shanahan made clear his government's disapproval of
apartheid, emphasizing that "the Assembly should make
clear the concern which the international community felt at
the policy of apartheid followed by the Union Government."[83] Thus there was agreement on the preamble, but not
on the operative paragraphs.

By the end of the committee debate on November 9, more
than fifty delegations had spoken, more or less to the issue.
The United Kindgom did not speak, its position of generally
standing with South Africa on votes, despite opposition to
apartheid, being well known. The USSR, indicating its
distrust of what schemes might be behind the words of the
United States delegate,

> saw no need for operative paragraph 2, which might create
> the false impression that all Member States were being
> reminded of their obligations to respect human rights and
> freedoms in accordance with the Charter, whereas the Assem-
> bly was considering the question of racial discrimination in
> the Union of South Africa.[84]

Accordingly, the USSR and eight Eastern European countries planned to abstain on operative paragraph two. The
range of attitudes toward the draft resolution was thus quite

broad. Outright opposition could be expected from neighbors and allies of South Africa (Britain and Portugal) as well as from strict legal constructionists (France and Belgium). Abstention or noninvolvement characterized only the Communist bloc. Support for the resolution ranged from passive acquiescence by the United States, to the reformist desires of the Scandinavians and the zeal of the Afro-Asians. Overall, however, the spectrum was limited compared to its shape ten years later.

The most specific solution to the problem was offered by the innovative Haitian delegate, who recommended, among other things, a trip to South Africa by the secretary-general to voice the concern of the UN, the establishment of a UN information center in South Africa, the creation of an international university for blacks not admitted to South African universities, and, appealing to the technology-minded, the establishment of a powerful UN-operated radio station aimed at South Africa. But none of his original proposals was to come to pass soon, as a thirty-six-power draft resolution was introduced at the same meeting, with provisions basically the same as those of the previous year's resolution.[85]

The draft resolution circulated among members of the committee after November 3, and picked up enough support to ensure its passage; indeed, the only dissenters appeared to be the Communist bloc, on operative paragraph two, and certain Western European countries, on legal or special political grounds (Britain, France, Portugal, and Belgium). The voting was on a paragraph-by-paragraph basis, as requested by France so that it could register its dissent on certain parts. The resolution voted on by the SPC on November 10 was as follows:

The General Assembly

Recalling its resolution 1248 (XIII) of 30 October 1958 on the question of race conflict in South Africa resulting from the policies of apartheid of the Government of the Union of South Africa,

Deeply convinced that the practice of racial discrimination and segregation is opposed to the observance of human rights and fundamental freedoms,

Considering that government policies which accentuate or seek to preserve racial discrimination are prejudicial to international harmony,

Noting with concern that the policy of *apartheid* is still being pursued,

1. *Expresses its opposition* to the continuance or preservation of racial discrimination in any part of the world;

2. *Solemnly calls upon* all Member States to bring their policies into conformity with their obligations under the Charter of the United Nations to promote the observance of human rights and fundamental freedoms;

3. *Expresses its deep regret and concern* that the Government of the Union of South Africa has not yet responded to the appeals of the General Assembly that it reconsider governmental policies which impair the right of all racial groups to enjoy the same fundamental rights and freedoms;

4. *Appeals* to all Member States to use their best endeavours as appropriate to achieve the purposes of the present resolution.[86]

The voting on each paragraph progressed easily, with the greatest dissent shown on operative paragraph two, when the vote was a lopsided 61–1–14. The abstentions represented a combination of the Communist bloc and Western Europeans. The resolution as a whole passed easily, 67–3–7, and was sent to the General Assembly.

Little time was spent in the General Assembly considering the arguments, as all countries had had an opportunity to speak in the SPC. Few countries showed any interest in rehashing the issue, and thus, "pursuant to rule 68 of the rules of procedure, it was decided not to discuss the report of the Special Political Committee."[87] Voting on the resolution took place immediately, and the vote was almost identical to that in the SPC, 62–3–7.[88] Thus Resolution 1375 was entered in the books in the relatively calm, orderly, and well-mannered fashion of the 1950s.

The inability of the anti-apartheid movement to achieve its ultimate goal in the early years (1952–59) reflected several factors whose reversal would be important in the succeeding decade. Hesitant leadership by the Asians meant that the apartheid dispute was not widely discussed outside the General Assembly. The Cold War climate which pervaded the UN was also detrimental to progress on the apartheid issue. The killing of the Commission on the Racial Situation in South Africa in 1955 at the insistence of South Africa was only one instance of that country's parlaying its rigid anti-Communism into political capital at the UN. There was also the honest unwillingness of many members to continue the commission without the cooperation of South Africa.

The commission, however, was representative of a passing fad of international organizations: a commission of inquiry composed of individuals chosen for their expertise, not their citizenship. During the early years of the UN, commissions were almost consistently composed of government representatives, especially commissions dealing with political questions. Thus the General Assembly Commission on the Racial Situation in South Africa was rather unusual, as virtually the only commission established by the assembly that was composed of experts to deal with a political dispute.[89] In the era since 1955, however, which has seen the politicization of much of the work of international organizations, it might have been expected that members of commissions of inquiry would be chosen more for the political blocs they represented than for their expertise: one more manifestation of "bloc politics" in international organizations. The Commission on the Racial Situation in South Africa must be recognized for the rare bird that it was, an independent commission attempting a moderate and balanced investigation in an immoderate environment.

The inability of the movement against apartheid to achieve institutional linkages, too, was not recognized until the end of the decade. As seen in the 1959 treatment of the issue, the agenda item moved from organ to organ; there was no simultaneous treatment to raise the question of conflicts between organs. Only with the establishment of an African grouping at the UN, designed to serve as spokesman for the independent African states, do we see a consciousness of one organization addressing another organization to solve the common political problem of apartheid. Bandung was an episode of personal diplomacy, without the institutional machinery to affect the actions of other organizations. The independent African states, on the other hand, undertook steps for implementation of policies, especially after 1960. And at that point, as we shall see, the drive against apartheid became a powerful and meaningful effort.

2

From International Concern to Increasing African Opposition

The apartheid conflict grew during the period 1960–62 as a result of two principal factors: the dramatic Sharpeville shootings, and the upbeat of African organizational efforts. The crisis of 1960 is a turning point in the apartheid dispute for a number of reasons. Most superficially, it blew open the ivory curtain for a moment to give the world a glimpse of the nature of apartheid. For the UN, the crisis jerked the issue out of the routine that had continued from session to session of the General Assembly, and dumped it on the table of the Security Council. Inevitably, then, the secretary-general became involved, with the combination of these elements giving the apartheid dispute a new impetus. The new direction came largely from African states and African regional conferences.

The apartheid dispute received its second major impetus with the appearance of serious African organizational efforts. These efforts were apparent on the African continent and, even more importantly, in African caucuses at the UN, the International Labor Organization (ILO), and the World Health Organization (WHO). These UN family members were largely unaware of proper responses to the African initiatives, and for that reason, we shall examine the efforts by the African bloc in terms of their possessing the initiative during 1961–62 without organized opposition.

The initial stages of the conflict between South Africa and the African states developed naturally from the policy decisions of the Conference of Independent African States (CIAS) and the publicity given the Security Council meetings on Sharpeville. Important support for the African cause appeared periodically, often unpredictably: the exclusion of South Africa from the Commonwealth and the effects of this on British votes in the UN, the publicity on the South West Africa issue, and, in 1962, the combining of the "Indian" and "apartheid" issues in the General Assembly. These random events never affected the basic African strategy, which depended largely on good luck for its implementation. Only gradually was the African group able to impose its interpretation of events on organizations: first on the Special Political Committee (SPC) and eventually on the General Assembly. The process culminated in the creation of the Special Committee on Apartheid. Obtaining a secure "base of operations" was essential to the African cause if other organizations were to be prodded into action. This was a time, after all, when no African continental organizaton existed.[1]

The Africans utilized two primary tactics, punishment and isolation, against South Africa, much as if they regarded it as a criminal. Punishment consisted of a movement to institute economic sanctions against South Africa. This tactic encountered significant opposition, even among African states, for nearly every state had something to lose by ending economic ties with South Africa. Other opposition came from states concerned about violence that could result from enforcement of sanctions. The latter objection raises the question of whether economic sanctions would have helped, in this case, to control violence or would merely have exacerbated the situation. The use of economic sanctions against South Africa would clearly have to be considered a "negative" sanction,[2] i.e., enforcement of a norm that the government and white citizens of South Africa did not regard as legitimate. Because enforcement of economic sanctions almost certainly would have entailed the use of some force, the possibility of economic sanctions, although not necessarily the African pursuit of them, was negative for the purposes of controlling the conflict in South Africa.

Isolation of South Africa, on the other hand, was essentially a social sanction, and did not necessitate the ending of economic and political relationships. The theme, instead, was exclusion from international organizations, the interna-

tional equivalent of exile.[3] Social sanctions, in contrast to
economic sanctions, were easily voted in, since they cost little
and South Africa had been an international recluse since the
coming to power of the Nationalist Party in 1948. The use of
social sanctions had more "positive" elements than other
forms of sanctions, in that South Africa withdrew from as
many organizations as she was ejected from in the course of
the dispute. In other words, South Africa understood the
norm of behavior that required termination of membership
when basic values were in conflict.

What is most striking about 1961–63, perhaps, is the
extraordinary naïveté with which the African group pursued
its quarry in organization after organization, without an
overall plan, but confident as long as South Africa was on
the defensive. In the game of diplomatic poker, the Africans
could place their bets without other players knowing whether they were bluffing. The result was success in many arenas,
as measured by the goals set out in African organizations
during 1961 and 1962.

International organizations had their own relationships
during this period, but they were largely confrontational,
and derived from two sources. Constitutional factors required the Economic Commission for Africa (ECA) to
appeal to ECOSOC for a change in South Africa's status.
Political choice would lead the African political organizations to take their case against South Africa to the General
Assembly of the UN, the Commonwealth, and the ILO.
None of the organizations, in any case, helped to control the
conflict, as it escalated from the extraordinary events of
Sharpeville.

Sharpeville and Its Aftermath

The drama opened in Sharpeville, South Africa, on March
21, 1960, when South African police killed and wounded a
significant number of unarmed black Africans who had
gathered to protest new legislation by the government.
International reaction was strong, immediate, and adverse to
South Africa. The Asian-African group at the UN recognized it as an opportune moment. On March 25, twenty-
eight African and Asian members of the UN submitted a

request to the Security Council for an emergency meeting:

> Under instructions from our Governments and in accordance
> with Article 25(1) of the United Nations Charter, . . . we
> consider that this is a situation with grave potentialities for
> international friction, which endangers the maintenance of
> international peace and security.[4]

This was the moment for which the Asian and African
leaders of the anti-apartheid group had been waiting. Public
opinion was aroused; the Security Council could not refuse
to hear the issue. Some optimists even hoped that coercive
action might be instituted against South Africa, but in any
case, the precedent for Security Council handling of the issue
would be established.

The complaint was placed on the agenda on March 30,
and the Council began its consideration under the chair-
manship of United States representative Henry Cabot
Lodge. Immediately reservations to the agenda vote were
submitted by Britain, France, and Italy, all concerned about
the possible clash with Article 2(7). After the appropriate
expressions of outrage had been read into the record by the
concerned parties, and South Africa had made its statement
(and departed), the debate began to focus on the proper
action to be taken. There was little inclination on the part of
Western members to invoke the powers of Chapters VI or
VII; the issue did not appear that serious, despite the elo-
quence of the Asians and Africans.

By Thursday afternoon, March 31, a consensus appeared
possible, and Ecuador submitted a draft resolution which,
apart from minor changes resulting from early translation
difficulties, was later adopted by the Security Council as its
conclusions on the following day.[5] The key element, as far as
operative paragraphs were concerned, was that the Security
Council chose to involve the secretary-general in the question: "*Requests* the Secretary-General, in consultation with
the Government of the Union of South Africa, to make such
arrangements as would adequately help in upholding the
purposes and principles of the Charter and to report to the
Security Council whenever necessary and appropriate."[6]
That this was the extent of the Security Council's concern
was disappointing to the Africans. As the Tunisian delegate

pointed out, in voting for the resolution:

> The Ecuadorian draft resolution does not seem to us to be entirely in keeping with the gravity of the situation on the one hand, nor on the other hand to be what the conscience of the world, which still has faith in this Assembly, expects as a result of this debate.[7]

But he was able to vote in favor of the resolution as a "minimum." The USSR was not particularly happy to give discretionary power to the secretary-general, as the Soviet delegate said ironically, "in whose judgment and political acumen we all have full confidence," but voted for the resolution.[8] The vote on the whole resolution was 9–0–2, with Britain and France abstaining.

The complaining parties had not obtained all that they felt was due, but operative paragraph one was in itself an important step: "*Recognizes* that the situation in the Union of South Africa is one that has led to international friction and if continued might endanger international peace and security."[9] With this use of the language of Chapter VI, the Security Council legitimized the view of the Asians and Africans that the apartheid issue could properly be handled in all aspects by international organizations.

Given a general mandate by the Security Council in S/4300, Dag Hammarskjöld applied his "quiet diplomacy."[10] The first report on his task was sent to the Security Council in less than three weeks; in it he discussed his communications with the South African minister of external affairs.[11] Louw had taken a rather accommodating tack, agreeing to talks with Hammarskjöld in London after the conclusion of the Commonwealth Prime Ministers' Conference in May. Much groundwork was covered: the talks were considered mere preliminaries to the secretary-general's visit to South Africa in late summer, after the "Judicial Commissions [investigating Sharpeville] will have completed their inquiry and submitted their reports." As a concession to South Africa's sensibilities, Hammerskjöld assured Louw that his visit "would not require prior recognition from the Union Government of the United Nations authority."[12] At this point, the Security Council did not interfere with the secretary-general's diplomacy; it merely awaited the course of events.

The second report to the Security Council provoked little controversy, merely giving a brief description of the talks in London on May 13-14, 1960. Apparently the two men reached agreement "on the character and course of the further consultations to take place in Pretoria [at which time] no restrictive rules were to be imposed on the Secretary-General."[13]

Not all action, however, was centered in New York. The second Conference of Independent African States (CIAS) in June 1960 was an occasion for self-congratulation on the issue of apartheid. South Africa was on the run, and with one all-enveloping operation, many African leaders felt, apartheid would be dead.[14] Even the conservative Liberian delegate allowed his optimism to rise to the surface: "The situation [in South Africa] has now become so abhorrent that the conscience of the world has been touched, and I believe that concerted action will bring about a change."[15] The tone of a delegate's rhetoric was inversely proportional to the distance between his country and South Africa. The Sudanese foreign minister announced that his country had been boycotting South African goods for two months already, and proclaimed that "master-races have always paid the price of delusion."[16] A few delegates became concerned with a larger strategy, especially the Guinean, Achkar Marof, who insisted that strong resolutions were not enough:

> De l'avis de la Délégation de la République de Guinée le renforcement de notre unité d'action, à l'O.N.U. et au sein des organismes internationaux, serait pour nous d'une importance capitale sur tous les plans. Il est indispensable, en effet, que les Etats africains forment un front uni, à l'O.N.U. et dans les Conférences internationales, pour la defénse de leurs intérêts.[17]

Even more sober was the view of Tunisia's Taieb Slim, who described efforts in the Security Council in March, where Slim was the sole African representative. Obviously dissatisfied with the unwillingness of the Security Council to institute sanctions, he was not terribly hopeful about the secretary-general's mission: "Nous espérons que le Secrétaire Général reussira dans sa mission plutôt délicate. Sans être pessimiste il nous semble permis d'être sceptique."[18] The next step, then, was for the conference to define a strategy for obtaining approval of sanctions in the UN.

The resolution passed by the conference reflected an awareness that other powers and organizations would have to be enlisted in the battle on the African side. Many aspects of the resolution are noteworthy:[19]

1. The resolution recalled as precedents the declaration of Bandung, resolutions adopted at the Conferences of Independent African States held in Accra in 1958 and at Monrovia in 1959, General Assembly Resolution 1375 (XIV), and Security Council Resolution 134 of April 1, 1960. The legitimacy of their position was important to the African states, and they drew strength from many sources.

2. The resolution called upon all African states to sever diplomatic relations with South Africa, institute a total trade and communications boycott, and deny South African planes the use of their air space.[20] These operative paragraphs went further than any proposed by other international conferences.

3. It asked the Arab states to institute an oil suppliers' boycott of South Africa. Presumably this would have been accomplished through the Organization of Petroleum Exporting Countries as well as Western oil companies.

4. It invited the African Commonwealth members to expel South Africa from that organization. This was, in a sense, a response to the meeting of the Commonwealth Prime Ministers in early 1960, where no decision was taken on the question of South Africa's remaining a member in the event of its becoming a republic. The CIAS did not expect to have a direct impact on the Commonwealth, but rather to draw public attention to the fact of South Africa's precarious position in that body.

5. It also addressed one operative paragraph to the Security Council, in calling for action "by the United Nations in accordance with Article 41 of the Charter." This reference to Chapter VII was bit of hyperbole, for it was well known that more than one permanent member of the Security Council was resolutely opposed to Chapter VII measures. It did, however, indicate the intensity of the feelings of the African states, if not a reflection of reality. This relationship of

African organizations vis-à-vis the Security Council became, in time, a frozen posture.

In a tangential resolution, the CIAS indicated where the action for the immediate future would be: at the UN. The Informal Permanent Machinery was maintained in New York until a new home in Africa could be found.[21]

The CIAS in Addis Ababa was merely the highlight of African conference diplomacy for the year.[22] Two earlier conferences that had received little attention were the Afro-Asian Peoples' Conference (AAPC) in Tunis on January 25–31, 1960, and the Accra "Positive Action" Conference on April 7–10, 1960. Neither conference had permanent organizational machinery. The AAPC, which was noted for a relatively radical stance among "third world" groupings, had decided to establish a committee to organize a boycott of South African goods.[23] This committee of the AAPC was summarily put out of business by the sweeping measures of the CIAS in June. The rapid sequence of events demonstrates just how radicalizing the Sharpeville shootings were.

The "Positive Action" Conference of Kwame Nkrumah suffered the same fate in the whirlwind of events.[24] That conference not only called for a boycott of South African goods and severing of diplomatic relations, but also the expulsion of South Africa from the Commonwealth. Even those measures could not be considered respectable in nationalist African circles two months later at the CIAS, as more fertile minds were at work devising strategies to end the presence of apartheid on the African continent.

Events in New York, in the meantime, moved very slowly. By the time of the secretary-general's second report, he and the Security Council had become totally immersed in the problems of chaos in the Congo. The council left the secretary-general to his own devices on the apartheid question. He could obtain little support from the African group, which was growing larger every day, and fragmenting over the Congo question. The Africans at the UN, in any case, were becoming disenchanted with the Secretariat as organized by Dag Hammarskjöld. For many, he was too much of an activist in outlook, which especially troubled those African states with sensitive sovereignties. Thus they defended the secretary-general only halfheartedly against Soviet attacks in the Fifteenth Session.[25] There were tensions between the African ambassadors and the Secretariat at lower levels as well; apparently many of the staff were personally disagreeable in dealing with Africans who were inexperienced with the complex diplomatic protocol of the UN.[26]

Low-profile diplomacy produced rather meager results in Hammarskjöld's South African trip of early January 1961. Most disappointed, perhaps, were the Bantu and Indian groups in South Africa who had hoped for signs of dramatic leadership. The secretary-general refused to accept memoranda from victims of apartheid (even when smuggled to him in wreaths of flowers), and spoke only with the official Advisory Council and government-appointed chiefs. Chief Albert Luthuli represented the moderate view of Hammarskjöld's visit when he said that "until Mr. Hammarskjöld makes a public statement, his visit will remain under a cloud."[27] Hammarskjöld made no public statement in South Africa. The Indian groups were also active in pushing for more extreme action by the UN. As the South African Indian Congress said at the time:

> In this hour of crisis, we appeal to the UN not to continue as it has done annually since 1946. . . . We appeal to the UN to resolve that its member states immediately apply economic sanctions against the Union Government and outlaw it from the world organization.[28]

Hammarskjöld himself considered his talks with the South African government a failure; he reported to the Security Council that "no mutually acceptable arrangement has been found."[29] Thus the entire episode of utilizing the secretary-general in this matter was unsatisfying, except for those who wished to delay consideration as long as possible. Hammarskjöld helped to control the conflict for a short time, but at the expense of his own prestige.

Despite the failure of Hammarskjöld's efforts, and the lack of interest by the Security Council, the African conferences— especially the CIAS in Addis Ababa—were to have a continuing importance in exacerbating the conflict not only in 1960, but also in 1961–62. The course was set for three years, and little more coordinated stimulus was provided from Africa until the formation of the Organization of African Unity (OAU) in 1963. However, the anti-apartheid movement did not decline during the years 1960–63; the momentum building up in the wake of Sharpeville was tremendous, and the African states were able to carry their campaign to the conference halls of UN organs and several specialized agencies. The movement was so strong that even would-be defectors voted with the African bloc for at least five years. The fact remained, however, that coordination of the African bloc remained centered in New York, enhancing the bloc's impact at the UN, but underscoring its lack of continent-wide cooperation at home.

The Sharpeville crisis itself had serious effects on the progress of the apartheid dispute. In publicity terms, it "educated" a large segment of the public to the existence of apartheid. Perhaps more importantly, the General Assembly could no longer pass ritualistic resolutions; the involvement of the Security Council established the ability of that body to deal with the apartheid issue, notwithstanding Article 2(7) of the UN Charter. The secretary-general became involved for the first time. The dispute had thus entered a new phase, with important backing from African regional conferences.

The relationships established by the African group in New York with African regional conferences were simply tentative indicators of future developments. The African group, in bringing the apartheid issue to the Security Council, was clearly dependent upon the angry chorus of public outrage against South Africa from various African regional conferences. With that mechanism established, the Africans began to use other intergovernmental organizatons, as described below, in the effort to score points against South Africa.

African Organizational Efforts at Home

The year 1961 witnessed the appearance of what has been described as the African "alliance system,"[30] with many repercussions on the apartheid conflict. Even as primitive a strategy as was devised by the Africans in 1961–62 posed serious problems for the arbiters of peace in international organizations. With the rush of nations to independence in 1960, the African continent lost all semblance of unity, and was unable even to meet together in one conference, owing to severe divisions over the Congo, ideology, boundary disputes, modes of political and economic development, and subversion. The most remarkable feature of this period of fragmentation was the essential unity of the various African blocs on the question of apartheid; this common feeling, of course, had little effect on the African continent itself, and was manifested simply in the UN, specialized agencies, and the Commonwealth.

The first grouping to establish a separate identity was the Casablanca Group, created in January 1961 at a conference in that city; it became known as a "radical" group for its stands on the Congo, Algeria, and colonial questions. Concerned with African problems more pressing than apartheid, the initial conference hardly went beyond the second CIAS, in recalling the resolutions of the UN, condemning South Africa, and calling for action by the UN. It did condemn, as well, "the imperialist powers who continue to lend moral, political, military support to the racialist government of the Union of South Africa."[31] Essentially the same resolution was cleared by the subsequent meeting in Cairo in June 1962. The Casablanca Group, however, was not destined to last; its organization was poor, and the volatility of the members (Ghana, Algeria, Guinea, Mali, UAR, etc.) made it difficult to maintain harmony.[32] The group had an extremely informal organization at the UN, but that became less important when Ghana obtained a seat on the Security Council in early 1962. Ambassador Quaison-Sackey of Ghana thereby gained a prominent place in which to publicize the Casablanca view of South Africa.

The most important competitor faced by the Casablanca Group was the Union Africaine et Malgache (UAM), composed of former French colonies, and moderate in inclination.[33] By 1960 it was a coherent grouping, and received its institutional form in 1961 at the conferences of Yaoundé and Tananarive. Although deeply opposed to many positions of the Casablanca Group, the UAM did not retreat from the line on South Africa laid down at the second CIAS at Addis Ababa. The conferees harshly condemned apartheid, and advocated the breaking of all relations with South Africa.[34] The UAM survived in somewhat better form than the Casablanca Group, even if mainly in those areas where coordination was provided by the French government. Its political power in international organizations may have been reduced by the fact that members of the UAM were more interested in events in Paris than in New York or Geneva, and yet it still created an impressive degree of coordination at the UN. The group financed an office in New York at a cost of more than $100,000 per year, and sought to maintain the unity of the bloc of votes as much as possible.[35]

There was a third African voice in world affairs: sometimes weak or nonexistent, but dominant in the long run. The moderate non-French-speaking group that included Ethiopia, Liberia, and the East Africans gradually became more important on the African scene. One can see as early as May 1961, at the Monrovia "Reconciliation" Conference, which failed to unite Africa, that a third way did exist. That conference took a strong stand against South Africa, asking for sanctions, and in a sense was the true perpetuator of the centrist spirit in Africa: radical on external issues, and conservative on purely black African issues. In this way pressure was maintained on non-African organizations to take action on apartheid, as it became clear that even the most moderate of African gatherings would push for severe measures.

African Organizational Efforts Abroad

For the time being the most potent factor abroad was the African group at the UN. Independent of their foreign ministries to a large degree, the ambassadors to the UN from African countries were able to maintain effective pressure on South Africa in several international bodies. The stands taken by the group in the UN, adhered to by African delegates almost without exception, were formulated simply as a result of personal diplomacy, without the institutional backing they were later to receive from the OAU.

The UN and UN subsidiary bodies were the principal foci of African action during this period. Only tentative efforts were made in the ILO, and seemingly simply in a move to create publicity and added pressure for the UN struggle. Only the diplomatic moves in the UN, in any case, were at all coordinated, thus causing other efforts to have a merely sporadic effect, sometimes called "spillover." The effect of anti-apartheid resolutions in the ILO on other organizations, for instance, would depend upon informal communication among African diplomats. There was no African clearinghouse for the campaign outside the UN, and the ILO and other organizations wanted to reduce publicity as much as possible. The first stage of the campaign outside the UN, however, came in the British Commonwealth, when South Africa applied for readmission. After success in that forum, the Africans realized that there were other organizations in which South Africa could be pressured.

The Commonwealth was the first major organization to take the step of exclusion, but many others were to follow.[36] The Commonwealth is a club; it remains exclusive, somewhat inclined to privacy, and tied together by weak threads of common background: the British colonial experience, and varying degrees of allegiance to the Crown. In the days of white exclusiveness before World War II, the Commonwealth functioned much like upper-class clubs of London's West End. Its representatives' quiet conversations were recessed for tea and a formal portrait with the King, and publicity was not sought. After some meetings, no communiqué appeared, and the conversations made only slight ripples in the memoirs of retired statesmen. Even after World War II, with the entry of India, Pakistan, and Ceylon into membership, and as late as Ghana's entry in 1957, the pattern continued unchanged.[37] The outward calm of the grouping was undisturbed by internal upsets such as South Africa's treatment of Indian citizens, at a time when the issue was causing displays of ill temper in the UN forum. Nehru accepted the ground rules of the club.[38] Thus until 1960, the Commonwealth was a tranquil organization, if one can use that term to describe a grouping without a secretariat (to be created later),[39] voting body, or collective security arrangements, and its transformation in the period 1960–70 is all the more extraordinary if one considers its initial posture.

The club underwent a number of significant internal changes at the beginning of the 1960s that were to have an important bearing on its future direction. Its membership was changing rapidly, becoming more African in composition, and the effect of that was unpredictable. Not only were the Africans different from Asians, in being "active and extrovert," with unknown consequences, but as J. D. B.

Miller says, the African leaders tended "to overstate their
cases and to use the Commonwealth as a direct bargaining
venue, rather than as the place of indirect or person-to-
person negotiation which it had traditionally been, and as
which the Asians had, on the whole, accepted it."[40]

With the growth in membership, and the introduction of
new tactics by some members, recognizable divisions began
to appear in Commonwealth meetings. While formal caucuses were not held until the discussion of the Rhodesian
issue in 1966, the divisions in 1961 were clear enough for
observers to be able to predict the stances of members. On one
side was the "Old Commonwealth" (Britain, New Zealand,
Australia, and South Africa), and on the other side was the
"New Commonwealth" (India, Pakistan, and the African
states); holding them together and performing mediation
were a few members such as Canada, Malaya, and Ceylon.
These ideological divisions gained importance because they
were made public, which was the second important innova-
tion. The meetings were not public, but preliminary publicity and lobbying became an important activity, making
private bargaining that much more difficult. Some writers
go so far as to maintain that Commonwealth discussion of
issues and the accompanying publicity exacerbated difficulties;[41] this, however, is part of the more general question of
the helpfulness of discussing problems for which solutions
may not be found very easily. What was clear, though, was
the emergence of a degree of polarization in the Commonwealth as racial and "North-South issues" became more
prominent.

Most crucial to the development of the apartheid issue in
the Commonwealth in 1960–61, however, were external
pressures. This meant not only the publicity mentioned
above, but also the resultant public concern. African diplomats pressed for action on all fronts against South Africa in
the wake of the Sharpeville incidents. Various nongovernmental organizations were educating public opinion, and in
the forefront was the Anti-Apartheid Crusade in Britain.
The UN was itself an important factor; Nkrumah of Ghana,
for instance, decided to take a moderate line on South Africa
while he awaited the fate of the secretary-general's mission
under Security Council Resolution S/4300. Thus he tempo-
rized during the Commonwealth meeting in late April 1960,
but by May, after the meeting, appears to have decided for

South African expulsion.[42] In a more general sense, the General Assembly was instilling in its members, and especially its African members, a set of values that some members felt would have to be applied in all international organizations. In other words, the fact that the Commonwealth had scrupulously avoided discussing matters of domestic policy in the past was not important to the African members. To them the General Assembly was a legislative body that could create standards to be enforced by *all* international organizations, including the Commonwealth. Anglo-Saxon qualms about the advisability of applying this doctrine to South Africa were eventually overridden.

As a confluence of these internal changes and external pressures, as well as South Africa's truculent attitude, events in 1960–61 rolled toward a predictable outcome. At the Prime Ministers' Conference in the spring of 1960, the South African government presented its plan for a referendum of white voters on the issue of becoming a republic. The Union of South Africa hoped to follow the pattern of India and Ghana after achieving republican status, namely, to be readmitted to the Commonwealth. Being under a great deal of public pressure after the Sharpeville incident to take some action, real or symbolic, the prime ministers indicated that they could not promise continued membership for a Republic of South Africa; implicitly they were saying, "Proceed at your own risk and we shall see how the winds are blowing at the next meeting." South Africa went ahead with the referendum, which gave the government a majority for its republican scheme.[43]

The 1961 meeting of Commonwealth statesmen was not, as it turned out, a friendlier environment for the South African point of view. The enthusiasm of the anti-apartheid movement was at a higher pitch, and the African members correctly saw an opportunity to make an effective stab at South Africa. The initiative of the secretary-general had, by this time, been classified as a non-event, and dramatic progress was needed somewhere. On the other side, Prime Minister Verwoerd saw few reasons to compromise, since the material benefits of Commonwealth membership were not based on remaining a member, but on mutual agreements with Britain, making South Africa's exclusion largely a symbolic act.[44] The discussion before the vote was not educational, as both sides had made up their minds. The only stalwarts for keeping South Africa in the Commonwealth in order to exert a gradual influence on her policies were Harold Macmillan (Britain) and Sir Robert Menzies (Australia).[45] Verwoerd thus left the meeting satisfied that the Commonwealth had cut off its nose to spite its face, and the Asian-African bloc felt that it had administered the first of a series of body blows to the South African apartheid policy.[46] Indian Prime Minister Nehru, in a speech in the Lok Sabha, expressed pleasure with the result:

> This was a very significant step that the Commonwealth took, but I believe that it has strengthened it and certainly not weakened it. It has even wider significance than it might appear at first sight, because thereby the question of racial equality has been put on the highest level in the world context. As a matter of fact, the United Nations Charter itself concerns this . . . .[47]

As a result of this London confrontation in March 1961, South Africa did not attend another Commonwealth meeting, but little else changed for the outcast. It continued to benefit from Commonwealth preferences, and from membership in the sterling zone, both based upon bilateral agreements with Britain. It also enjoyed close diplomatic consultation with the British government until Harold Wilson became Prime Minister in 1964.[48] The Simonstown agreement continued in force, providing the material for a later controversy in the Commonwealth; little had in fact changed, and apartheid's shadow remained to darken later deliberations of that body.[49]

The Commonwealth, on the other hand, was affected in strange but profound ways by the departure of South Africa. In the short run, there was one less Anglo-Saxon vote, and the meetings were somewhat more tranquil until the Rhodesian crisis. In the long run, however, the Commonwealth's ability to resolve the issue was severely damaged. The tactic of confrontation had been given sufficient legitimacy through success, in African eyes, to cause its general adoption by African caucuses. As some writers express it, the Commonwealth was no longer a "family."[50] Even more, the obvious ineffectiveness of Commonwealth actions, as opposed to expressions of sentiment, has led Miller to point out that

> since success was more often measured in rhetorical than in real terms at each of these bodies, and since the Africans had little power of pressure apart from their threats to disrupt the Commonwealth or resign from it (threats increasingly discounted by British opinion as the years went by), the performance of African leaders in Commonwealth gatherings became increasingly rhetorical.[51]

The Commonwealth action did, at least, turn the attention of the Africans away to other organizations for some time, as they refocused their attention on the UN organs and specialized agencies in searching for ways to censure and punish South Africa. Exclusion from organizations as a tactic received more respect from the Africans, for it did obtain concrete results, and thus it became their favorite approach. More generally, the South African issue indicated that black Africa was a new kind of force that the Commonwealth would see more of—a force that would mean greater involvement of the Commonwealth with the UN and African organizations:

> Whereas it was usual for an Asian minister to return home after a Commonwealth meeting and say that he had secured Commonwealth support for some national policy . . ., after a meeting in the 1960's each African leader was expected to say what he had done for Africa as a whole. . . . He was also expected to report to non-Commonwealth Africans at the OAU and the United Nations; success was needed here too.[52]

What made an impact in diplomatic circles was that Britain was now free to vote as it pleased in the UN. In the past, believing that apartheid was governed by the *inter se* doctrine, Britain and Australia had been in the embarrassing position of voting with South Africa or abstaining on resolutions concerning apartheid in the General Assembly.[53] Following the 1961 Commonwealth meeting, Britain felt free to cast its vote against South Africa. It was the least expected, but most welcome, result of the exclusion for the African states.

The Commonwealth incident exemplifies the power of "spillover" on political affairs, for while the Commonwealth had no formal ties with other international organizations, it clearly had an important impact on them and the future of the apartheid dispute. The example of exclusion (or expulsion) of South Africa was to be lavishly imitated in international organizations. The Commonwealth also demonstrated the dilemma of an organization without internal constitutional checks and balances; only tradition kept a significant proportion of the membership from imposing its standards of political legitimacy on the other members. The UN, on the other hand, had control mechanisms against spontaneous movements to expel South Africa, the Security Council being the only body competent to deal with such questions. The Commonwealth could only accept the will of a majority, and pass the question on to other organizations better equipped to control it.

Postponing substantive discussion until the completion of the secretary-general's efforts and the Commonwealth meeting, the UN General Assembly finally tackled the problem of apartheid in the second part of the Fifteenth Session (spring 1961). The Africans were still at fever pitch after the Commonwealth victory, and the Special Political Committee immediately faced serious divisions on the issue.[54]

At this session Quaison-Sackey of Ghana, the most effective spokesman for the African caucus, stood up to speak for the second CIAS, held in June 1960. Outlining the measures endorsed at the conference, he called for the rupture of economic relations, diplomatic relations, and communications with South Africa, under Article 41 of the UN Charter. Rehabilitating an old institution, he also asked that the Commission on the Racial Situation in the Union of South Africa be re-formed, with new members, and new terms of reference.[55] By remaining within the terms of the resolution of Addis Ababa, Quaison-Sackey kept the African forces united; he did not invoke the resolutions of the Casablanca meeting of January. The Casablanca meeting was in fact mentioned by India as an indication of African feeling, but more often the Commonwealth expulsion of South Africa was alluded to as the proper model of action.[56]

The basic division within the SPC, and in the General

Assembly as well, was over the question of sanctions. The legal arguments dwelt on Articles 10, 11, and 12, in an effort to determine the proper role of the General Assembly in acting against a recalcitrant member, when the Assembly has no power to require members to apply sanctions. The discussion eventually became more pointed, as it was clear that only certain powers would apply the measures, causing other countries to feel that it would be useless to pass ineffective sanctions. The result was two separate resolutions, one submitted by twenty-five African states,[57] and the other a five-power Asian resolution that did not call for sanctions, except to "request all States to consider taking such separate and collective action as was open to them to bring about the abandonment of these policies."[58] Most of the Western European states and many Latin American states were against both or merely abstained, indicating that although the sentiments were well expressed, they would not apply sanctions.

Because voting in the SPC is done on the basis of a simple majority, both resolutions passed, the African resolution by 47–29–18, and the Asian resolution by 93–1.[59] The difference between the resolutions at that point was that the African resolution called for a series of diplomatic and economic sanctions, and asked the Security Council to aid in enforcement, whereas the Asian resolution did neither.

This militancy of the African group in comparison with the Asian states was hardly a new phenomenon. The disillusionment of Africans with the Asians on the decolonization issue had come early, dating back to the investigation of the Cameroon in 1958.[60] The so-called Afro-Asian bloc became, in fact, simply an ad hoc coalition on certain issues, and its cohesiveness declined as the years passed. What happened, in effect, was that the Asians, and especially India, maintained the positions staked out in the 1950s, considered radical at that time. As the Asians encountered the revolutionary states of the 1960s, however, their old radical views seemed pale by comparison with those of the African newcomers. The Asians are not necessarily unhappy with this position; it simply leaves them open to occasional attacks by younger, generally African, radical states.

The General Assembly could not pass both resolutions, for if it adopted the African resolution, it would, as the

stronger of the two, supersede the other. The problem faced
by the Africans in the plenary session was the two-thirds
majority requirement for passage of the resolutions. As the
critical moment approached, African unity began to break
down; the Ivory Coast decided to absent itself from the hall,
foreshadowing more obvious African divisions of the late
1960s. Then, as the vote was taken on operative paragraph
five of the African resolution, which contained the sanctions, Togo defected to the ranks of the abstainers, and the
Africans found that they had only a simple majority, 42–34–
21, and not the required two-thirds. At that point Quaison-
Sackey and the Ethiopian delegate rose to withdraw their
resolution from further consideration. There were no objections. The Asian resolution then passed essentially without
opposition.[61]

The result of the Fifteenth Session, then, was to indicate to
the African group that they did not yet determine the posture
of the General Assembly on the apartheid question. It would
take more than one effective spokesman to persuade the
members of the wisdom of sanctions, especially when it came
to Asian powers such as India, which was making a last
effort to negotiate before resorting to the tactics of confrontation.

The Sixteenth Session, on the other hand, saw the appearance of several significant trends. The first, beyond our
purview, was the growing importance of South West Africa
as an issue; it had clear legal handles that anti-apartheid
forces could grab, and it was an area in which the Western
nations had few direct interests, thus neutralizing somewhat
that source of opposition.[62] As discussion of new tactics
arose, this discussion might have been evoked by either the
South West Africa issue or the apartheid issue. The prolonged discussions in the Fourth Committee in late 1961, for
example, while concerned with the agenda item of economic
sanctions to wrest South West Africa from the grip of South
Africa, implicitly involved the issue of apartheid, since the
principal contestants in each case, South Africa and the
independent black African states, were identical.[63]

The interaction between the International Labor Organization (ILO) and the UN over apartheid began at an early
stage. At the International Labour Conference of June 1961
in Geneva, a tremendous controversy had erupted over the

presence of South Africa, and Quaison-Sackey, in his annual speech to the SPC, capitalized on that unrest to advertise the disruptive role of South Africa to the world.[64] The ILO was the first specialized agency involved with the apartheid issue, and it made several precedent-setting decisions. The ILO, for instance, was virtually the only organization outside the UN to be shaken by the Sharpeville shootings of 1960. Requests for South African withdrawal from the organization were approved by the general conference as early as 1961, indicating the early concern of delegates to ILO conferences.

As in many organizations, the first sign of tension in the ILO concerned the African regional conference. The first African regional conference, convoked by the Governing Body of the International Labour Office, was scheduled for Lagos, Nigeria, in December 1960. South Africa, extremely sensitive to the general hostility at that time, declined the invitation extended to thirty-five European or self-governing political authorities in Africa, and thus no incident occurred at the conference.[65] Resentment against South Africa was building up, however, and it all spilled out at the General International Labour Conference in the summer of 1961. Conferences of the ILO are unusual among intergovernmental organizations in that they have four delegates from each country: one representative from the workers, one representative from the employers, and two from the government. The most volatile element on political issues is the worker or trade union element, and in order to pass a resolution, it need obtain only 34 percent of the employer and government representatives. In 1961, Resolution I dealt with the presence of South Africa. Not only did it condemn South Africa's racial policies, but it also declared that the continued membership of South Africa was "not consistent with the aims and purposes of the Organization." It went on to request the Governing Body "to advise the Republic of South Africa to withdraw from membership" until apartheid was abandoned.[66] The Governing Body forwarded the resolution to South Africa without formal comment, but no response from South Africa is on the record.[67] When a similar resolution was adopted at the 46th Conference in 1962, it was becoming apparent that the drive for expulsion was no passing fancy, and that something would have to be done.

The theme of caution was played up by many forces within the organization, and one of the most influential was that of Director-General David Morse:

> It might sometimes be highly desirable that ILO views on such questions should be expressed to the United Nations by reason of their economic or social implication or aspects, but the value of such a view will tend to depend on the extent to which it represents a general consensus of opinion within the ILO, and this is an added reason for hesitation before submitting to the Conference proposals which are likely to divide rather than to unite it as regards such matters.[68]

In fact, no concrete decisions were taken before the 47th Conference in June 1963. Even in this first phase of the dispute in the ILO, the direction of events was not yet clear. There were forces for radical change, and for intransigence in the face of calls for such change. The clear articulation of both forces ensured, at least, a continuation of the dispute.

At the Sixteenth Session of the UN General Assembly, the African states mounted a determined drive to obtain sanctions against South Africa, even at the risk of alienating previous allies (in Asia) and potential friends (in northern Europe). The Africans demonstrated their will to seize the initiative in subsidiary committees, and then to take the fight to the floor of the plenary. In the SPC, as in the previous year, two resolutions were submitted.[69] The African resolution, similar to the 1960 version, eventually passed the SPC, 55–26–20.[70] The eight-power resolution, introduced by Afghanistan, Ceylon, Denmark, India, Malaya, Norway, Togo, and Venezuela, was the object of three amendments that made it in effect as action-oriented as the African resolution.[71] In the procedural environment of the SPC, where only a simple majority was required, all the amendments passed, and the General Assembly was presented with two resolutions that offered more of an echo than a choice.[72]

As the representative from Denmark complained in the plenary session, the eight-power draft resolution had been so drastically amended that he had been forced to abstain on the resolution he had cosponsored when it came to a vote in the SPC.[73] The plenary session, therefore, took on an importance that it had not displayed in years, as the sponsors of the eight-power resolution attempted to restore it to its original condition. The first step was to defeat the African resolution, by denying it a two-thirds majority.[74] The Danish representative then called for separate votes on the inserted paragraphs of his resolution, concerning the Security Council, a petroleum boycott of South Africa, and economic sanctions, all of which failed to obtain a two-thirds majority.[75] In its original form, and reduced to the statements of the previous year, the resolution passed 97–2–1.[76]

The most remarkable thing about the whole session, in retrospect, was the way in which the African and Communist states tried to pit a subsidiary committee against a parent organ, the General Assembly. It was a foreseeable possibility, in view of the different majorities required for passage of resolutions in the plenary and committee meetings. An important factor in this show of militancy may have been the controversy over the routine speech of Prime Minister Louw of South Africa in the general debate of the General Assembly. The Liberian representative was so incensed by Louw's routine defense of apartheid that he moved that the speech be stricken from the record. With clamorous support from many of his colleagues, the motion almost passed over the protests of the parliamentarians, until the Nepalese delegate pressed for adjournment.[77] Tempers cooled in the delegates' lounges. On their return, the delegates agreed merely to pass a vote of censure against Louw, although many members remained in the corridors and did not record a vote.[78] The Africans were obviously not satisfied, and their resentment may have surfaced in the SPC, where they used their numerical strength to alter the Asian-Scandinavian resolution. The General Assembly, in any case, was able to resist the African demands, but for the last time.

There was yet another principal branch of the UN to be drawn into the conflict: the Economic and Social Council (ECOSOC) and its subsidiary organs. The organ most immediately relevant to the Africans was the Economic Commission for Africa (ECA). The relationship of South Africa with the ECA had always been somewhat uneasy, before it blossomed into active hostility in 1962. At the time of the formation of the ECA, South Africa indicated its preference for the old colonial institutions concerned with economic affairs in Africa, such as the Commission for

Technical Cooperation in Africa south of the Sahara (CCTA), and initially chose not to join ECA:

> It is the view of the Union Government that the commission's term of reference may well make overlapping with the functions of these bodies [the CCTA, etc.], which are doing valuable work, inevitable, and it would wish to study this matter further. For this reason the Union Government has decided for the present not to participate in the work of the Commission.[79]

South Africa did not maintain that position for long, however, as the colonial powers decided to work in the commission, and so, despite its misgivings, South Africa could not remain outside.

Changes in the membership of the ECA soon had their effect; the role of the Europeans declined, and by 1961 the ECA had taken up the question of "the economic and social consequences of racial discriminatory practices." Needless to say, South Africa was tremendously irritated by this turn of events, and with the issuance of the first report on the above topic,[80] to be presented at the annual meeting in February 1962, South Africa decided not to send a delegation to Addis Ababa, in light of the "hostile attitude adopted against South Africa."[81]

South Africa's refusal to attend the meeting did not stop the other members from discussing apartheid at great length. They were insulted by South Africa's refusal to hear their attacks in person, but decided in the end that it might be better to expel South Africa from the ECA. The only hitch was that the ECA could not do it; only ECOSOC could determine the membership of regional commissions. Nevertheless, the ECA resolved "that the United Nations Economic and Social Council should deprive the Republic of South Africa of its membership on the Commission until such time as it puts an end to its policy of racial discrimination."[82] ECOSOC, at that time, was still controlled by advocates of universality in international organizations, and chose not to act on the ECA's recommendation.[83]

By the fall of 1962, however, the UN was giving the apartheid issue a new role. The topic of apartheid, appearing in the Seventeenth Session of the General Assembly as agenda item eighty-seven, was the object of a merger. On the surface, the issue of apartheid and the situation of Indo-Pakistanis in South Africa had been combined. Even more, the political forces behind the two issues had been combined in a way that gave the African states the initiative. It is difficult to say why this occurred: certainly India was distracted by other crises that needed attention, such as the border war with China and the assimilation of the Portuguese colonies in India. Additionally, the African states were not reluctant to submerge the issue of overseas Indo-Pakistanis, in view of their increasingly apparent problems with their own South Asian minorities, especially in East Africa. In any case, the Asian states quickly assumed a secondary role, in the SPC and the General Assembly, as conciliation gave way to confrontation.

All attempts by Guatemala to soften the Afro-Asian draft resolution by amendment in the SPC failed by solid majorities, and the draft passed to the General Assembly by a vote of 60–16–21. The Africans had devised a tough resolution, one that proposed action in a number of areas broached by African regional organizations:

The General Assembly. . .

4. *Requests* Member States to take the following measures, separately or collectively in conformity with the Charter of the United Nations, to bring about the abandonment of those policies:

(a) Breaking off diplomatic relations with the Government of the Republic of South Africa, or refraining from establishing such relations,

(b) Closing the ports of each State to all vessels flying the South African flag,

(c) Enacting legislation prohibiting the ships of each State from entering South African ports,

(d) Boycotting all South African goods and refraining from exporting goods, including all arms and ammunition, to South Africa,

(e) Refusing landing and passage facilities to all aircraft belonging to the Government and companies registered under laws of the Republic of South Africa;. . . . [84]

Thus the long-sought sanctions were finally entered into the books of the UN.[85] In order to keep tabs on the progress of the sanctions, and keep pressure on South Africa:

The General Assembly. . .

5. *Decides* to establish a Special Committee. . .

(a) To keep the racial policies of the Government of the Republic of South Africa under review when the United Nations General Assembly is not in session, and

(b) To report either to the General Assembly or to the Security Council or both as may be appropriate from time to time;. . . . [86]

With the creation of the Special Committee on Apartheid, we see the recognition that there might be a long, drawn-out battle; in this way, it was hoped to establish an institution, more aggressive than the short-lived (1952–55) Commission on the Racial Situation in South Africa, to keep the pot boiling. At the close of operative paragraph five, however, is a hint that the African states were aware that the General Assembly might not be the scene of the crucial battle. The focus of attack was already being shifted to the Security Council, where Africans had obtained a seat (Ghana), and were bargaining for another in the 1963 reorganization. The last paragraph of the resolution was pointed in its intent: "The General Assembly . . . *Requests* the Security Council to take appropriate measures, including sanctions, to secure South Africa's compliance with the resolutions of the General Assembly and of the Security Council on this subject, and, if necessary, to consider action under Article 6 of the Charter."[87] The threat of applying Article 6 to South Africa refers to expulsion from the organization, and clearly was not taken seriously by most permanent members of the Security Council.[88] It was a theme that, when later formulated into a policy by the OAU, was applied liberally to organizations outside the UN, but only occasionally heard within the General Assembly and the Security Council. It was derived, as a successful course of action, from the Commonwealth experience. With little debate, the draft resolution from the SPC was approved by the General Assembly in a vote of 67–16–23.[89]

The Special Committee on Apartheid was to become an essential weapon in the hands of the group trying to combat apartheid on the battlefield of the UN. Originally designed to be a watchdog body, the Special Committee appeared to lose its head of steam shortly after its formation, in the process of defining its goals and when it was challenged by the more powerful Group of Experts of the Security Council. Even in difficult times, however, it remained a useful focus of the scattered anti-apartheid forces, even some nongovernmental forces being brought into the fracas. In addition, it took the burden of the apartheid issue off the General Assembly and its regular committees, which was helpful to the General Assembly but, in a sense, also weakened the anti-apartheid movement by isolating it in a committee of its own. Before it developed into an active arm of the General Assembly in 1964, however, it did have a life of its own, and the results are remarkable in a number of ways.

At the first meeting of the committee in April 1963, the acknowledged leader was Diallo Telli of Guinea. Its initial mandate was to coordinate implementation of Resolution 1761, especially the provisions for boycotts and sanctions. The committee began this task by sending out questionnaires, and obtained replies from a majority of UN members, indicating to what degree they would comply with the resolution. A second important function at all times was the collection of testimony and views on apartheid from interested individuals and organizations. This broadening of access to the UN by petitioners was important in focusing outside attention on the General Assembly. Several international trade union groupings thus obtained an opportunity to indicate their solidarity with the campaign. The International Confederation of Free Trade Unions rightly pointed out that it had organized the first boycott of South African goods; the World Federation of Trade Unions (WFTU) also pledged its help,[90] serving as a clearinghouse for African views as well. Naturally all decisions of specialized agencies, such as the ILO and WHO, that were concurrently in the midst of crises over South Africa were communicated to the Special Committee. Other nongovernmental organizations, such as the World Council of Churches and the International Commission of Jurists, were occasional participants in the work of the Special Committee.

Expulsion as a tactic within the UN, however, was not yet dead, for the battle in ECOSOC had hardly begun. With the strong stand taken in the General Assembly in the fall of 1962, ECOSOC became the momentary center of attention. The ECA meeting in February–March 1963 went predictably, except for the introduction of one novel proposal. The expected resolution asked ECOSOC to reconsider its decision not to expel South Africa.[91] An additional resolution widened the gap between South Africa and the ECA:

> The Economic Commission for Africa. . . Invites all African states members of the Commission to take into consideration the policies of the Governments of South Africa and Portugal when granting to representatives of those two countries visas or entry permits for the purpose of enabling them to participate in the conferences or meeting of the Commission or of the specialized agencies, which may be organized in any African State member of the Commission.[92]

All meetings of the ECA, of course, were held in African countries, and thus South Africa was unable to participate, even if it had wanted to. This "undiplomatic" tactic was applied on a much broader scale thereafter.

The most important aspect to the Africans, however, was the symbolism of expelling South Africa, and so the battle in ECOSOC was crucial. Undermining the African case, however, was a letter received in the middle of July, in which ECOSOC was informed by South Africa that it "decided not to attend any ECA Conferences in the future nor to participate in the other activities of the Commission while the hostile attitude of the African States toward South Africa persists."[93] Discussion in ECOSOC began immediately, in an attempt to resolve the uncomfortable impasse.

Appointed as spokesman for the African group, Ethiopian representative Wakwaya made it clear at the start that the withdrawal of South Africa was not sufficient punishment for the crime; it must be expelled. Opposing him at the meeting, the British representative proposed a formal acceptance of the South African letter, and a joint United States–Argentinian resolution proposed "suspending South Africa from participation" rather than "expelling" it.[94] The Argentinian delegate argued that expulsion was too radical a step: "It was therefore much wiser to assume that South Africa had accidentally violated the United Nations Charter and would ultimately be reintegrated into the community of nations. . . ."[95] Of importance to his argument was the fact that the relevant guideline for action was not the recent action of the ILO, which had effectively ended South African participation, but rather Resolutions 1663 (XVI) and 1761 (XVII) of the General Assembly, which had made South Africa the object of penalties while retaining it inside the organization.[96] The merits of the argument were heeded less and less as the Asian, African, and Communist members lined up against the rest of the council. Some saw a possibility of compromise in preambular paragraph four of the African draft resolution, which read, "*Noting* further that new developments relating to the membership of the Republic of South Africa in the Economic Commission for Africa make reconsideration of the Council's decision necessary."[97] One member asked if "new developments" referred to South Africa's letter. No, replied Wakwaya, they referred to the progressive steps taken against South Africa at the ILO and the OAU Summit Conference at Addis Ababa, and the attacks in the Security Council. In the resulting votes, when all attempts at compromise had failed, the British and United States resolutions were defeated, and, in a vote of 6–6–6, the African resolution also failed to pass.[98]

When it became obvious that the Africans could not obtain all that they wanted, they left the task of framing a compromise resolution to the United States; this was accomplished by the end of July. Unobjectionable to nearly everybody, but arousing no enthusiasm, Resolution 974 (XXXVI) passed 6–2–10, with the Africans abstaining:

The Economic and Social Council

1. *Decides* to reconsider its decision on the recommendation of the Economic Commission for Africa in respect of the membership of the Republic of South Africa:

2. *Decides* that the Republic of South Africa shall not take part in the work of the Economic Commission for Africa until the Council, on the recommendation of the Economic Commission for Africa, shall find that conditions for constructive cooperation have been restored by a change in its racial policy.[99]

It is quite apparent that the Africans thus gained the substance of their quest, even if South Africa's suspension from the ECA was probationary, not permanent. The most remarkable, precedent-setting aspect of the resolution was the delegation to the ECA of authority to determine South Africa's fitness to rejoin the ECA. In a sense, ECOSOC decided that if the Africans wished to politicize the economic and social activities of the UN, then they would have greater responsibility for what happens. In this way, the ECA became responsible for determining South Africa's membership, an issue that had served merely to upset the subtle equilibrium of ECOSOC and its relationship with the ECA.

In the final resolution, too, all mention of other organs and organizations was eliminated, even references to General Assembly resolutions. This indicates the touchiness that the issue was causing in the UN, the specialized agencies, and beyond. The decision taken in ECOSOC was not to be quoted extensively at other meetings either, for it was a victory for no one, a solution that neither side would claim with pride.

What is most important about the ECOSOC-ECA dispute, however, is that a compromise solution was reached that satisfied the substance of both African and South African demands, without further exacerbating the conflict. This difficult position was reached by avoiding the broader question involved (the nature of apartheid), and concentrating on the specific problem at hand: the role of South Africa as a member of the ECA. This approach to conflict settlement, while effective, was a product of the rare, perfect balance of forces that existed in ECOSOC. Without the tie votes that forced such a solution, ECOSOC would undoubtedly have chosen another path, and it did so at a later date, when its composition had changed.

One can see in the transition from the Fifteenth Session to the Sixteenth, and then the Seventeenth, the gradual breakdown of any defense for South Africa, culminating with the institutionalization of the anti-apartheid forces in the Special Committee. The measures to be overseen by the new committee were among the most severe that can be directed against a member state by the General Assembly. Because of this, all that followed was, as far as South Africa was concerned, essentially harassment.[100] Most important to our treatment of this issue, however, the African states were able to take the initiative in the General Assembly on this issue; they then used that body to prod recalcitrant states and other international organizatons into action on the apartheid issue. Exactly how that happened we shall see, for up to 1962, it was basically a question of an attempt by the General Assembly and the Africans to establish some common view on the issue, through personal and institutional channels. That was done; the movement then became more widespread.

Other organizations were not yet heavily involved in the African-South African dispute. The Governing Body of the ILO, with no enthusiasm, had accepted the resolution addressed to South Africa by the International Labour Conference, but had not kept the question on its agenda. For the time being, organizatons outside the UN were showing little interest in the dispute between the Africans and South Africa.

Within the UN, the Africans looked beyond the General Assembly and ECOSOC to the Security Council, where the real power lay. On a broader scale, the Africans could see easy targets in the specialized agencies, where one country had one vote, giving them a solid bloc even before the debate began. Perhaps most importantly, however, the African diplomatic scene was reaching a maturity that would permit the formation of the Organization of African Unity, giving the anti-apartheid effort a new basis of public support as it fought South Africa on a broader front of international organizations.

3

OAU Momentum and the Retreat
of South Africa

The direction of the apartheid dispute in 1963–64 is notable for the role of the Organization of African Unity (OAU), formed in Addis Ababa, Ethiopia, in May 1963. The new organization was an important force affecting the apartheid issue in international organizations, but only as long as African diplomats remembered the spirit of Addis Ababa. Thus this period saw not only the most impressive successes of the anti-apartheid drive, but also the ebb and flow of OAU strength. As the Africans achieved success, and occasionally met failure, the lesson they learned was that only Africa could lead the fight against apartheid. This realization led, by the end of 1964, to a realignment of tactics: a de-emphasis of the sometimes unwieldy OAU in favor of institutionalizing the anti-apartheid effort in the UN.

International organizations were forced into a posture of reaction, in which the results only occasionally contributed to dampening the dispute. One frequent response, given the unwillingness of either side to compromise, was flat rejection of African demands—a move that could be sustained only in certain organizations not governed by the majority vote. This brutal form of socialization of the Africans eventually produced the desired results in some organizations, in the sense that violent disruptions of ongoing programs ceased.

During 1963–64 the South Africans showed little ability to deal imaginatively with the radicalized climate in which they were being pressured to withdraw from organization after organization. Such universal application of a diplomatic weapon had rarely been seen before, and certainly the South African government, which habitually responded slowly to international events, had a difficult time understanding the nature of its enemies. South Africa had not yet conceded the legitimacy of international concern with race problems in South Africa, and its response was generally to retreat in the face of diplomatic adversity, leaving the field to the enemy, while attempting to devise a counter-strategy. In this case, it meant withdrawal from a number of specialized agencies before it could be expelled, to avoid having to meet the arguments of the anti-apartheid forces. South Africa's psychological posture was still weak in the wake of the Sharpeville incident and the resulting outflow of Western capital. A more liberal wind, too, was blowing in the United States, fanned by the rhetoric of the Kennedy administration. South Africa, thus uncertain of Western attitudes toward continued Nationalist Party rule, took a passive attitude toward African attacks.

If the previous period of anti-apartheid activity, 1960–62, could be characterized as successful because of naïveté and good fortune in certain forums, the victories of 1963–64 were achieved through dynamic African leadership, diplomatic momentum from the OAU, and publicity about events in South Africa. One important lesson for the African states came from the coincidence of their greatest triumph and greatest disappointment. Most African statesmen had long hoped for a pan-African organization; once the OAU was formed, they found that to obtain a consensus, nearly all members had had to sacrifice some principles, and they were unable to police fellow members.[1] Out of this realization that the OAU's strong point would not be centrally enforced sanctions, the principal members chose to carry the struggle against apartheid to other groups.

With the advantage of hindsight, the degree of unity manifested at Addis Ababa in May 1963 on the apartheid issue seems remarkable. The South African racial policy was an issue on which African heads of state could fairly honestly agree, despite their fundamental disagreement on numerous other issues that imperiled the conference. In effect, apartheid represented a useful outside enemy for increasing internal African unity.

Without detracting from the large areas of agreement at the conference, it should be noted that some disharmony existed on the question of means of attacking South Africa. Proposals for combating apartheid were forthcoming in the preliminary Foreign Ministers' Conference: creation of a fund for the liberation of South Africa, coordination of economic sanctions by the OAU, support of recommendations of the Special Committee, dispatching of a delegation of foreign ministers to the Security Council, and appeals to national governments for aid.[2] Yet no one member felt strongly enough about any particular tactic to foment serious disagreement. Instead, most chroniclers of the OAU portray this initial meeting as a compromise between the radical Casablanca bloc and the conservative Union Africaine et Malgache (UAM). In this context, the policy on apartheid was designed so that "in exchange for the predominance of moderate theses on intra-African relations, the radicals obtained greater attention to the problems of colonial Africa, particularly the Portuguese territories and South Africa."[3] In May 1963 a Liberation Committee (also known as the Committee of Nine) was formed to coordinate the distribution of aid, men, and supplies in the "war for southern Africa." The Liberation Committee, however, becomes important only in a later context.

The resolution adopted by the Addis Ababa Conference, in fact, involved few responsibilities for the African members, but alluded to the UN a great deal. On the one hand, it supported and enthusiastically endorsed the recommendations of the Special Committee as well as the sanctions voted by the General Assembly in Resolution 1761 (XVII); on the other hand, the OAU decided "to despatch a delegation of Foreign Ministers to inform the Security Council of the explosive situation existing in South Africa."[4] As indicated above, this latter action was serious, in indicating the inability of the OAU to speak in coercive terms. The OAU could not fight South Africa on its own. It could lead the battle, and indeed would have to, as the rest of the world became less interested, but it needed the UN to supply the initiative to end apartheid. Thus it hoped to use the instrumentality of the Security Council to achieve the OAU goals in South Africa. The OAU also had plans to create a defense

commission, but in the chaos of African politics following
Addis Ababa, it did not even approach the vitality of the
moribund Military Staff Committee of the UN Security
Council.

The tactics actually used after the Addis Ababa meeting
were of only two types. In those organizations where no
provisions existed for sanctions (except for financial reasons), the OAU chose to press for expulsion. That group
included virtually all specialized agencies, and some UN
organs as well. These sanctions are described as "social"
because they sprang from the Africans' resentment at South
Africa's refusal to be socialized, i.e., to accept the General
Assembly definition of international good behavior. Indeed,
the sanctions, as voted by most specialized agencies, had
little economic or political effect, but merely banned South
Africa from public gatherings, affecting the appearance
rather than the substance of international relations.

The second group of tactics applied in the international
community appeared primarily in the UN, in the effort to
use Charter-provided sanctions to bring South Africa into
line. Because provisions for sanctions existed in Chapter VII
of the UN Charter, the OAU felt an obligation to ask for their
implementation, since it was clear, in any case, that South
Africa could not be expelled from the UN before other
methods of compliance were tested. In this spirit, the leaders
in Addis Ababa designated the foreign ministers of Liberia,
Tunisia, Malagasy Republic, and Sierra Leone to plead their
case before the Security Council and obtain whatever puni-
tive sanctions were possible. The Security Council sessions
began in July.

No longer was the African campaign at the UN to be the
independent effort of a few diplomats unchaperoned by their
foreign ministries. The African Group still existed, although its condition was doubtful after the liquidation of
the UAM machinery in New York. The foreign ministers
designated by the OAU infused some centralized direction
into the anti-apartheid effort.

For the Security Council, on the other hand, the mid–1963
apartheid dispute occurred in a much different climate from
that of the previous encounter in 1960. The General Assembly had recommended virtually to the limits of its powers,
even establishing a Special Committee on Apartheid. The

OAU was attracting attention for the African diplomatic stance in general. Thus the Security Council was ripe for being drawn into the maelstrom.

No one crisis, strangely enough, precipitated consideration of the issue by the Security Council. The Africans simply decided that the general atmosphere was propitious for a confrontation, and sent a letter to that effect to the Security Council president.[5] It was clear on whose behalf the subject was brought to the Security Council, as Dr. John Karefa-Smart of Sierra Leone opened the debate:

> The Heads of African States and Governments who met in Addis Ababa from 22 May to 25 May 1963, were very much concerned over the policies of apartheid. . . . They gave instructions to their Permanent Representatives to the United Nations to request that the Security Council be convened urgently to consider the explosive situation which exists on the African continent as long as South Africa adheres to the policy of apartheid.[6]

Equally stimulating to the African governments was the work of the Special Committee on Apartheid, whose reports were sent to the Security Council and circulated among its members.[7] The speakers, in fact, spent little time rejecting the South African position regarding Article 2(7); it was regarded as an ineffective argument by all, since the Security Council had previously dealt with the question. The general thrust, instead, was one of documenting the intensity of the crisis in South Africa and the threat from South Africa to the independent African states. For this reason, supporting evidence from the Special Committee, the OAU, and specialized agencies was of importance. The investigative powers of the General Assembly, as implemented in Resolution 1761 (XVII), ultimately had an effect on the functioning of the Security Council; the accumulation of evidence by the Special Committee could not be dismissed out of hand.

The Security Council was not convened merely to berate South Africa; the African states wanted mandatory implementation of the recommendations in the General Assembly resolutions and the expulsion of South Africa from "the comity of nations," as had recently been accomplished by the ILO.[8] Quaison-Sackey argued that no harm would be done to the organization if South Africa withdrew, citing the Commonwealth and the temporary withdrawal of South Africa from the Eleventh Session of the General Assembly. Implicit in the proposals of the Africans was a threat that the Africans could no longer compromise. As Mongi Slim later reported to the OAU foreign ministers:

> I assure you, Mr. President, that we needed to bring forth all our arguments and all the pressure we could, making full use of the psychological fact that thirty-two African States, all the African States, were appealing to the Security Council. All our Latin American, Asian, and Filipino friends were considerably impressed by this.[9]

The Philippines had been represented on the Council and the Special Committee, and therefore felt strongly about the issue at the moment.

Enthusiasm for the African cause was not universal around the horseshoe-shaped table. As the Africans later lamented:

> When Africans were pleading a cause so close to them, the United States Government, the Government of the United Kingdom, and the Government of France all openly showed a kind of disdain for 32 African States. . . .
>
> Similarly, the Government of the USA considered NATO of such great importance to them that they said quite openly that if it came to a vote, their alliance with NATO was of much more importance to them than their friendship with Africa.[10]

Adlai Stevenson of the United States was somewhat less explicit in his public statements, maintaining that "the founders of the United Nations were very careful to reserve the right of the Organization to employ mandatory coercive measures," as found in Chapter VII, in "situations where there was an actuality of international violence or such a clear and present threat to the peace as to leave no reasonable alternative but resort to coercion."[11] Clearly, the disagreement in the council was as to whether any reasonable alternative existed; the Africans saw none. Nevertheless, it was obvious that the African demands would have to be tailored to the feelings of the states with veto power.

One issue that all could agree upon was the rapid buildup of arms in South Africa, and what it might imply for black Africans if they were to respond. The United States had unilaterally announced the cessation of military shipments to South Africa, and it was unlikely that either France or Britain could publicly dissent from an arms ban. Building on that slim consensus, Quaison-Sackey of Ghana submitted a draft resolution, "the first step to be taken by the Security Council in the hope that by 30 October we would have seen a change in the attitude of the Government of South Africa."[12] The key provisions included:

> *Being convinced* that the situation in South Africa is seriously disturbing international peace and security, . . .

> 3. *Calls upon* all States to boycott all South African goods and to refrain from exporting to South Africa strategic materials of direct military value;

> 4. *Solemnly calls upon* all States to cease forthwith the sale and shipment of arms, ammunition of all types and military vehicles to South Africa;

> 5. *Requests* the Secretary-General to keep the situation in South Africa under observation and to report to the Security Council by 30 October 1963.[13]

Quaison-Sackey quickly pointed out that paragraph five was not meant to undercut the Special Committee. In fact, he *wanted* duplication of effort, hoping to keep both the Security Council and the General Assembly concerned about the question.

Any possible controversy over the preambular paragraph had been settled out in the corridors before its submission. The Africans obviously wanted to label South Africa a "threat" to the peace (Chapter VII), but had to settle for a "disturber" of the peace, at the insistence of the Western powers. Paragraphs four and five engendered no outright opposition from other members, but paragraph three involved too big a step for a majority of the council. When voted on separately, it was not adopted, receiving only five affirmative votes (Ghana, Morocco, Philippines, USSR, and Venezuela), with the others abstaining.[14] When the rest of the resolution passed easily, the Africans consoled themselves with having achieved a suspension of some military sales to South Africa and, perhaps more important in the long run, having involved at least one person in the Secretariat on a full-time basis.

During the traditional explanation of votes, much was said by the Africans about the failure of operative paragraph three, indicating that the OAU would still continue its economic boycott. It was thus somewhat ironic when, at the OAU Foreign Ministers' meeting a few days later, Karefa-Smart of Sierra Leone made clear one of the principal problems:

> We tried of course to go further and to obtain a decision from the Security Council stipulating measures of an economic nature against South Africa. . . . We felt that certain countries seemed to be hinting to us that, before making such a request to the Council, we ought to make sure none of the African countries had any interests in or economic relations with South Africa.[15]

In the end, the OAU, which wanted to apply economic sanctions, was unable to do so; at the same time, the Security Council was unwilling to adopt the sanctions it had the power to invoke.

This session of the Security Council was, in a sense, only temporarily adjourned. By giving the secretary-general a mandate to report back to the council on progress concerning the resolution's implementation, the African states hoped to involve the Security Council in the anti-apartheid cause once again in the near future.

The OAU during its first year experienced growing disunity on internal questions, and needed a notable success on external questions to provide cohesion. The OAU's internal problems derived, by and large, from serious differences between members over the means and pace of achieving African unity. The issue of apartheid, on the other hand, provided a respite from disunity in the meetings up to 1965, except for minor differences, and thus gave a hopeful, but somewhat distorted, view of the OAU in general. Out of 125 resolutions passed by the OAU during the 1963–65, 33 dealt with southern African affairs and 16 with UN matters, which is indicative of which subjects provided areas of agreement.[16]

The lessons learned by the OAU from the campaigns of May–August 1963 were few, for it was time of exploration. How much success could they achieve simply through boldness? Clearly it would take more to overturn apartheid, as the foreign ministers realized when they compared notes at the August 1963 OAU meeting in Dakar. Because there had been some successes, however, the gathering was a time for boasting. The OAU Secretary-General's report summarized the steps taken unilaterally by African states, as well as progress in international forums such as the ILO and ECOSOC. On the question of South African membership in the ECA, the report states: "No doubt equal and even more success can be expected in the fight against apartheid in South Africa."[17] It was also an occasion for setting new goals; the Tanganyikan delegate demanded more:

> Are we satisfied with just that? Can we direct our activities towards trying to arouse the people living in those countries to struggle for themselves . . . ? We are bound to enlist the help of all those nations which are now considered powerful and which profess to side with us in our cause. . . .[18]

The highlight, however, was the arrival in Dakar of the African delegates to the Security Council meeting (just completed), who made their reports to the OAU. In this way, one begins to see the close interrelationship, in African eyes, of the two organizations. The case had been taken to the Security Council by Tunisia and Liberia, not for themselves, but for the OAU. In general, the Africans were dissatisfied with the lack of progress in the Security Council, both in defining the problem and in taking action; witness the remarks of the delegate from Liberia:

> One particularly important fact of which we have been conscious is that the Security Council has not resolutely committed itself to examine and take charge of the situation in South Africa.[19]

> I must tell you that the USA made some difficulty with regard

to the course to be followed in chapter 7 as well as in chapter 6 of the Charter.[20]

Right from the beginning, the Western Press did everything either to cause disunity among the African countries or to minimize the importance of what we were charged by the African Heads of State to bring to the Security Council.[21]

Perhaps most depressing of all was the apparent futility of the action finally taken:

In addition to that, the Americans and Britons have openly told us, whatever the report of the Secretary-General will be in October, that they will not change their position and that their economic links with South Africa are much more important to them than our condemnation of the policy of apartheid.[22]

The African drive against South Africa was, however, only temporarily blunted.

One point of disunity relevant to the effort at the UN, and not mentioned at the OAU meeting, was the dispersal of the UAM machinery in New York. Its well-staffed secretariat was formally transferred to the OAU, despite misgivings on the part of the Ivory Coast and Madagascar.[23] The effort to utilize UAM personnel for the new African caucus, however, broke down before long as a result of their policy differences with the OAU Secretariat, and certain longstanding difficulties: language barriers, procedural disagreements, personal antipathies (such as that between Achkar Marof of Guinea and Arsène Usher of Ivory Coast), and, eventually, the formation of the Organization Commune d'Afrique et Malgache.[24] The long-term result of the breakdown was a more direct link between the OAU and the UN, since the intermediary caucus was ineffectual on many issues. In this situation, the OAU's policy on apartheid may have had a greater effect, being implemented in the UN in a manner unfiltered by the caucus at the UN.

The actual impact of the OAU Foreign Minister's meeting in August was not important in terms of policy design. There was little planning undertaken for the fall meeting of the Security Council that the Africans planned to call as soon as the secretary-general released his report. They still had the unfulfilled goals of the previous meeting (economic sanctions), and planned simply to press for their adoption. The foreign ministers did not plan to send a formal delegation, expecting the permanent delegations to enter the ring for the next round.

On another level, however, the OAU had more ambitious plans. In the General Assembly, the OAU heads of state wanted to make their presence felt in the fall session, and hoped for a universal condemnation of apartheid. As a result, the General Assembly temporarily assumed greater importance in the OAU's planning.

The Eighteenth Session of the General Assembly was a watershed for the apartheid issue. In one sense it was the moment of most intense concern on the part of the members, as measured by the number of meetings dealing with apartheid.[25] Another way of viewing the 1963 session is as the moment when the General Assembly left the realm of the possible, and began legislating measures that many members had no intention of carrying out. However one views it, this was a time of virtual unanimity on a mandate, but discord on the implementation of that mandate.

The normal proceedings of the Special Political Committee (SPC), which was being guided by the Special Committee on Apartheid and by the policy of the OAU, and the General Assembly were interrupted by the so-called treason trials in South Africa that caused almost as much indignation as the Sharpeville shootings of 1960. As the trials were proceeding posthaste, and sentencing was imminent, the African bloc pushed through a resolution that requested South Africa "to abandon the arbitrary trial now in progress and forthwith to grant unconditional release to all political prisoners and to all other persons imprisoned, interned or subjected to other restrictions for having opposed the policy of apartheid."[26] The lopsidedness of the 106–1 vote was the significant factor; for the first time in General Assembly history, South Africa was absolutely isolated.[27] The Africans were delighted; form had triumphed over substance, and the South Africans, although unaffected and unchastened, had been soundly defeated in the Assembly Hall.[28]

The General Assembly had clearly been the object of a prolonged and intensive campaign before that symbolic near-unanimity was attained. The Africans felt that it signaled a new trend in UN voting. For the Eighteenth Session, the OAU had mobilized all the political power at its disposal, and thirty-two African heads of state planned to attend.[29] This power was directed, however, not to obtaining effectiveness, but to obtaining a formal consensus, a general commitment to the view that South Africa's stand was immoral. In this way, the OAU provided a misleading model for the Africans, for there too the Africans had tended to accept the rhetoric of unity without the substance, assuming that the practical mechanisms of unity would automatically follow. Therefore, the Africans had scarcely received their near-unanimous vote in the UN General Assembly when they were reminded that only the Security Council could possibly provide them with the force to back up the intentions of the General Assembly. This came about when Guinea departed from OAU policy to urge South Africa's expulsion from the UN, a step heretofore prescribed primarily outside the UN. Expulsion, of course, could only be accomplished on the recommendation of the Security Council, but Guinea wished to apply pressure by having the General Assembly invalidate the credentials of the South African delegates.[30] It was not done, and Guinea had to be satisfied with making a reservation to the report of the Credentials Committee.[31]

As the major product of agenda item 30 on apartheid, the SPC recommended two resolutions to the General Assembly, both introduced by the Afro-Asian grouping. The first resolution indicated that the initiative had moved to the Security Council, on the one hand, and the Special Committee on Apartheid, on the other.[32] It urged full compliance with the sanction measures voted by the Security Council on December 4, 1963, and asked the Special Committee to "continue to follow the various aspects of this question constantly." Of a more subtle nature was Resolution 1978B (XVIII). It called upon the secretary-general "to seek ways and means of providing relief and assistance, through the various international agencies, to the families of all persons persecuted by the Government of the Republic of South Africa for their opposition to the policies of apartheid," and asked all member states to contribute generously.[33] Not only did this resolution involve the secretary-general in the anti-apartheid fight to a greater degree, but it also created another continuing body that could apply pressure. It later received the blessing of the General Assembly in 1965 as the permanent UN Trust Fund for South Africa. The fund became a center for coordinating and centralizing the disbursement of funds for the education and welfare of South African exiles.

The entire Eighteenth Session was shaken by the tremors in other organizations. The crisis of the ILO in the summer of 1963 was especially troubling,[34] as many Africans made public their feeling that South Africa should be banned from all organizations. One could not be certain that the Great Powers, in their rush to curry favor with the young African states, would not agree to expel South Africa from the UN, thereby reversing its long-term trend towards universality. Even more ominous to the nations that were dedicated to "peaceful change" was the new tone of the rhetoric coming out of African and Afro-Asian regional organizations. In February 1963, for example, the Afro-Asian Peoples' Solidarity Organization called for the use of violence in southern Africa.[35] The OAU sanctioned violence when it established the Committee of Liberation.[36] The members of the General Assembly could not at that point predict the future ineffectiveness of that committee, and felt that they might be called upon at any moment to lend assistance to the guerrilla struggle in southern Africa. The trend was disturbing to many, as confrontation took center stage.

By September 1963, the Special Committee had accumulated an enormous mass of information, testimony, and opinion that was boiled down to a report to the General Assembly running somewhat more than 200 pages.[37] The report indicated how literally the committee interpreted its mandate to watch over the internal situation in South Africa. At that time South Africa was at the boiling point, thanks to the heavyhanded implementation of various treason laws, and so the question of the actions of other organizations took second place to developments in South Africa itself. Within a short time, however, the Special Committee began to play an active role in the moves against South Africa, submitting a report on trade patterns in late 1964, and sending a delegation to the nongovernmental International Conference on Economic Sanctions held in London in April 1964.

The relationship of the Special Committee with the

Security Council remained somewhat ambiguous, perhaps because the two groups did not agree on the proper course to be taken in the dispute. In its original mandate, the Special Committee was instructed to submit its reports to both the General Assembly and the Security Council. It did so religiously. As the General Assembly quickly reached the limit of its effective powers, however, the Security Council became the focus for the Special Committee's demands for action. As Haiti pointed out during preparation of the March 1964 report, the committee's language was becoming "somewhat peremptory and should be made more moderate." The Haitian representative went on to say that "the Committee must be careful not to give the impression that it was attempting to dictate to the Security Council."[38] Haiti was clearly in a minority of one, however, as Guinea's Diallo Telli insisted that the wording was already a compromise that many states regarded as too weak. Most members, therefore, saw the Special Committee as a prod for further action by the Security Council.[39]

The Africans were concerned when the Security Council created the Group of Experts in late 1963. They feared that the group, headed by Alva Myrdal of Sweden, would undercut the role of the Special Committee. This apprehension was brought up in the Special Committee, for instance, in connection with a letter from the Special Committee to the Organization of Petroleum Exporting Countries. Carlet Auguste of Haiti, the perennial dissenter, suggested that it might be best to let the Group of Experts monopolize discussion of oil boycotts. Diallo Telli asserted that "no aspect of the matter was outside its competence [the Special Committee's]" and was roundly supported by the committee.[40] The issue was not raised again. It came as a pleasant surprise, therefore, when the Group of Experts issued its report in late 1964 and it was not a whitewash.

The Security Council discussion at the end of 1963 did not depart markedly from the pattern set in the July meetings. There was a continuing effort by the Africans to include Chapter VII language in Resolution 182 (again unsuccessful), but in general they did not attempt to create a crisis atmosphere. Treatment of the issue was leisurely, with meetings held on November 27 and 29, and December 2–4.[41] References to the dedication of OAU members were becoming increasingly ritualistic at this time, as that organizaton was clearly having trouble with the implementation of sanctions by its own members. There was, instead, a greater tendency to speak of apartheid as a UN problem that would have to be solved by UN organs. The Africans recognized that both GA Resolution 1761 (XVII) and Security Council Resolution 181 of August 7, 1963, had failed. The African rationale for further UN action then became the fact that "the United Nations cannot allow itself to be openly flouted [by the South African Government] in this way."[42]

The points of departure for these meetings of the council were ostensibly the reports of the secretary-general regarding implementation of the earlier Security Council resolutions. These reports began appearing in October, and the African states requested the meeting on October 23. It is quite interesting to review the Security Council action on the apartheid issue, since it obviously did not fall within the realm of its "fire brigade" function as envisaged by President Roosevelt. Instead, it is as if the Security Council, in response to complaints that the wiring in the house was a fire hazard, took its time in investigating, since it could see no flames, and the question of when the wiring would actually start a fire was obviously a matter of opinion. For this reason, the Security Council meetings on apartheid had a somewhat restrained atmosphere; the Africans could not cite open conflict, since some of the violence in South Africa had been abetted by them. On the other hand, the non-Africans hated to see the Security Council involved in situations of internal tension, especially after the chastening experience of the Congo.

There was never any quarrel about the constitutional right of the Security Council to investigate the apartheid dispute. Under Chapter VI of the Charter, after all, the council can examine any "situation" that might lead to international violence. The primary difference between the Africans and the Western states, when it came to problem definition, appeared when the Africans demanded consideration of the issue under Chapter VII, which assumed the existence of a "threat to the peace," and opened the possibility of mandatory sanctions. The question of defining the situation, then, became the first and most important step in the familiar scenarios of examining the apartheid conflict.

The solution chosen by the majority of the Security Council in this case was framed by the Norwegian delegation in a draft resolution that was later adopted.[43] In most areas it hardly went beyond the measures of July 1963. In addition to banning the shipment of arms to South Africa, it prohibited the sale of equipment for manufacturing arms. That measure, considering the advanced state of the machine tool art in South Africa, was more a statement of principle than a practical political measure. The Security Council repeated its request to the secretary-general to keep the situation under observation. What the Norwegians proposed, however, was the device chosen by most organizations faced by an unpleasant decision: creation of another committee. The structure would be somewhat different—a committee of experts—but the purpose would be essentially the same, "to examine methods of resolving the present situation in South Africa through full, peaceful, and orderly application of human rights. . . ."[44]

The Africans were not entirely happy about the Group of Experts, as was pointed out at the subsequent meeting of the OAU Council of Ministers: "We said we would not accept the setting up of this Committee . . . [although] we finally accepted the setting up of this Committee for tactical reasons."[45] The Africans objected to it as a delaying tactic; they had a plan to end apartheid, and simply needed the Security Council to enforce it. As Benhima of Morocco insisted, "The existence of the group of experts must not be used as a procedural argument for delaying or preventing such a meeting [of the Security Council]."[46] A second fear of the Africans was that they would not control the Group of Experts as they did the Special Committee of the General Assembly. Quaison-Sackey was quite blunt:

> What is more, we fear that any agreement on our part to a special group of experts would commit us in large measure. Supposing the group advocated the partition of South Africa—which we all oppose—what, then, would the position of African states be in regard to such a recommendation?[47]

Directly related to this difficult problem was the fact that many saw the proposed Group of Experts as competing with the African-controlled Special Committee. In a sense, they feared that the Security Council, controlled by the great powers, might try to suppress the issue by consigning it to a committee that would make the Special Committee appear redundant, and that might then do nothing to implement measures against South Africa. These fears turned out to be false, as we have already seen, but were worrisome at the time, when the African states felt they finally had South Africa on the run.

The moderate and conservative states from the Western bloc in the Security Council tried to allay the fears of the Africans, for the disagreement was not over goals, but over the means to be employed. Sir Partick Dean of Britain attempted to be conciliatory, taking note of the overwhelming sentiment of the General Assembly expressed in Resolution 1881 (XVIII) of October 11, 1963.[48] At the same time, the basic disagreement between the two groups was clear:

> We have to proceed now, recognizing that the situation in South Africa still does not constitute a threat to the peace, a breach of the peace or an act of agression within the meaning of Chapter VII of the Charter. In that respect the situation is unchanged since last August.[49]

This position was supported, of course, by France and the United States.

The debate closed in a show of harmony despite the obvious disagreements among factions. Ghana, which had asked for a separate vote on the paragraph concerning the Group of Experts, agreed to withdraw its request in exchange for Dean's withdrawal of a reservation regarding implementation of the previous resolution of the Security Council. In this way, the Security Council passed the resolution unanimously, traditionally a point of importance to the African states.[50]

Disappointment in the progress of the Security Council was pervasive among the Africans following the meeting. They had no faith in the Group of Experts, and they knew that the question of sanctions represented only a small step in the right direction. One hopeful note constantly cited by African representatives was the introduction of the resolution by a European power, Norway. They thought it indicated that a non-African state had finally committed itself to the anti-apartheid drive.[51] But the Africans missed the point of the Norwegian intervention. What motivated the Norwegians in this case was a real concern for the future of the Security Council and the UN in general. The confrontations resulting from African draft resolutions had not helped the UN at all, and been damaging to the functioning of the Security Council, which relied to a large degree upon consensus. Thus it becomes clearer why Norway applied so much pressure on Ghana, the USSR, and Britain to withdraw their requests for separate votes; the resolution designed by Norway was a finely honed attempt to control the conflict, and it could not have been successful if any operative paragraph had been eliminated. In this way, the politics of gradualism became involved in the apartheid issue.

African Drive for Social Sanctions

Beyond the confines of the UN, the OAU Summit Conference at Addis Ababa was having an impact on the specialized agencies. The 1963 Conference of the ILO began shortly after the OAU Summit Conference, and the effect of increased African coordination was clear: the 1963 ILO Conference was a shambles.[52] Not only did the Africans demand the withdrawal of the South Africans, but they also refused to participate in the conference until the Governing Body took some action. The tenth sitting, on Wednesday afternoon, dissolved in pandemonium when the Africans asked the president to eject employer delegate Hamilton of South Africa. The point was that he was next on the speakers' list, and the Africans did not even want him to approach the rostrum to withdraw his name from the list. When nothing could be accomplished, the adjournment motion for the day was finally made by Mali.[53] By Friday morning, most parties thought they had arrived at a compromise, and so the eleventh sitting commenced. Nigeria immediately moved that South Africa be removed from the speakers' list: "Here is a government which has been condemned not only by us but by the United Nations and other international bodies."[54] The president, nevertheless, ruled that South Africa could speak, whereupon all the African delegates, Arab delegates, and worker delegates walked out. After the South African speech, all plenary sessions were suspended, as those who had walked out were not willing to rejoin the meeting.[55]

Director-General David Morse attempted to take control at this point, urging the African bloc to submit resolutions that would condemn apartheid, and seize the UN of the problem. He hoped in this way to obtain a definitive ruling from the Security Council as to South Africa's fitness to remain in the UN family.[56] The Africans, however, voted in their caucus not to shift responsibility away from the ILO.

Little more business was accomplished, and yet the meetings that were held revealed a great deal about the functioning of the ILO in political disputes. In a letter to Morse, and at a meeting of all the delegations the following Tuesday, J. M. Johnson, the government representative from Nigeria, submitted his resignation as president of the conference, to protest the continued presence of South Africa. Speaking for all the Africans, he expressed total disillusionment with the organization, indicating that the African group would abstain from further participation.[57] The accusations he directed against the ILO, however, seemed mild by comparison with the statement of Director-General Morse, who stood up to answer Johnson and the African bloc as a whole. He accused them of deceit, dishonesty, and a total lack of good faith in dealing with the Secretariat.[58]

The Africans had been caucusing all weekend, and had refused to discuss their views with Morse, who was attempting to mediate a solution. He was especially concerned about the misinterpretation of the fact that the South African had been allowed to speak; apparently a meeting of the conference officers had concluded that the South African should speak, and no one had dissented. Yet Johnson took great offense that his name had been associated with the decision. He explained later why he had not objected at the time to allowing the South African to speak: "I knew that a lone dissenting voice would have no effect at these meetings, so I kept my peace, and if silence meant consent, I was guilty of that."[59] There was, in any case, a total breakdown of communication and trust by the end of the session. Everybody was stunned by the crisis in the organizaton, and yet no easy solution presented itself, since the ILO constitution had no provision for expulsion.

Taking the initiative into his own hands, Morse drew up some possible plans of action which were approved shortly thereafter by the Governing Body.[60] As he clearly pointed out, the governing principle of the ILO in the past had been that, "as an organization at the service of all its members, [the ILO] should remain aloof from political controversy in the United Nations and other international organizations between nations or groups of nations. . . ." Indeed, he felt that this principle remained valid except in the case of apartheid, which had "stirred such universal reprobation in the International Labour Conference that it has become both possible and necessary for the ILO to give vigorous expression to the general attitude of the Conference. . . ."[61] He foresaw, for instance, complete cooperation with the Special Committee on Apartheid in the General Assembly as a means of implementing this policy.

Needless to say, the Governing Body took up the controversy at the first opportunity (late June 1963), and became involved in prolonged debate over Morse's proposals. In the relative calm of that body, the African and Arab delegates continued to press for the immediate expulsion of South Africa. Akrouf, as the spokesman, maintained that "it had never been the intention of the Arab and African delegations to destroy the ILO in protest against the Republic of South Africa," and yet expulsion was the only course of action.[62] Indeed, if necessary, the ILO should ensure that the Security Council was seized of the proposal for expulsion. An additional argument often heard was that the ILO was obliged to help implement General Assembly Resolution 1761 (XVII).[63]

There was strong opposition to the proposed expulsion. Italy's Robert Ago, a professor of international law at Rome University, pointed out that it was simply not constitutionally possible to expel South Africa. As he saw it, there were only three possibilities: not invite South Africa to any ILO meetings, amend the constitution to allow expulsion, or ask the International Court of Justice for an opinion.[64] Alexandre Parodi, the French government representative, answered Akrouf's suggestion concerning the Security Council: the ILO could not seize it of the matter, for the ILO had no standing before it. He suggested that the UN Secretary-General might be able to aid them in that respect.[65]

The possibilities for legitimate action were thus quickly narrowed down, with the Africans, as usual, being restrained by the constitutional stance of the Western states. In the first resolution, the Governing Body decided that South Africa would no longer be invited to ILO meetings where membership was determined by the Governing Body. It also asked the director-general to offer the International Court of Justice all possible help in the South West African cases then pending before the court. Resolution II was principally concerned with the relationship of the ILO with the UN, and urged close consultation with the secretary-general:

(ii) bearing in mind the close relationship that exists between membership of the United Nations and that of the International Labour Organization, to emphasize, and jointly seek a solution appropriate to each organization of, the problems posed by the membership of the Republic of South Africa so long as it continues to maintain its present policy.[66]

Despite the definitive tone of these resolutions of June 1963, the battle had hardly begun. The Africans wanted *de jure* expulsion of South Africa as well as *de facto* withdrawal. Harsher words were exchanged at the November meeting of the Governing Body. A special mission authorized by the Governing Body in June had accomplished little in consultations with the UN Secretary-General. The patience of some delegates was wearing thin as they waited for the UN to act, as exemplified by the speech of Diarra, Minister of Labor for Mali, and spokesman for the African group in the Governing Body:

But if we have to choose between the I.L.O. and human dignity, we shall choose the latter.[67]

This [that no member of the UN introduced a motion to expel South Africa] meant that some governments had two policies—one for the United Nations and one for the I.L.O. Such a situation was quite inadmissible.[68]

The Indian delegate pointed out that Britain was pledged to veto any effort to expel South Africa from the UN; as a result, the ILO had a choice of harmony with the UN or expulsion of South Africa. The point was that no solution yet existed to satisfy a significant majority, and invocation of UN authority could help to delay consideration of the matter.

Action in the ILO was formally delayed until early 1964,[69] but the Africans were already beginning to see some of the hurdles their plan for social sanctions would have to clear. The greatest procedural problem was that the secretariats of most specialized agencies were controlled by Western Europeans; they were also committed to the concept of universality of international organizatons, prompting them to obstruct any effort to expel South Africa. In a matter of greater substance, however, the Africans realized that taking the question of South Africa to the Security Council did not merely involve the ILO, but brought into question the entire ILO-UN relationship. That link was inserted into the question for tactical reasons, but for whatever reason it was introduced, once activated, it became a live issue. The Africans were initially in favor of strengthening the ILO-UN ties, so that the ILO would be able to pressure the Security Council for action. When they realized that those ties were being used against their cause, they quickly moved to reassert the independence of the ILO. In other organizations, however, the Africans were careful not to unsheath the weapon of the UN relationship, for it was indeed a two-edged sword.

For those attempting to find a temporary solution for the apartheid conflict, the ILO episode demonstrated the difficulty they would have in reaching a compromise with the Africans. When South Africa was suspended from future meetings, the Africans demanded formal expulsion. In a sense, the Africans were trapped by their group formation of tactics. The use of caucuses at the ILO assemblies in 1963 imposed a rigidity on the African stance that eliminated public compromise. The bloc of African votes at any international gathering was significant, and other organizations would have to deal with it.

The problem of South Africa's role in the World Health Organization (WHO) began before the adrenalin provided by the OAU Summit Conference, but the crucial action took place in May 1963 and early 1964. It was something of a shock for the WHO leadership to be faced by a crisis over South African membership, because the organization had a history of avoiding political issues. When the Middle East had been transformed politically in the late 1940s into an area of permanent hostility, WHO simply dissolved the administration of the Eastern Mediterranean Region, expressing the hope that more competent organizations would settle the political questions of the area.[70]

For WHO, the apartheid issue gave no warning of its explosiveness; South Africa was a respected supplier of dues and technical knowledge in a field highly relevant to all of Africa. In the fall of 1962, however, there was a wildfire quality to the issue that engulfed even WHO. The WHO Regional Committee for Africa had a meeting scheduled in Dakar, but the Senegalese government refused to give a visa to the South African representative. This forced a change of venue to Geneva, but the Africans were not happy, and asked for some guidance from the World Health Assembly (WHA) for future steps.[71] The initial solution proposed appeared quite feasible, that is, to continue meeting in Geneva or to choose some African capital, such as Brazzaville, that was not so arbitrary in its visa policy. South Africa even offered to build a $200,000 headquarters for the committee on its territory in January 1963, but the offer was not encouraged.[72] In any case, the WHA meeting in May 1963 disposed of the issue surprisingly calmly, using working parties that proposed no real solution. They simply called attention to General Assembly Resolution 1761, urged South Africa to renounce apartheid, and asked for no further impediments to "the effective functioning of the African regional organization."[73] The greatest concern in the meeting seemed to be that implementation of Resolution 1761 might interrupt the flow of medicines and drugs to South Africa. Senegal carried the flag for the African troops, trying to maintain that "certainly, WHO was a technical organization, but certain conditions had to be fulfilled before it could achieve its technical aims."[74] But even the Africans could not achieve a united front; the OAU Summit Conference was occurring at exactly the same time in Addis Ababa.

Following the events of the OAU in May 1963, and the succeeding turmoil at the UN that fall, the spillover of militancy to WHO increased. There was a contagious enthusiasm in the African diplomatic corps that flowed from other successes. Their drive to be the first in expelling South Africa

merely increased the degree of militancy. And nowhere did
that become stronger than in all-African organizations that
could not function without their black African members.
The fall meeting in Geneva of the WHO Regional Committee for Africa was a shambles; every black African nation
boycotted it following a confrontation between the Africans
(led by Dr. Somme-Dolo of Mali) and Britain, France, and
South Africa. The WHO Director-General attempted to heal
the rift, but the meeting adjourned *sine die* on September
24.[75] The organization was on the verge of total ineffectiveness in the African region, and the parent group was bound
to be affected, too.

Even organizations with almost no public visibility were
affected. The UN Regional Cartographic Conference for
Africa opened in Nairobi on July 1, 1963, and lasted for
nearly two weeks, with the delegates engrossed in discussions of the problems of producing reliable maps of Africa.
Although nearly all African countries and colonial authorities sent representatives, there was none from South Africa. It
later came to light, although it was not publicized at the
time, that the Kenyan government (not yet independent) had
declared any South African representatives to be "prohibited
immigrants."[76] In other words, they would receive no visas if
they arrived at Nairobi Airport, a tactic inspired by the ECA
and OAU Addis Ababa Summit Conference.

The UNESCO-sponsored International Conference on
Education, holding its conference in Geneva from July 1,
1963, onward, bowed to the pressure and decided not to
invite South Africa to the meeting. That move did not
remove political problems from the conference. The African
delegates then demanded that Portugal leave the conference;
with a majority vote, Portugal was ejected.[77]

In organizations of both major and minor importance, the
effort to implement social sanctions against South Africa
continued. In technical conferences with almost no previous
public visibility, the Africans asked for expulsion of South
Africa: the UN Conference on International Travel and
Tourism, establised by ECOSOC in Resolutions 813 (XXXI)
and 870 (XXXIII), opened in Rome in August 1963 with a
challenge and was constantly punctuated by pandemonium.

Fifteen African nations submitted a resolution on August
26 that would have excluded the South African delegation

from the conference. Conference President Alberto Folchi of Italy saw no merit in the motion, since he was presiding over a technical, not a political, conference, and ruled it out of order. He made it quite clear, with the backing of Secretary-General U Thant, that the membership of conferences was determined by ECOSOC, not the conferences themselves.

As might be expected, parliamentary order rapidly dissolved into disorder. Delegates shouted at one another, there were innumerable unsuccessful calls for adjournment, and the assembly hall reverberated with cries of "point of order!" To add to the general confusion, whenever the South African delegate tried to speak, the Africans all left the hall. After two days of disorder and corridor conferences, the assemblage finally passed a resolution (38–25–9), deeming the presence of the South African delegate undesirable and inviting him to leave.[78] Somewhat surprisingly, the South African did not accept the invitation, and on August 29 he rose to make a point: "The floor was given to the South African delegate, but his voice was drowned by the continuous banging of desks which ceased only when he had finished his statement. . . . The South African delegate did not speak again."[79]

In a similarly small, but illustrative incident, the International Union for Conservation of Nature and General Resources Conference discovered at its September 1963 meeting in Nairobi that the South African delegates had failed to appear. It was a surprise in view of the important role South Africa had played in the organization in previous years. On inquiry, it turned out that the Kenyan government, in its host role, had once again chosen not to give the South African delegates visas.[80]

For a major specialized agency of the UN, the Food and Agriculture Organization (FAO) handled the apartheid issue with skill and dispatch. It suffered little impairment of functions despite attempts by various members to introduce confrontation tactics.

A few months previous to the 12th session of the FAO Conference in late 1963, Ghana proposed an amendment to Article II of the FAO Constitution that would provide for exclusion of a member by a vote of two-thirds of the conference. This suggested amendment was considered by Commission III of the conference in late November, when some familiar disagreements appeared. Several Western European

states and the United States posed an alteration in the
wording which would have allowed exclusion "only if they
[the proposed expellees] have already been excluded from the
United Nations Organization."[81] The argument followed
the lines of the ILO discussions. Ghana and a majority of the
commission refused to water down the amendment, however, and so it went to the plenary session of the conference
with an endorsing vote of 52-28-2. For a constitutional
amendment to be adopted, as in most bodies, a two-thirds
majority is required by the FAO, and by the time the
amendment was presented, enough votes had been changed
(47-36-11) to ensure a solid defeat without discussion.[82]

There was a second solution to the apartheid problem in
the wings, however, and that was the report of the 2nd FAO
Regional Conference in Africa of May 1963. With the
recommendation of the director-general, the conference
decided to implement one suggestion:

> *Decides* that . . . the Republic of South Africa shall no longer
> be invited to participate in any capacity in FAO conferences,
> meetings, training centers, or other activities in the African
> region, until the Conference decides otherwise.[83]

Although the resolution did not exclude South Africa
from meetings of the General Conference, South Africa was
not reassigned to another regional authority. Following the
conference, South Africa apparently decided that there was
little reason to remain in the organization, and notified the
director-general on December 18, 1963, that it was withdraw-
ing from the FAO, as provided for by Article XIX, effective in
one year. No further action was necessary.

In the ILO, the final decision could be delayed no longer.
At the 158th Session of the Governing Body, the Africans had
a concrete proposal for a constitutional amendment permit-
ting expulsion or suspension.[84] In opposition, the Western
Europeans expressed strong reservations, insisting that the
UN would have to act first. The Canadian government
representative felt it was particularly unfortunate that the
ILO should take any substantive action on a political issue
just when the Security Council was dealing with that issue.
The most telling points, however, were probably made by
Brazilian representative Josue de Castro:

the question arose as to whether the I.L.O. should concern
itself with such a highly political issue. The answer as he saw
it could only be affirmative. . . . Just as the United Nations
Security Council has jurisdiction in political matters as such,
so the I.L.O. acted as a sort of security council for social
questions.

It was wrong to rely entirely on the United Nations to take
necessary action; indeed General Assembly Resolution 1904
(XVIII) called on the specialized agencies . . . to promote
energetic action which, by combining legal and other practical measures, will make possible the abolition of all forms of
racial discrimination.[85]

His point was taken, and the ILO decided to devote its
energies to the attack on apartheid as a social question. In the
final resolution, the proposed amendment was worded to
allow expulsion of a member *after* similar action by the UN.
In this way, the relationship of the ILO with the UN
remained formally the same, since it conceded the greater
authority of the UN in political matters; it was done,
however, only by redefining as social certain issues that the
membership felt should be attacked by the ILO. The Governing Body also decided to examine all credentials at the
beginning of the conference session, which meant that South
Africa would obviously not be accepted. Lastly, a campaign
for the elimination of apartheid was initiated, with the
object of using the social tools at the command of the ILO, in
coordination with the relevant committees of the UN.[86]

The ILO did not have to wait for the ratification of its
amendment to see the elimination of South Africa from the
organizaton. In a letter to the director-general dated March
11, 1964, the government of South Africa indicated that it
would withdraw as a result of hostile acts on the part of the
conference, the director-general, and the Governing Body.[87]

The interaction between the ILO and the UN was intense
throughout the period of tension in more than one sense.
The first problem was whether the ILO should give primacy
to the UN in the solution of a political problem; it did this by
redefining the issue as social. The second problem faced by
the ILO was timing. The gravest point of the internal crisis

was at the beginning of 1964, which also happened to be the time when the General Assembly and the secretary-general were attempting new approaches to South Africa. Should the ILO have awaited their outcomes, and deferred action so as to not jeopardize the UN initiatives? As it happened, there was too much tension in the ILO for action to be delayed. The last problem was the precedent-setting power of the ILO. The 1963 decision to cease inviting South Africa to ILO meetings was widely quoted and praised by African delegates as they sought to elicit similar moves by other organizations. In a sense, the ILO, as a model, became more active in the fray than participants may have expected. But it could not be avoided. In its quest to save its own functions and structure, the ILO could do little to mitigate its impact on other organizations.

The Seventeenth Assembly of WHO, in March 1964, was faced with a draft resolution similar to that of the ILO, submitted by the African states, that posed unprecedented political problems for WHO. There were only two operative paragraphs:

> 1. *Decides* to apply to the Republic of South Africa provisions of Article 7 of the Constitution relating to voting privileges; and
> 2. *Requests* . . . formal proposals with a view to the suspension of exclusion from the Organization of any Member violating its principles and whose official policy is based on racial discrimination.[88]

Discussion, of course, was intense. On one side were the defenders of universalism in international organizations, especially technical organizations such as WHO. They cited in defense of their cause a letter from U Thant recently received by the ILO, in which he said:

> I should like to emphasize how important it is that the organizations in the United Nations family should avoid divergent action in matters gravely affecting their constitutional processes. I am accordingly confident that full regard will be given by the agencies to whatever position is taken by the principal organs of the United Nations, and that a course will be followed which will enable your constructive work of

human betterment to proceed unimpaired.[89]

Leading the opposition to this traditional, functional view of the WHO was Dr. Ba of Senegal, the principal African speaker at the assembly on this issue. Taking away South Africa's voting privileges and services seemed quite straightforward to him. What WHO lacked and needed most desperately, in his view, was a provision in its constitution permitting South Africa to be expelled, or at least suspended. If the FAO, the ILO, and ECOSOC (on behalf of the ECA) had managed to do so, then WHO should, too. The argument did not sway many votes, however, as the margin of victory for the Africans was clear. When the vote was taken, the result was a lopsided 66–23–6.[90] At that point, South Africa withdrew from the session.[91]

Even though the ostensible purpose of the anti-apartheid group (withdrawal of South Africa) had been accomplished at that point, the Africans were determined to implement the second half of Resolution WHA 17.50. Responding to a general letter of the director-general in late 1964, all submitted an identical suggestion for the revision of Article 7 which would provide for the exclusion of a member deliberately practicing racial discrimination.[92] When this proposed amendment to the constitution was taken up at the Eighteenth Assembly, it provoked one of the most interesting discussions to arise in WHO concerning its relationship with the UN. The British delegate suggested an amendment making expulsion contingent upon prior expulsion from the UN. That maneuver, of course, would have given control to the permanent members of the Security Council, where all movements for expulsion in the UN must originate (Article 6 of the UN Charter). In this case, Britain had the support of Secretary-General U Thant, who had suggested inserting a provision similar to that in UNESCO's constitution.[93] The Africans, however, could control two-thirds of the votes, which meant that the amendment was sent to the government of each member for ratification.[94]

The strangest element of the continuing WHO debate over South Africa was that the opposing sides could not even agree on what the central question was. The Africans asked whether any member could be tolerated in their ranks who practiced racial discrimination. For their antagonists, primarily the Western Europeans and Americans, the essential question was the possible effect of apartheid on the effectiveness of WHO's health programs. Through 1963, there had been no damage; when the Africans insisted on making an issue out of it, however, thereby crippling the African services, it became a choice as to which part of the program would have to be sacrificed: South Africa or the rest of the continent.[95] The withdrawal of South Africa was discussed in terms of who would make up the $200,000 in annual dues that it had paid WHO.[96]

The African states, in subsequently taking their campaign to the International Atomic Energy Agency (IAEA), were faced with a tricky problem. They had to face up to the fact that when a state is expelled from an international body, it not only loses the privileges attached thereto, but it is also freed from most of the responsibilities involved with belonging to the organization.[97] The issue was quite important in the case of the IAEA, since South Africa was the only African country capable of producing nuclear weapons within a short time. In addition, one project of continuing concern to African leaders was the denuclearization of the African continent, and one useful way of achieving that goal would be through the IAEA.[98] It was, therefore, crucial to decide on what tactics to follow in the IAEA, since expulsion of South Africa would place it beyond the restraining reach of the organization.

At the seventh session of the General Conference in 1963, the African states contented themselves with submitting a joint statement that condemned South Africa's policy of apartheid, and asking for a review of South Africa's role in the IAEA.[99] No further action, however, was taken at that time. By the 1964 General Conference, the Africans felt somewhat more confident, and submitted a declaration that South Africa could not represent Africa on the Board of Governors; they asked for its removal.[100] Again, however, it was treated as a mere expression of sentiment, allowing South Africa to remain a prominent member of the atomic energy community. The Africans seemed to realize, in the case of the IAEA, that they had plunged in over their heads, and were just barely treading water. Because of the OAU's vested interest in the IAEA, they did not dare splash too much, for South Africa might quit if it got too wet, which would be worse than having it remain in the organization.

The Universal Postal Union (UPU), in fulfilling another essential international function, produced an entirely different result. It has two official purposes, laid out in Article I of the Ottawa Postal Convention (1957):

1) to form a "single postal territory for the reciprocal exchange of correspondence."

2) "to secure the organization and improvement of the postal services and to promote in this sphere the development of international collaboration."

The scope of the union is made rather clear in the title: it was meant to be universal, that is, all governmental units were to be included. The post–World War II period has not been an easy time for maintaining these basic precepts of the UPU. One problem has been to find a formal way of including the divided countries (China, Germany, Vietnam, and Korea); it has not been accomplished for all, and yet all those governmental units do abide by rulings of the UPU. Furthermore, the ideal remains alive, as the director-general wrote to the Special Committee of the General Assembly in early 1964:

I venture to remind the Special Committee . . . of the purely technical nature of the Universal Postal Union and of the fact that the provisions of the Universal Postal Convention defining the functions of the Union and in particular its essential aims, stress the universality and unity of the postal world.[101]

The question of UPU's cooperation with the UN had remained equivocal since 1945, especially for an organization dating back to the middle of the nineteenth century. The UPU was hesitant about sacrificing any degree of independence. "Relations with the United Nations were not established without certain misgivings," one observer of the UPU has said. "However, as long as the UPU stresses the independent and technical aspects of its activities and avoids unnecessary immersion in political problems, this fruitful but limited cooperation will probably be maintained."[102]

The conflict over apartheid was impossible to avoid. In late 1963, the regionally based African Postal and Telecommunications Union (APTU), an offshoot of the moribund Commission for Technical Cooperation in Africa (CCTA), was faced with the announced withdrawal of Kenya, Tanzania, and Uganda. It was a logical step, since the APTU was based in Johannesburg, and did not, strictly speaking, represent any change for the UPU. It did, however, indicate that postal organizations would be arenas for political conflicts.

In June 1964 the UPU Congress was held in Vienna; the Africans introduced a resolution condemning apartheid and formally expelling South Africa from the organizaton. Although there was no provision in the convention for expulsion of a member, the resolution was put to a roll-call vote, and passed 58–30–26. The South African delegate refused to leave his seat, invoking legal arguments, until the president of the conference asked him to leave. The delegation departed. The Africans also introduced a second resolution, proposing that South Africa not be allowed to adhere to the new convention then being drawn up. That resolution, however, when put to a secret ballot at the request of several members, was rejected, 56–58–5.[103] The difference between publicly held and privately held opinions is notable. Thus South Africa joined that mixed company that hovers around the UPU, honoring its conventions, maintaining membership without attending the conferences. Once again, the Africans had defeated South Africa with a majority vote, in removing its physical presence from UPU conferences, but had not changed the continuity of international transactions.

Shift of Emphasis to the UN

The changes occurring in African thinking in early 1964 were logically derived: the OAU was a difficult place from which to coordinate action against South Africa, and various groups in the UN, especially the "captured" Special Committee of the General Assembly, were closer to the essential action in the Security Council. The result was a gradual alteration in the role of the OAU, which was given the difficult task of aiding liberation movements in southern

Africa as its main object. Resolutions in regard to the effort in international organizatons became increasingly hortatory.

The Lagos Conference of the OAU in February 1964 revealed a continuation of the pattern of frustration for the African states in international bodies. As the Guinean delegate said, "There is no longer any measure, moral or otherwise, that has not been attempted and [that has not] failed . . . by the United Nations to call an end to the policy of apartheid. . . . The next step to take will be the use of violent means."[104] There was some comfort to be gained from the unanimous votes in the 1963 session of the General Assembly, and the December 1963 meetings of the Security Council, but they were far outweighed, for many Africans, by the obvious ineffectiveness of the measures taken.[105]

The problem facing the Africans, as the Guinean delegate pointed out, was that "as long as there is no threat to international peace and security, sanctions will not be voted for at the Security Council."[106] The object, therefore, became one of establishing the threat without unduly antagonizing neutral states: "As far as possible it would be better to arm the nationalist movements in order to allow us in the Security Council to be better equipped though at the moment there would be condemnation."[107] Thus the only way of establishing a "threat to the peace," in Western terms, was that of provoking South Africa to overt hostile action. This view is not as Machiavellian as it might sound, since, for the Africans, the South African regime has always been a threat to the peace, simply by existing, by discriminating, and by maintaining apartheid. They believe in a theory of "static aggression." They did recognize the importance, however, of how Western states would interpret the arming of the nationalist movements in southern Africa.

One lesson that the African states were learning from pushing the issue in the UN was self-reliance: "I would like to say that from now onward the source of inspiration, the source [of] every action against apartheid, is the OAU."[108] In that bit of hyperbole there is an element of truth, even if one later had to substitute the Special Committee on Apartheid or the African caucus for the OAU. Only the Africans cared enough about the issue to keep it in prominence in international organizations. It was reflected in the final resolutions of the conference, where six out of eight operative paragraphs dealt with actions in institutions other than the OAU.[109] The Africans were keenly aware that, even if they were to remain the inspiration of action against apartheid, the vehicle would necessarily be more powerful organizations and states.

While the impact of these OAU meetings was becoming more and more difficult to judge,[110] as the Special Committee on Apartheid became more prominent, the effect on Africans was significant in many ways. The self-confidence of African diplomats in discussing the apartheid issue in other organizations was boosted immeasurably, simply as a result of the OAU consensus.[111] The OAU endowment of the anti-apartheid cause with legitimacy, and its semiannual renewal, made a difference.[112] This became clear in the series of disruptions that followed at various meetings. African caucuses were held regularly at meetings of specialized agencies. Agreement on tactics was another important result; it is difficult to imagine the lack of communication between African capitals in ordinary circumstances, and in the period of strained relations before 1963, the only common contact was the UN. With the advent of the OAU, both communication and some decisionmaking could be in the same place, namely, in the heads of state meetings. Thus action against South Africa, as one subject upon which all agreed initially, provided a point of agreement even at meetings where nothing else could be done.

By early 1964, the leadership of the African effort at the UN had virtually passed out of the hands of the OAU to the Special Committee on Apartheid. The momentum of the Addis Ababa Summit Conference was about to dissipate and, partly because of that, the apartheid issue seemed to drift without direction in UN organs during the first half of 1964. The Special Committee was attempting, however, to forge new links and find new allies in the fight. The specialized agencies, for instance, had a fluctuating importance in the work of the Special Committee. The ILO and WHO had observers at meetings after March 1964, and UNESCO, FAO, and IAEA occasionally sent observers. There was an obvious reluctance on the part of the agencies, however, to expend much of their thin budgets on an apparently endless dispute. After passage of GA Resolution 1978 (XVIII), Achkar Marof, new chairman of the Special Committee, called a meeting of representatives of the specialized agencies to see how they could aid in implementation. The only result was that UNESCO agreed to report on the educational, scientific, and cultural effects of apartheid.

Of more importance to the future of apartheid and the OAU campaign, the Security Council was under unusual pressure during the first half of 1964. Tensions were creating havoc in the specialized agencies, which placed the Western countries in an embarrassing position, and various nongovernmental events, such as the conference on sanctions held in London in April, served to undermine the South African position even further. The conference was officially nongovernmental, even though the list of patrons included eleven African heads of state. The most important stimulus for the Security Council, however, was the Special Committee, which submitted two comprehensive reports in the six months before the Security Council meeting of June 1964. In each case, the Special Committee made clear its feeling that the Security Council's actions to date had been totally inadequate:

> The Special Committee feels that the Security Council, as a principal organ of the United Nations endowed with effective enforcement Powers under the Charter, should assume its decisive responsibilities in connection with the situation in South Africa.[113]

> The Special Committee wishes to emphasize again the urgent need for mandatory action under Chapter VII of the Charter, with the active cooperation, in particular, of Governments that maintain close relations with the Government of the Republic of South Africa.[114]

With its reports to the Security Council, the Special Committee also managed to bring to its attention resolutions of the OAU, and events in other international organizations and interested nongovernmental pressure groups.

Within the structure of the Security Council there was an active body examining possible solutions to the dispute: the Myrdal Group, appointed in December 1963. This Group of Experts had a difficult time attempting to fulfill its mandate.

Initially South Africa refused to cooperate with it in any
way, even refusing it admission to South African territory.
As a result, it limited its field work to interviews with African
leaders in New York and London.[115] It received aid from the
Special Committee, holding formal consultations with it at
least once, and informal contacts at other times.[116] The
report of the Group of Experts, having been produced under
the direction of the group's prestigious chairman, Alva
Myrdal, was clearly capable of stimulating far-reaching
change.

The resulting report was a compromise that included
elements from all points of view except that of the South
African government. The Africans received their share in an
endorsement of economic sanctions:

> The Security Council, in December 1963, expressed its strong
> conviction that "the situation in South Africa is seriously
> disturbing international peace and security." This situation
> has deteriorated further due to the actions of the South
> African Government. If no satisfactory reply is received from
> the South African Government by the stipulated date, the
> Security Council, in our view, would be left with no effective
> peaceful means for assisting to resolve the situation except to
> apply economic sanctions.[117]

The solution proposed by the Group of Experts for the
apartheid problem was drawn principally from Western, not
African sources. The first step was a national convention for
South Africa, where all elements of the population could
decide peacefully on a new form of government that would
provide for fair representation of all groups. If that failed, a
result the odds tended to favor, the second step would be
mandatory economic sanctions enforced by the Security
Council.

With the report of the Group of Experts in hand, as well as
the reports of the Special Committee mentioned above, the
African countries felt that it was time for another meeting of
the Security Council; an additional factor was that Arsène
Usher of the Ivory Coast was due to assume the presidency of
the council in June 1964. The Africans were more comforta-
ble with an African diplomat in the presiding officer's chair.
It was clear by this point, as well, that the inspiration for the

council meeting had to come from within the UN caucus. The concern of the states calling the meeting was the continuing trials of "political prisoners" in South Africa, a question that the Africans had found to be useful in mustering unanimity in the Security Council. As a result, the report of the Group of Experts was temporarily set aside to allow discussion of the more pressing humanitarian problem of the prisoners on trial. After discussion on June 8, 1964, Morocco introduced a draft resolution that included clauses such as "Invites all States and Organizations to exert all their influence in order to induce the South African government to comply with the provisions of this resolution."[118] The words "and Organizations" were deleted on the following day at the request of some states, and the Africans complied, hoping for eleven affirmative votes on the resolution. They were to be disappointed, since, when the vote was taken on the following day, it passed by only 7–0–4, with the United States, Britain, France, and Brazil abstaining on the ground that the trials were still in progress, and therefore the council should not interfere.[119] For whatever reason, the prisoners were not executed; they were given life sentences at hard labor.

Having passed that resolution, the Security Council could get back to the broader question of apartheid, and the solutions recommended by the Group of Experts and the Special Committee. The OAU was no help; it was simply a source of legitimacy, mentioned only by the Africans; for instance the Liberian representative spoke "in pursuance of a mandate we have received form our Heads of State and of the Governments who met in Addis Ababa in May 1963."[120] The suggestions of the other organs were definitely piling up in one direction. The Special Committee report stated that what was needed was action by the Security Council.[121] The Myrdal Group of Experts was inclined toward sanctions as a solution. The International Conference on Economic Sanctions against South Africa, held in London in April, was generally regarded as seeing sanctions as practicable.[122] With regard to choosing among the various recommendations, however, the Ivory Coast representative may have touched upon a rather crucial point: "My delegation considers that the recommendation of experts appointed under a Security Council resolution cannot be rejected lightly."[123]

The only problem was that no opinion had changed since December 1963, and the task of designing a compromise resolution fell upon the same Norwegian representative. Sanctions under Chapter VII could not be included; they would be vetoed by a permanent member. Thus there were three important operative paragraphs in terms of our focus;

> 3. *Notes* the recommendations and the conclusions in the report of the Group of Experts; . . .

> 8. *Decides* to establish an expert committee, composed of representatives of each present member of the Security Council, to undertake a technical and practical study . . . ; . . .

> 11. *Invites* the Secretary-General in consultation with appropriate United Nations specialized agencies to establish an educational and training programme for the purpose of arranging for education and training abroad for South Africans.[124]

Paragraph eleven was especially important to Norway's Nielsen. The new committee seemed to be nothing more than a stalling device, since it could hardly expect to be any more productive than the Security Council as a whole, given the fact that membership would be the same. There was, of course, tremendous disappointment on the part of non-Western countries. Indonesia considered it a sellout; the Ivory Coast indicated that "this draft resolution is not ours. It does not express our views, and is far from representing what we have asked of the Council."[125] The USSR found it "extremely weak and unsatisfactory"—enough so to abstain, with Czechoslovakia, on the final vote, where the resolution was adopted easily. France also abstained for reasons which were the opposite of the USSR's,[126] for France probably still used her concern for Article 2(7) to make sure that her arms shipments to South Africa would not be interrrupted by the UN.

The report of the Group of Experts was thus effectively ignored, shelved for possible future use. Rather than give the Africans what they wanted, the Great Powers agreed merely to keep the dispute under active consideration by another committee, clearly not the solution the Africans were looking for when they brought the issue to the Security Council. Many segments of the UN, however, opposed any more enforcement adventures. The financial crisis resulting from the Congo intervention was approaching its painful conclusion, and so for some the primary question was the survival of the UN rather than the morality of its stand on apartheid. Thus on this question the Scandinavians took the lead in producing a temporary solution. The Africans, however, could not abandon the Security Council; it was the only organ able to prescribe mandatory sanctions, and so even after June 1964 the Council remained a focus of tension over apartheid, as the one organ that could adopt mandatory economic sanctions against South Africa.

At the OAU Summit Conference of July 1964 in Cairo, in the heat of the Egyptian summer, the effort against apartheid wilted. Or, viewed from another perspective, the OAU decided that the only method of defeating South Africa was with economic sanctions, which only the UN could apply effectively. One milestone in African thinking was the unofficial conference on sanctions in London in early 1964.[127] Several African heads of state attended the conference, and came away convinced that adoption of economic sanctions was essential to the end of apartheid. Another impetus to shift all responsibility to the UN, however, was the absence of armed revolt in South Africa. The possibility of armed action against South Africa was looking less practical all the time, as the Liberation Committee was not functioning properly, and nobody knew when it would be straightened out.[128] Thus a movement began for the OAU to initiate its own centralized campaign of economic sanctions against South Africa and, specifically, to create a special unit in the OAU Secretariat for that purpose. There were objections, of course, such as duplication of organs; but they were brushed aside. More serious was the general shift of OAU feeling to the view that, now that independence was won for most of Africa, the greatest threat might be one's own neighbors. Even in an agreed-upon issue such as apartheid, many states did not want other Africans snooping in their national affairs, especially since quite a few African countries had not completely eliminated trade with South Africa, and did not see how they could in the near future. One has, therefore, the example of Ghana's objection to the new unit:

The proposed permanent body, whether in Addis Adaba or the
United Nations, should act as an informatory body, not a
control commission, making recommendations, not trying to
accomplish the impossible task of tracing traded goods to
their sources.[129]

In fact, no state could yet divulge in public its reasons for
objecting (Malawi was still rather reserved), and so the new
machinery in the OAU Secretariat received a broad mandate,
from the planning of sanctions to the "strictest implementation" of OAU resolutions.[130]

Africa, however, moving into turbulent times, was to be
successively plagued by the second Congo crisis, the Rhodesian Unilateral Declaration of Independence in 1965, and
finally the Nigerian civil war. In this atmosphere, the anti-
apartheid campaign moved hardly at all, and resolutions of
the OAU were strictly ritualistic. The meeting of the foreign
ministers in Nairobi in early 1965 once again asked African
states to implement the sanctions voted two years before. It
reaffirmed the support of the OAU for the Special Committee on Apartheid, and even gave a special endorsement to the
concurrent campaign in the International Civil Aviation
Organization (ICAO), where South Africa was under attack.
But there were no new proposals, and the escalating rhetoric
on apartheid had temporarily reached a plateau.[131] The
African offensive had reached its high point.

It is clear that the first year of the OAU had a significant
impact on the apartheid dispute, even though its effect
dwindled thereafter. The African efforts resulted in acceptance of their position by most organizations as the best
means of defusing the conflict. Clearly some accepted the
role of condemning apartheid with more grace than others,
but nearly all reflected a general awareness of the impact of
their decisions on other organizations. Each specialized
agency, however, saw the conflict only in terms of threats to
its own functions, not of imperiling the other members of
the community of international organizations. The apparent political strength of the OAU caused each organization
to leap for its own safety.

There were, however, other factors which limited the
extent of the conflict. Several non-African states, especially

the Scandinavians, chose to take leadership roles in offering compromise solutions to the dispute. Because their good faith could not be doubted, these states could create the finely honed resolutions that supported the principle of sanctions without their implementation.

Of equal importance, though, was the gradual realization by Africans of the advantages of not pursuing some sanctions, as in the IAEA. Even within their own organizations, such as the OAU, the enforcement of economic sanctions became increasingly difficult, as vested economic and trading interests in African countries became aware of the value of South African trade. In a sense, socialization was having a greater effect on the Africans than on the South Africans.

4

Counterattack by
the South Africans

By the mid-1960s, international organizations were ranged across a whole spectrum of policy responses to the apartheid conflict. Those taking the African line in resolutions, including the UN General Assembly, the ILO, and UNESCO, continued their efforts to reverse South African policies. In other organizations, such as the World Bank group or the IAEA, on the other hand, African initiatives were rejected, not so much as an expression of alignment with South Africa, but out of a belief that these latter organizations should not be used as battlefields for African conflicts.

The only organizations that might be said to be occupying a middle ground were those that had previously expelled South Africa, and thereafter remained outside the dispute. Most specialized agencies had arrived at that position.

The greatest disappointment for the African diplomats, however, and the greatest implicit support for the South African position, came from the unwillingness of key international groupings to pass mandatory sanctions: the Security Council in the political-military field, and the World Bank in economic affairs. With those two institutions failing to adopt policies in favor of mandatory sanctions, the tactic was clearly in trouble.

The international environment appeared to be turning against the Africans, too, in terms of specifically African problems with significant effects on the progress of the apartheid dispute: Rhodesia after 1965, and Nigeria after

1966. Both Rhodesia and Nigeria broke down African solidarity, a break symbolized at the UN by the re-creation of the
African Francophone grouping in late 1965.[1]

Some natural forces were also at work. By 1965, the African
states had been around long enough to have lost friends;
endemic tensions existed between the Africans and Latin
Americans, especially over trade matters after the 1964 UN
Conference on Trade and Development (UNCTAD), as well
as competition for political spoils in the General Assembly.
An even more serious indictment by observers was that
qualified Africans were disinclined to take posts of influence
in the Secretariat.[2] Africa, of course, had few trained diplomats to spare for service in the UN; only later, when African
governments became somewhat less stable, did African
diplomats find that employment in international organizations was a safe refuge. The Africans at that time apparently
subscribed to Conor Cruise O'Brien's theory that because the
UN was just a stage, the General Assembly must be the real
seat of power.[3] All those factors weakened the African
position as they argued for economic sanctions against
South Africa.

A more complete explanation, however, would have to
include the change in South Africa's posture. No longer
passive, it even demanded to be admitted to the Western
caucus in 1965, and was admitted. It made increasingly
successful overtures to black African countries for economic
agreements and, implicitly, political agreements to live and
let live. South African foreign policy, which had always been
formulated as an extension of domestic policy, began to be
formulated in a fashion that envisioned "national interests"
that lay outside its national boundaries.[4] In the case of
Rhodesia, for instance, the entire weight of South African
diplomacy was thrown into the effort to obtain a negotiated
solution. Verwoerd feared that the UN would establish the
precedent of enforcement by sanctions, and he wanted to take
the spotlight off southern Africa by ending the Rhodesian
dilemma.[5] Faced by a changing environment, therefore, the
Africans found that the militant tactics of the early years did
little to achieve the end of apartheid, the substance of what
they sought.

Following the confusion of 1964–65, when the UN was
virtually paralyzed by the financial crisis, the Africans faced

up to the need to improvise a new attack on apartheid. They still needed international organizations to implement their policies, and with the de-emphasis of social and economic sanctions as a tactic, the role of education became foremost.

Education, as implemented by the Special Committee on Apartheid with the aid of several other UN organs, became diffuse both in terms of methods and target groups. Propaganda, public testimony, traveling committee meetings, international conferences, issuance of postage stamps, and publication of tracts on apartheid all became a part of the effort to "educate" the general public on the African view of apartheid. The educational campaign, in fact, had become too disorganized by 1969, and the UN was unable to evaluate its effectiveness; its repudiation of any plans to expand funding for education was clear in the decision of ECOSOC not to fund another commission on apartheid, especially one designed primarily to produce more propaganda.

A second emerging trend after 1965 was continual testing of the effectiveness of violence against the South African government. Violence was sanctioned by the Special Committee on Apartheid, but had to be implemented by others, presumably the OAU.[6] That which was still useful to the African cause in international organizations had been institutionalized: the Secretariat Unit on Apartheid for education; the Special Committee on Apartheid for liason with the UN; and the fact of South Africa's expulsion from most international organizations.

To see the gradually diminishing role of international organizations, we shall examine sequentially, as they characterized the apartheid dispute, the problems caused the Africans by the paralysis of the General Assembly (1964–65), the failure of economic sanctions, the virtual completion of the campaign for social sanctions, and the efforts to create a viable educational center on apartheid. The culmination of this analysis will be the failure to institutionalize the anti-apartheid drive in ECOSOC in 1969, symptomatic of a mutual disillusionment.

The Nineteenth Session of the General Assembly, opening in the fall of 1964, held meetings, but produced nothing, in that no resolutions could be voted upon in the face of the financial crisis of the organization. As far as the apartheid issue was concerned, however, events could proceed almost as usual, since most action was taking place outside the plenary session of the General Assembly. There was simply no final resolution, except to indicate receipt of the report of the Special Committee. All substantive resolutions were carried over to the Twentieth Session.

It was unfortunate for the anti-apartheid forces to have the General Assembly mechanisms break down, as international pressures were becoming significantly stronger. In May the International Press Institute of Geneva issued a strong attack on a report of the South African Press Commission that called for government censorship of the press. The institute labeled the report "a step toward political control of the press." Further adverse publicity for apartheid came from the London Conference on Economic Sanctions in April and the spring meeting of the Heads of State or Government of Non-Aligned Countries, which endorsed OAU resolutions on South Africa.[7] All the diplomatic movement, however, faded in importance as the Soviet-American confrontation over budgetary questions paralyzed the General Assembly.

The Special Committee on Apartheid, however, continued its work under the leadership of another Guinean, Achkar Marof. It submitted regular reports, expanding its recommended actions against apartheid with each report. On the basis of Resolution 1978B (XVIII) of December 16, 1963, the Special Committee had the secretary-general contact the International Red Cross and the UN High Commissioner for Refugees (UNHCR), to examine their potential role in the dispute. The resolution had expressed special concern about the "families of all persons persecuted by the Government of the Republic of South Africa for their opposition to the policies of apartheid." The International Committee of the Red Cross could offer little; in South Africa, all their activities were carried out by the South African Red Cross, which indicated that all aid to such families was available from the "competent authorities," and so little more could be done.[8] Of more interest was the reply of the UNHCR, who indicated that he was ready to give any help needed to refugees from South Africa, but had received no requests for aid from any African countries.[9] In any case, the Special Committee continued to look for weak spots in the South African armor, but few were found in the report submitted to the General Assembly in the Nineteenth

Session, where it was duly noted along with all other questions without a vote.[10]

As the time for the Twentieth Session of the General Assembly approached, the Special Committee was certain that at least some of its suggestions would come up for a vote, since the UN had temporarily shelved the financial problems imperiling its existence. The Special Committee's first report of the year, however, was not concerned with the General Assembly, but rather with stimulating some action in the Security Council. The reports that appeared in June 1965 dealt primarily with the buildup of military forces in South Africa, and the nature of foreign investment there, especially by certain permanent members of the Security Council. The intent of the Special Committee was plain: the former topic was a reason for action, having been the subject of previous Security Council discussions, and the latter was the means to a solution; for the Africans at this stage, only economic sanctions supported by the United States, Britain, and France could end apartheid. As was mentioned in the June 16 meeting of the Special Committee, it was felt that the African group could then ask for a meeting of the Security Council, with the document in hand. They did not expect the meeting to be held, in fact, until September.[11] At the end of June, the committee also persuaded the UN Secretariat's Office of Public Information to publish a booklet entitled *The United Nations and Apartheid*, to be circulated in all member countries.

The work for the upcoming General Assembly went ahead, despite concurrent developments in the Security Council, and the results were summarized in the committee's report to the General Assembly and Security Council in August 1965.[12] In this report one could see a number of substantive new proposals that were to affect the course of the dispute in the next few years. One point, held over from 1964, was that the Special Committee should be enlarged "to include the permanent members of the Security Council and the present major trading partners of the Republic of South Africa."[13] It was an optimistic reflection of faith on the part of committee members that the friends of South Africa could be "educated" to the point of approving economic sanctions by participating in the Special Committee. Another sweeping recommendation, which combined efforts for publicity and education, was the creation of a three-year program in connection with the celebration of the International Year of Human Rights, scheduled for 1968. The program, initially proposed by Nigeria, was to include publication of booklets and monthly news bulletins, symposia in different countries, issuance of stamps, preparation of posters, contact with mass media—all dealing with the policy of apartheid.[14] The dissemination of information would be easy enough; the General Assembly could direct the secretary-general to take care of that. Cooperation with the International Year of Human Rights, however, meant that some relationship would have to be established with ECOSOC, inasmuch as the Year of Human Rights "belonged" to it.[15] Since ECOSOC's previous encounter with the apartheid issue, its membership had changed; with the increased African membership, ECOSOC welcomed the Special Committee tie.

The Special Committee clearly wanted to involve as many outside organizations as possible with this question. The role of specialized agencies and intergovernmental and nongovernmental organizations was mentioned many times, in connection with the dissemination of information, implementation of economic sanctions, and rendering of humanitarian assistance. The committee was encouraged by resolutions and statements of groups such as the Inter-Parliamentary Union and Amnesty International.[16] The most comprehensive statement of the year came from the International Commission of Jurists, which had investigated restrictions on the movements and residence of nonwhites in South Africa; the Special Committee circulated that report among UN members.[17] The new direction of effort by the Special Committee was notable in that it indicated, on the one hand, a certain disillusionment with the notion of prodding "effective" organs, such as the Security Council; on the other hand, it meant a massive broadening of the anti-apartheid campaign for education, not of a few, but of the world, with the intention of overwhelming the powerful few with numbers. In this sort of campaign, each organization, governmental or nongovernmental, became one more valuable soldier.

During the following few years, the Special Committee obtained the most active help and consultation from the ILO and UNESCO. Occasionally, the WHO would also offer consultative help. The other specialized agencies, however strongly their memberships may have expressed their opposition to apartheid at various times, chose to refrain from participation in the committee's work. Such a tendency did not indicate residual sympathy for apartheid; rather, the nonparticipating agencies eschewed all "political" questions.

The August report of the Special Committee on Apartheid was sent to the Special Political Committee of the 1965 session of the General Assembly to have the conclusions and recommendations boiled down to a workable resolution. The SPC was not, of course, an unfriendly forum for the Africans, and essentially all the original recommendations were included in a package of two resolutions that went to the General Assembly for passage without discussion. An exchange of letters, related to later developments, took place in the course of the SPC proceedings, when the Nigerian delegate suggested that South Africa be encouraged to participate once again in the SPC debates—or, as Chairman Carlet Auguste of Haiti wrote to the South African representative, there was a "desire of everyone to engage in a really fruitful dialogue."[18] The South Africans did not rise to the bait, as they found it difficult to correlate the indicated feeling of the SPC, as expressed by Auguste, with the fact that more than half of the General Assembly walked out when the South African representative rose to speak in the plenary session. In any case, discussions were becoming shorter every year in the SPC, as the Western countries made only ritualistic objections to the draft resolutions, enough to indicate that the provisions would be ignored, especially by the major trading partners of South Africa. The resolutions themselves, 2054A and 2054B (XX), demanded little new from other organs, except for increased dissemination of information by the Secretariat. The establishment of the UN Trust Fund for South Africa actually reduced the secretary-general's work load, since the problem of humanitarian assistance was thus entrusted to an independent body.

The General Assembly was able to achieve symbolic victory over South Africa on the question of credentials, an issue under discussion since 1963.[19] At the Twentieth Session, the attempt to reject South African credentials in the Credentials Committee was defeated 5–4, but in the General

Assembly the African states proposed a resolution, based on the precedent of Hungary, "to take no decision on the credentials submitted on behalf of the representative of South Africa."[20] But the victory for the Africans was only symbolic—it affected South Africa's standing in the organization no more than most of the resolutions on apartheid adopted to date had altered those discriminatory policies.

The reassessment occurring in African thinking was a natural result of the traumas the UN was experiencing, the organizational problems of the nascent OAU, and a growing awareness of the realities of the international political process on the part of the Africans. The results, as we shall see in more detail, were virtual abandonment of several militant goals in favor of the educational campaign tentatively tried out during this period of reassessment. Education, it appeared, was the only viable alternative. In other UN forums, discussions were moving in the direction of establishing a juridical basis for ending apartheid, namely in the Declaration and Convention on the Elimination of All Forms of Racial Discrimination.[21] The declaration had been embodied in General Assembly Resolution 1904 (XVIII) of November 20, 1963, and was followed by a carefully constructed Convention on the Elimination of All Forms of Racial Discrimination.[22] The enforcement procedures of the convention are notable for being both strong and precise,[23] providing for the creation of an eighteen-member Expert Committee on the Elimination of Racial Discrimination to perform a good offices function with respect to alleged incidents of racial discrimination.

The intent of the authors of the convention was clearly to remove some of the contentiousness surrounding human rights proceedings in the UN. It is still too early to judge their success. The question of apartheid could not be brought before the committee until South Africa adhered to the convention.

South Africa did not participate in the creation of the convention and, it may be assumed, will not adhere to it in the foreseeable future. Article 3 of the convention fairly well ensured South Africa's absence, in condemning apartheid explicitly. There had been sixty-five ratifications, including those of thirteen African states, as of September 1972, and the convention is in force.[24] It is to be hoped that the relatively small number of African states ratifying the convention reflects upon the uncertainty of their legislative processes rather than a lack of zeal to abolish racial discrimination everywhere.

The development of the convention illustrates the non-African sources of strength for the anti-apartheid drive. The Commission on Human Rights and its Sub-Commission on Prevention of Discrimination and Protection of Minorities were deeply disturbed in 1959–60 by a serious outbreak of incidents of anti-Semitism in many parts of the world. With the approval of the General Assembly, and the support of the Western bloc, the Sub-Commission began to search for ways to prevent such cases of discrimination. The preferred method appeared to be an international convention. By 1962, the African states had prevailed upon the relevant organs, including the Third Committee of the General Assembly, to describe the problem as one of "racial discrimination." Because of divergent viewpoints, however, it was agreed to issue a declaration in addition to a convention. Because the original issue of anti-Semitism was rapidly being obscured, it was agreed to draw up separate documents for that problem, in the form of a declaration and a convention to prevent religious discrimination.[25] With due speed thereafter, the Declaration, and later the Convention, on Racial Discrimination were produced.[26]

A second aspect of the convention's development to recall is that the use of an international convention to outlaw discrimination had precedents. The ILO had produced the Discrimination (Employment and Occupation) Convention in 1958, and UNESCO had adopted the Convention against Discrimination in Education in 1960.[27] Some states, therefore, saw the UN convention against all forms of racial discrimination as a natural sequel to the two earlier conventions.

Of potential importance to the future effectiveness of the convention was an amendment by the African states to the effect of banning reservations to ratification or accession by a state if two-thirds of the states party to the convention objected to the ratification. The amendment was included as Article 20 (2). In this way, the committee would presumably not be paralyzed by reservations. The African contribution thus may be deemed, in the long run, to be quite valuable.

Campaign for Economic Sanctions

The effort to obtain economic sanctions against South Africa reached its climax in 1965, but it resulted in total failure for the Africans. The outcome was particularly stunning because public opinion appeared strongly mobilized by the end of 1964. Groups outside the UN, especially nongovernmental organizations, gave support to the movement for sanctions and the use of force. In the Security Council, however, the result was deadlock, and in the World Bank it was intransigent opposition.

During late 1964 and early 1965, the Expert Committee of the Security Council was devoting a great deal of time and effort to its task, in the face of the original skepticism of the African states, who saw the committee as merely another delaying device. Thirty-eight meetings were held between July 21, 1964, and February 27, 1965, with all members of the Security Council represented except France, which continued to question the committee's competence. It became clear within a short time, however, that a committee constructed in this fashion was as ill-suited to compromise and peaceful solution of this issue as a session of the entire Security Council. As the committee began its working session, various forces caused severe divisions. The United States, for instance, wanted to have the secretary-general undertake massive studies of the South African geography, people, and economy. The USSR and Czechoslovakia pointed out that enough reports by the Special Committee on Apartheid already existed to permit conclusions to be drawn.[28] The move by the United States was viewed by many as a delaying tactic. The final compromise on that particular squabble was to commission new reports on South African external trade and industrial structure.

As the committee approached its deadline, there were three groups of conclusions submitted for adoption by it, from Czechoslovakia–USSR, Ivory Coast–Morocco, and the United States. Britain seemed to be closest to the position of the United States, leaving the Latin Americans as the floating group. The Communist summary was rejected at the start, by a vote of 6–4. The African summary was rejected as well, 5–4–1, with the Chinese delegate abstaining. Repeated appeals were made by China and the Latin Americans for alterations in the text, but the Africans would compromise no further—an impasse the Latin Americans solved by drawing up a new report that took their objections into account. At this point, rather than accept an inevitable defeat, the United States withdrew its report in favor of the Brazil-Bolivia report that combined the substance of the United States report with the rhetoric of the Africans. Thus, while condemning apartheid as an evil worthy of the strongest sanctions possible, it also pointed out the strength of the South African economy and the fact that the committee could not assume implementation of Article 41—only the Security Council itself could do that. In the conclusion, for instance, the question of economic sanctions was treated very conditionally: "Although it was pointed out South Africa would not be readily susceptible to economic measures, the Committee agreed that South Africa was not immune to damages from such weapons."[29] The report was accepted by the committee, 6–4, with the Communists and Africans in the minority.

The African states refused to compromise. They had not approved the creation of the committee and they saw no reason to endorse a report that did not satisfy a significant part of their demands: "The draft submitted by the two African delegations represented a minimum. . . ." Since the African report already said less than what the African bloc considered desirable, the other delegations should agree to it as a "compromise."[30] The rigidity of the African stance was, at least in part, a function of bargaining for the strongest possible report. The committee stage was not, in any case, the place to make significant concessions, since only the council could take decisions.

There was a rather unsettling quiet after the report was released; it had become an orphan nobody was in a hurry to adopt. Those who had drawn up the compromise saw little to implement. The African states chose to wait for the release of the Special Committee report in June 1965 to request a meeting of the Security Council.[31] Events were delayed slightly as the Africans also decided to await the report of the secretary-general in implementation of the previous Security Council resolution, especially the provisions for South African refugees. It turned out that the specialized agencies had been most cooperative in helping South African refugees obtain education and training, since they could fit into existing African programs of UNESCO, ILO, WHO, and FAO.[32] The Africans were beginning to stoke the fire under the boiler, and the session was expected in November, as five African states requested permission to participate in the debate in early November. The proceedings were abruptly suspended, however, by the Rhodesian declaration of independence on November 11, 1965, and the issue of Rhodesia went to the top of the African list in the UN:

> In view of the serious situation prevailing at present in Southern Rhodesia and the implications it will certainly have on the question of *apartheid* to be discussed in the Security Council, we request you to defer the debate on this question to a later date.[33]

The rest of the Council was only too happy to comply.

Projecting Economic Sanctions to the Specialized Agencies

The International Civil Aviation Organization (ICAO), with its power of regulating the world's airways, was one of the few organizations that could be useful against South Africa in enforcing social and economic sanctions. ICAO would not itself undertake the economic sanctions, but elements in the UN General Assembly saw the opportunity to act.

The relationship between the General Assembly and ICAO was characterized not only by wary coexistence, but also by clear conflict. One of the tactics utilized by the African states in their struggle in southern Africa was to deny the national airlines of South Africa and Portugal the right to land in their countries. An effort was made to universalize this tactic in General Assembly resolutions in 1962 and 1965.[34] The 1962 resolution, concerning South Africa, was ignored by the ICAO Secretariat, because the resolution was addressed to member states of the UN, and not to the specialized agencies. When the tactic was augmented by a resolution on Portugal in 1965, specifically including the specialized agencies, the ICAO Secretary-General sent a memorandum to the UN, pointing out the implicit contradiction for members of both ICAO and the UN. As far as he was concerned, the request to ICAO was "inconsistent with the terms of the Convention on International Civil Aviation."[35] He felt, therefore, that ICAO could do nothing to help implement sanctions against South Africa, as he stated in an internal memorandum to ICAO Council members.[36]

The council was not so convinced of his point of view, and at least six members (Kenya, Tunisia, India, Nigeria, UAR, and Czechoslovakia) were outraged by his action.[37] In a closed session of the council, they accused Secretary-General B. G. Twigt and the council president of making a serious error in refusing to cooperate with the UN on the apartheid issue. The General Assembly resolution had asked for dissemination of the resolutions; the ICAO Secretary-General felt that he had no "suitable" publication for that purpose, a point of view that enraged the Kenyan delegate in particular. The dissidents also disputed the strict interpretation of the resolutions by the secretary-general, who planned to continue to aid South Africa. They wanted to end all airline connections to that area.

The opponents of the ICAO Secretary-General could not overrule him, however, for they accounted for only six out of twenty-five members of the council. They were offered the chance to raise the issue for fuller, more formal, discussion at the next meeting of the council, but they eventually declined, realizing this would be futile.

The decision of the African group to wage economic warfare against South Africa certainly meant that the World Bank group would become involved at some time. The active leader of that group, the International Bank for Reconstruction and Development (IBRD), has traditionally avoided all questions of a noneconomic nature, despite the obvious implications of its loan policies in political and social matters.[38] As much as possible, however, the IBRD has pursued the ideals of a "functional" organization, operating by economic and financial standards, as illustrated by its provision for suspension of membership: *"Suspension of membership.* If a member fails to fulfill any of its obligations to the Bank, the Bank may suspend its membership by decision of a majority of the Governors, exercising a majority of the total voting power" (Article VI, Section 2). There are no provisions for suspension or expulsion on grounds other than those directly related to the financial operations of the bank, and there is no mention of the UN. One can see why, therefore, the president of the bank replied rather curtly to an inquiry of the Special Committee in early 1964: "I must frankly state that considering the nature of our functions I do not believe we are in a position to help in fulfillment of the mandate of the Special Committee. . . ."[39] The Special Committee was not pleased with that response, as they noted in a report to the General Assembly later that year:

> The Special Committee further suggests for the consideration of the General Assembly and the Security Council that
>
> (a) All international agencies, in particular the specialized agencies, including the International Bank for Reconstruction and Development and the International Monetary Fund, be requested to take all necessary steps to deny economic and technical assistance to . . . South Africa.[40]

The first formal communication between the UN and the bank on this issue did not appear until the end of 1965, specifically Resolution 2054 (XX), which requested the specialized agencies to help implement the measures against South Africa. The bank had a number of choices in this case, and it is interesting to speculate as to why it acted as it did. The events that followed were leading to a confrontation. The president of the bank circulated the resolution to the executive directors of the bank, with a covering statement of his own that political questions were not part of the bank's mandate.[41] As no decision was taken by the directors at that point, the president approved a loan of $20,000,000 to South Africa in September 1966. This antagonized the Africans tremendously, and in Resolution 2202 (XXI), the secretary-general was asked to enter into consultation with the bank to end such loans. An exchange of letters then ensued, through the summer of 1967, that demonstrated quite clearly the extent of the disagreement.[42] During the impasse that followed, the General Assembly passed resolutions in 1967 and 1968 castigating IBRD, and reiterating its request that the World Bank "deny financial, economic and technical assistance" to South Africa. The resolution concluded by expressing "the hope that the Bank will stand by its assurance that it will avoid any action that might run counter to the fulfillment of the great purposes of the United Nations."[43] It is clear, in any case, that they could find no way to settle their differences.

The motivations on each side are not clear, although much can be learned from an examination of this conflict. The states that focused UN attention on this question of the bank's behavior were not, in fact, the African states; it was the Communist bloc, by and large, most of whose members do not belong to the World Bank at all.[44] The discussion took place in the Fourth Committee, not in the Special Committee where the Africans held sway. The conflict with the bank, therefore, involved more than just apartheid, as the USSR had an ideological dispute with the bank group. On the other side, the structure of the bank explains a great deal about its actions. The voting power is distributed in proportion to subscriptions to capital, giving the United States and the Western European states a dominant position in the organization. Since those countries did not agree with the General Assembly's view of South Africa, it seemed likely that the World Bank would not go along with the United Nations. The president of the World Bank was an American, and the bank tended to reflect the Western preference for persuasion rather then confrontation to achieve social change in this case.

The legal position of IBRD is quite clear; according to the Agreement between the United Nations and the IBRD (Article IV, Paragraphs 1 and 2):

1. The United Nations and the Bank shall consult together and exchange views on matters of mutual interest.

2. Neither organization, nor any of their subsidiary bodies, will present any formal recommendations to the other without reasonable prior consultation with regard thereto. Any formal recommendations will be considered as soon as possible by the appropriate organ of the other.[45]

The bank felt that not only had the General Assembly failed to consult in an appropriate manner before issuing the first formal recommendation, but that in any case, the bank was not legally bound to abide by General Assembly recommendations.[46] In legal terms, the bank was right. Yet, was it proper for the bank to totally exclude noneconomic grounds in determining loan policy, since their loans had a political importance? In the case of apartheid, the bank refused to accept the recommendations of the General Assembly, on legal or political grounds, but defended itself on the basis of the legal agreement between the two organizations. The conflict had certain broader implications, to be discussed later, but it seems certain that the episode did little to harmonize relations between the two organizations during this period.[47]

The question of economic sanctions against South Africa thus passed not only from the agenda of the Security Council, but also from the attention of the General Assembly. The use of economic sanctions was not discredited, but any hope that key organizations would vote for the use of force against South Africa was dispelled. Apartheid still existed, of course, and economic sanctions would be debated later in the decade in other forms, such as its manifestation in Namibia or Rhodesia. Even with the emergence of the Rhodesian issue, however, serious consideration of economic sanctions against South Africa was dead. The desultory performance of the Group of Experts temporarily convinced many Africans that their solution to the apartheid problem would have to be implemented elsewhere, and with entirely different tactics. Thus sanctions as a tactic seemed to have reached a temporary impasse; the offensive continued in terms of ostracism and propaganda, for there were still some specialized agencies that had not yet faced up to the radical demands of the OAU.

The campaign for social sanctions against South Africa then moved in to the remaining areas of international life in which South Africa participated. Some efforts were oriented toward expulsion, as in the ICAO and the International Telecommunications Union (ITU); other moves, however, as in international sports bodies, appeared to be concerned with sensitizing public opinion to the apartheid issue as much as with the practical matter of South African participation. The point had been reached where organizations were becoming more adept at using their constitutional structures and relationships with other organizations to deflect the anti-apartheid effort.

The ICAO had an unusual problem in solving the crisis that by 1965 had gripped nearly all intergovernmental organizations.[48] The ICAO deals with a technical subject upon which the lives of airline travelers are dependent. It would apparently be, therefore, to the advantage of the organization, of members, and of travelers everywhere not to exclude any state from the ICAO regulations regarding airplane and airport safety. The provisions for expulsion of a member are therefore somewhat unusual, and indeed, ICAO would not have any provisions at all for expulsion if problems with Franco's Spain had not arisen in 1946. At that time, ICAO made an agreement with the UN, unique for specialized agencies, providing for expulsion from ICAO of a state that had been barred from the UN. The agreement was obviously aimed at Spain.[49] In the ICAO Constitution, the provisions for expulsion were in two parts: Article 93 (a)(1) provides for automatic expulsion from ICAO upon recommendation of the UN General Assembly to all specialized agencies; and 93 (a) (2) provides for automatic expulsion from ICAO of a state expelled from the UN.[50] Other than those provisions, the only form of punishment available was the suspension of voting rights, ordinarily for nonpayment of financial obligations.[51] In any case, the Africans recognized that suspension of voting rights would not be a particularly serious punishment, and would surely raise the constitutional hackles of many other members.

The first tactic to be tried was that of ostracism, or social sanctions. At the Africa–Indian Ocean Regional Air Navigation Meeting in Rome (November 23–December 18, 1964), the UAR delegate made a statement on behalf of the African states. Not only did he express regret at the presence of South Africa, but he also "stated that they did not desire to participate in any discussion which might be initiated by South Africa."[52] Operating under that social code, the conference proceeded smoothly.

The next general conference of the ICAO was scheduled for Montreal in July 1965, and it was in this setting that the real push to expel South Africa appeared. The necessary procedure was to have the convention changed to allow for the expulsion of members independently of expulsion from the UN. The African states introduced a resolution to that

effect, but failed to obtain the two-thirds majority necessary
for passage; the vote was only 42–30–15. One cannot be
certain how dedicated the African representatives were to the
goal of expelling South Africa. They were, for the most part,
not politicians, but people with a technical interest in
matters of aviation, to whom the question of expelling
South Africa may have seemed somewhat superfluous. In the
opening plenary speeches of the delegates, only one (the
Tanzanian) mentioned the need for expelling South Africa.[53] In the vote mentioned above, Malawi abstained, and
Algeria, Dahomey, Gabon, Zambia, and others were absent.[54] The African front was, if united, certainly not well
organized.

Instead of choosing to disrupt the conference, the African
delegates pressed for a symbolic slap at the South Africans,
by introducing a resolution that condemned apartheid, and
called on all states to "exert pressure on South Africa to
abandon its apartheid policy." That resolution passed easily, 39–1–40, although many countries, including all the
Western nations, abstained on the ground that it dealt with a
matter beyond the purview of the ICAO, i.e., a political
problem.[55]

ICAO was spared the worst of problems in its handling of
the apartheid dispute. What is ironic, though, is that ICAO
is often cited as having the closest ties to the UN, as shown by
its provisions for expulsion, and those very ties provided an
excuse for inaction, as members of ICAO urged that the
General Assembly initiate the expulsion recommendation.[56]
Indeed, those constitutional provisions protected the organization in another way, since the issue was still under active
consideration in the Security Council, and action could be
postponed until the results of that political process were
known.[57]

The ITU was one of the more intractable organizations on
the apartheid issue; it had provisions for neither expulsion
nor suspension, for any reason whatever. These legal factors
did not deter the African bloc from trying to expel South
Africa, but the attempt landed them in a good deal of trouble.
At the African Conference of the ITU in Geneva in the fall of
1964, Algeria introduced a resolution to expel South Africa.[58] It was approved, 27–9–2 (13 not participating in the
vote), but South Africa refused to leave, citing the unconsti-

tutionality of the resolution. A crisis ensued when the UN Secretariat insisted that it could not continue to provide services for a conference that operated contrary to the provisions of the International Telecommunications Convention. The Africans maintained their position, and so on October 19, 1964, the conference adjourned *sine die*, having lost Secretariat services and accomplished no business.[59]

Thus there were few ways in which to affect South Africa's position in the ITU. One means was found at the 1965 Plenipotentiary Conference in Montreux, during the controversy over the proposed reduction in membership of the International Frequency Registration Board, one of the central organs of the ITU. South Africa had served on that board since the founding of the ITU, as the representative of all of Africa. The Africans voted to give up their spot on the board, as part of an agreement to reduce the membership from eleven to five, since that was the only way to deprive South Africa of its position. As the Moroccan member stated, "The African countries did not wish to continue to be represented on the Board by South Africa,"[60] and the basic choice was to have no representative at all from Africa, or to have South Africa. They chose the former.

The second movement against South Africa at the conference was successful. In view of the fact that a member could not be expelled from the organization, it was felt that, under the rules of procedure, the membership could simply exclude South Africa from a particular conference. Many delegates fought this interpretation; the United States introduced a motion that the conference was not competent to consider questions of a political nature, on which basis South Africa was being excluded, but that motion was defeated, 58–51–2. The motion of the United Arab Republic to exclude South Africa from the Plenipotentiary Conference was put before the conference on September 15. Following protracted debate and several votes, the motion was finally carried on September 21 by a vote of 59–27–7 (15 not participating).[61] Thus South Africa left the conference in late 1965, retaining membership in the organization, and continuing to adhere to the conventions of the ITU.

The ITU was split, however, in its response to the anti-apartheid drive and the UN resolutions on that subject. The Secretariat wanted to avoid the subject entirely, which led to the problems in October 1964. The African members could affect South Africa's participation to only a limited degree, since the central functions of the organization were unassailable, certainly a factor in the unwillingness of the ITU Secretariat to press South Africa on the apartheid issue.

The UN Conference on Trade and Development (UNCTAD), a General Assembly subsidiary body, was the setting for several attempts to exclude South Africa, all unsuccessful. In 1964, the Afro-Asian group had declared that South Africa should be excluded from the conference, but they were frustrated by the lack of any constitutional provision for exclusion.[62] They were determined, in any case, to ignore the presence of the South Africans, and whenever a South African spoke, a majority of the delegates would walk out.[63] Nothing could be done after the conference, however, about the South African membership question, because the General Assembly was paralyzed by the financial crisis. Even when UNCTAD was established as a permanent organ of the General Assembly in late 1964, it had to be accomplished without objection, since a dispute over any provision, such as exclusion of South Africa, would have raised the question of voting rights in the General Assembly. The most obvious opportunity to exclude South Africa was thus missed. In the 1968 UNCTAD convened in New Delhi, the Africans staged a repeat performance, objecting to the South Africans once again. The Ugandan representative pointed out that the South African representatives were present, and suggested that the delegates be ejected. The Conference Secretary then read out the opinion of the UN Legal Counsel that supported the presence of South Africa for a number of reasons:

   1) There was no provison for exclusion in the establishing Resolution 1995 (XIX) of December 30, 1964, which says all members of the UN shall be in UNCTAD.
   2) UNCTAD was not affected by resolutions of the General Assembly on apartheid.
   3) "At no point has the Assembly given any indication that any State member of the Conference was to be excluded from the second session."[64]

Although frustrated for the duration of the conference, the Africans did persuade the other delegates to pass resolution

26 (II) of March 27, 1968, which asked the General Assembly to amend Resolution 1995 (XIX) to allow expulsion of South Africa.[65]

The real battle thus shifted to the General Assembly in the fall of 1968. The Second Committee went along with the resolution of UNCTAD, supporting the expulsion of South Africa by a vote of 49–22–23. At that point the UN Legal Counsel Constantin Stavropoulos advised the committee that he still felt that exclusion would be unconstitutional.[66] It was not a case of creating a "limited-membership" organ as some states maintained, he said, but rather of suspending South Africa. That would have to be done in conformity with UN Charter provisions for suspension, meaning that the action would have to originate in the Security Council, and be approved by the General Assemlby (Article 5 of the UN Charter). The recommendation of the Second Committee, however, was to suspend South Africa. In the General Assembly, each side had the time to marshal all the forces available, and the result was dependent upon a ruling of the president of the General Assembly as to whether it was an important question requiring a two-thirds majority. The president ruled it important, and the pressure applied to Asian and Latin American delegates by the British and Americans proved essential, as the General Assembly reluctantly supported the president, 56-48-13. When the motion to exclude South Africa was put to the vote, it received a majority of only 55–33–28, and thus failed.[67] The West voted against the motion, and the Communists plus some others abstained. The Africans had clearly lost on two strictly political motions.

The Africans had expected to lose the Western European states on those votes, but the Communist abstention was a blow. The Africans had not realized that the issue of representation of East Germany, North Vietnam, and North Korea was enough to defeat their motion. The response of many Latin American and Asian delegates to Western pressure could be expected. Even the African Group, however, proved that it was not a "bloc," as South Africa obtained the support not only of its economic satellites, but also of a few states particularly responsive to Western pressure (Central African Republic, Morocco).[68] The clearcut divisions in the General Assembly were becoming less distinguishable.

A curious factor in the votes on UNCTAD was the unwillingness of the Africans to compromise. When the Communist bloc (Hungary) offered an amendment to the motion that would have satisfied them by not closing the door against eventual admission of the divided Communist states, the Africans voted against it. The question of South Africa would not have been affected, and with the support of the Communists, the motion would have come much closer to the necessary two-thirds majority. As the Africans were accustomed to winning by overwhelming majorities in the General Assembly, however, their loss on this issue was the result of a clear miscalculation. They felt that they could reject the proposed compromise, entailing laborious consultation with the African delegations, and still obtain the necessary two-thirds majority. They were proven wrong by several votes.

South Africa's participation in international sports competitions illustrates the impact of nongovernmental, transnational factors in international politics. The exclusion of South Africa from various sports groups, in fact, is important only in part in terms of social sanctions; sports competition is also an area of tremendous visibility to the general public, and the measures taken against South Africa had an enormous impact on the public. The Africans felt that South Africa was not "playing fair" in the international system, and therefore deserved, so to speak, to be ejected from the game.

Sports federations are governed by various types of structures, but generally are controlled by self-perpetuating elites interested in the sport in question. They therefore tend to have few outside ties with other organizations, and have had little need for them, since political disputes enter their realms only rarely.

In the early part of the decade, South Africa was suffering exclusion from many international sport bodies.[69] To a people like South Africans, for whom sports are traditionally important, the exclusion from international competitions was painful. By the end of the decade, South Africa was out of nearly all international competitions on a team basis, except for some isolated Commonwealth matches and tours with old friends in Britain, Australia, and New Zealand. Even those occasions were unpleasant, generally being marred by serious protests.

South Africa's most publicized difficulties were with the International Olympic Committee (IOC), because of the prestige and honor associated with victories at the Olympic Games. The first problem came in October 1963, when the IOC was forced to shift a meeting scheduled for Nairobi to Baden-Baden because the Kenyan authorities adamantly refused to issue visas for the South African delegates. The Africans persisted, however, and on June 26, 1964, the IOC issued an ultimatum to South Africa that it would have to modify its policies by August, or be barred from the 1964 games. South Africa did not go to the 1964 Olympics. However, 1964 was not a good year for South Africa in other spheres of international sports, as the International Football Federation decided on October 8, 1964, to suspend all matches with South Africa. Immediately thereafter, a proposal for the expulsion of South Africa was presented to the International Amateur Athletic Federation Congress in Tokyo, but it was rejected as political by 145–82.[70]

The campaign to rouse public feeling against apartheid continued to have success in international sports organizations. With the approach of the 1968 Olympics, the Executive Committee of the IOC, under Chairman Avery Brundage, took great pains to find a satisfactory way around the impasse. A commission was sent to South Africa by the IOC to examine discrimination in sports; they found it to be serious, but not as serious as it had been, and on the basis of the report, it was initially recommended that South Africa be permitted to participate on the basis of its progress to date.[71] Many states objected, with some Africans indicating they would not compete in the 1968 Olympics in Mexico City if the South Africans did. The host organizing committee made clear its choice in the matter, and Avery Brundage and the IOC had to change its policy once again. South Africa was "disinvited."[72] The cumulative effect of being excluded from the Olympic Games twice was serious for South Africa, as the domino effect took hold in other sports: table tennis, football, track and field, gymnastics, swimming, and wrestling, among others. Even in tennis, South Africa was excluded from the 1970 Davis Cup competition by a vote of 24–8–3, and yet the Rhodesia issue was not affected, since the latter was a political question, whereas South Africa's exclusion was based solely on the issue of racial discrimination.

Little direct pressure, interestingly enough, came from UN organs—the movement to exclude South Africa originated largely within the international sports structure, and spread rapidly from the Olympic movement to other sports federations. The Special Committee, indeed, did not examine the question until they heard the testimony of Arthur Ashe, the black American tennis player, in June 1969. The committee was momentarily excited, but this gave little indication of the long-term possibilities of pressure in that sphere.

The fact that there were no visible links between the UN and the international sports movement indicated the degree to which public education had succeeded. The anti-apartheid movement had clearly moved beyond the stage where centralized direction was required, at least in the area of social sanctions.

Despite the failure of economic and social sanctions to end apartheid, the Africans perceived the value of the publicity accompanying those attempts. Indeed, they found that the transigence of the World Bank group, the IAEA, and the Security Council expanded the educational value of the episodes, in increasing public sensitivity to the apartheid issue.

The central theme of the anti-apartheid movement in the UN therefore became education. All other tactics had failed. The educational campaign against apartheid was wide in scope, using many weapons with varying effectiveness, with success often coming in unexpected situations, i.e., in the Olympic movement, where the embarrassment of South Africa reached more people than the rest of the campaign put together.

There was a professional side to the educational campaign as well, which involved the accumulation of evidence against South Africa by several UN organs. The process of obtaining testimony did not require the public to be educated, but the accumulated mass of words was released from time to time in UN publications or UN-sponsored conferences, with the hope that the impact would thereby be greater. Specialized commissions, such as the Commission on Human Rights of ECOSOC, were especially useful in being able to translate human dilemmas in South Africa into political advantage for the anti-apartheid cause; that commission's handling of violations of trade union rights in South Africa is particularly interesting.[73] Other organs were equally valuable, including the UN Secretariat, the Special Committee on Apartheid, plus the OAU.

The educational campaign did not have an inherently exacerbating effect on the apartheid conflict. The effect of the OAU efforts tended to increase tensions, but in general the educational campaign simply kept public attention focused on apartheid, without changing opinions in regard to goals and tactics.

One reason for the mixed effect of the educational campaign was that it was not one-sided in origin. The South Africans were abandoning their passive posture, and beginning to realize the power of propaganda as well as the Africans had earlier. And with the depth of their resources, they mounted a serious counteroffensive, concentrating upon their major trading partners and their neighbors in southern Africa. The voice of Radio South Africa could be heard worldwide; the South African embassies installed information offices. Nongovernmental organizations became especially important, with the South African Foundation, supported by Harry Oppenheimer, spreading a South African view. Thus, while one might tend to concentrate on the educational efforts of international organizations, all of which echoed the African line, or were silent, it must be recalled that there was also a strong counterforce from the south of Africa.[74]

The theme within the UN educational campaign was cooperation. The efforts were directed at public opinion, member states, and other international organizations. Its effect is difficult to measure since education is inevitably a long-term process, but in institutional terms, there were immediate rewards, in that various UN organs were drawn together in positive working relationships. The Africans were eventually to abandon this tactic as they had the others, but not before it was solidly institutionalized in the UN. In the meantime, all the resources of the General Assembly and ECOSOC were mobilized.

The OAU and the African group at the UN were suffering from divisions, all of which contributed to a slackening effectiveness in the apartheid battle. Disagreements within the OAU were becoming increasingly bitter; tactics over Rhodesia, finances, credentials of delegations, and, most importantly, the Nigerian civil war all caused serious fissures in an already fragile organization. Even on the question of South Africa, complaints could be heard concerning the inactivity of the Committee of Liberation and the ineffectiveness of sanctions.

Concurrent with the OAU's internal problems, however, there was an important increase in external institutional links, especially at the UN. In late 1964, the Special Committee established informal contact with the OAU, but the formal presence of the OAU at the New York headquarters had to wait another year.[75] With General Assembly Resolution 2011 (XX) of October 11, 1965, the OAU was given formal observer status in the General Assembly. The resolution also asked the secretary-general to promote cooperation with the OAU at all levels, such as exchange of representatives at meetings, continuous liaison at the Secretariat level, and technical cooperation in recruitment and training of staff. As an example, the OAU Secretary-General requested UN aid in obtaining secretaries and interpreters for the February–March 1966 meeting in Addis Ababa of the OAU Council of Ministers. This was accomplished through the Geneva office of the UN, and helped to alleviate some of the serious functional problems the OAU was having.[76] Another area where the UN could usefully support the OAU was in the exchange of information between the ECA and the technical commissions of the OAU. On the question of apartheid itself, however, the cooperation was much more tenuous. In March 1966, the Special Committee on Apartheid invited the OAU to send an observer to its meetings on a permanent basis, where the OAU representative made numerous contributions to the rhetoric of that committee.[77] The input from the OAU did not significantly change the orientation of the Special Committee, however, since it had been at all times an African preserve, pushing for adoption of the OAU program of action against South Africa.

Initiatives for action were even appearing in the formerly stalemated ECOSOC. Following its unhappy encounter with the issue in relation to membership on the ECA, ECOSOC had remained clear of apartheid until the expansion of its membership, as provided for in Resolutions 1991A and B (XVIII), tipped the balance in favor of the anti-apartheid forces. Nine new members were elected: seven from Asia and Africa, one from Latin America, and one from Europe. The seats were not actually filled until the Twentieth Session, in late 1965, and at that point ECOSOC became involved in the apartheid issue once again.

ECOSOC initiated the planning for a Seminar on Apartheid, scheduled for Brasília the following year. This was done in cooperation with the Special Committee on Apartheid of the General Assembly, the first instance of cooperation on the apartheid issue between ECOSOC and the General Assembly.[78]

At that point, too, the Commission on Human Rights, an active subsidiary of ECOSOC, became involved in the problems of southern Africa. It is not clear on whose initiative this new emphasis appeared in the commission, but it is likely that it was related to the expansion of ECOSOC membership, and the formation of new guidelines for action by the commission. In March 1966 ECOSOC invited the Human Rights Commission to consider the problem in southern Africa, particularly in the light of Rhodesian Unilateral Declaration of Independence and events in South West Africa. As might have been expected, the commission condemned the transgressions of liberty in southern Africa, and urged all members to implement sanctions against South Africa. This call was reinforced by ECOSOC in September 1966 in a report to the General Assembly.

The General Assembly, however, was not in a condition to respond quickly. The Special Committee on Apartheid underwent a serious identity crisis in 1966. External factors were jeopardizing its role, as Rhodesia and South West Africa crowded the apartheid issue out of the headlines. Even more serious, however, was its inability to persuade the main trading partners of South Africa to serve on the committee.[79] The expansion of the Special Committee had been an essential ingredient of Chairman Achkar Marof's program of education on apartheid: "By engaging in such a dialogue, the Committee would have entered a new and important phase in its efforts to discharge its mandate of assisting the General Assembly and Security Council to adopt the necessary measures."[80] Another object of this move was to bring the veto-holding members of the Security Council onto the Special Committee. The Secretariat spent the next six months trying to fill those six seats, but only the USSR, among the Great Powers, accepted the offer. It was quite clear that expansion of the committee would be impossible. Some members were ideologically opposed to the Special Committee, and did not want to be harangued further on the apartheid issue—but for smaller states, it was a problem of not having time for more committee meetings. By the end of the search, fifteen out of nineteen states approached had declined, including all of South Africa's main trading partners. The Special Committee was indignant about the refusals: "Such refusal, furthermore, seriously undermines the authority and prestige of the United Nations as an international forum for harmonizing the attitudes of Member States. . . ."[81] "Harmony" meant the acceptance of the Special Committee's viewpoint on economic sanctions, and this many states declined. The committee, at that point, decided to retain its original membership.[82]

The whole episode underlined the African dominance of the Special Committee, and the fact that it existed not to examine all approaches to a solution of the apartheid problem, but to carry out the solution that the Africans had decided was best. The committee's contention that the reluctant states were weakening the UN was probably an overstatement. What the committee members meant was that it damaged whatever prestige the Special Committee on Apartheid retained. As for the UN, the committee reflected an ideal view of the UN as one international community, a view that confused the ideal with reality. Thus the incident did not undermine the authority of the UN, but rather underlined the limited scope of UN authority. The only sense in which UN prestige was undermined was in African eyes, for if member states would not respond to a call to join a committee, the UN might not be worth much as a means of resolving the apartheid dispute. The Africans confirmed that conclusion some time later.

The South Africans could draw some comfort from the unwillingness of the Western Europeans and the United States to serve on the Special Committee. Thus it was made clear that the "Western caucus" in the UN, while continuing to offer verbal condemnation of apartheid, would not support active intervention of any kind.

Other organs were seizing some of the attention. The Committee of Twenty-Four (on the Situation with Regard to the Implementation of the Declaration on the Granting of Independence to Colonial Countries and Peoples) held some hearings on apartheid, as part of its concern about Namibia after the adverse judgment of the ICJ.[83] Of greater importance was the work of ECOSOC and its subsidiary, the Commission on Human Rights, which was engaged in building links with the Special Committee on Apartheid, as mentioned above.[84]

With the approach of the 1966 session of the General Assembly, the Special Committee applied itself to more substantive matters, expressing indignation over the IBRD loans to South Africa on July 29.[85] It decided to expend no further effort on the Security Council, hoping instead that South Africa might be harmed by the Rhodesia and Namibia issues then pending before the Security Council. The committee report was designed to enhance the long-range educational program, working with other organs as they became involved in southern Africa. According to the chairman, the committee "had opened up a new and dynamic phase in the handling of the problem of apartheid by the United Nations."[86] The Special Political Committee distilled the report of the Special Committee on Apartheid and presented proposals to the General Assembly which resulted in passage of Resolution 2202 (XXI). It not only chastised the IBRD for providing loans to South Africa, but enthusiastically endorsed the proposed educational goals, beginning with a conference on racial discrimination in Kitwe, Zambia, to be jointly sponsored by the Committee of Twenty-Four.[87] The UN Secretariat and its Office of Public Information, of course, were to be responsible for an expanded program of propaganda.

The Secretariat was continually involved in the anti-apartheid fight in the UN, especially as U Thant made an increasingly open commitment to the anti-apartheid forces. Its responsibilities were slight at first, involving communication between organs, or similar tasks already forming part of the routine work of the Secretariat. As the demands of the Special Committee grew, and research projects were devised that the committee could not take care of with its own resources, many people felt that some permanent unit should be established to coordinate research and action for the anti-apartheid movement. A good deal of discussion on the subject ensued at the Brasília Conference on Apartheid, where some delegates felt that "the task could not be left to a non-United Nations body whose operations would depend on voluntary contributions from organizations which might be tempted to exert various types of pressure on it."[88] In other words, the unit they had in mind must be: 1) independent of outside political pressures, 2) established permanently to carry on the fight against apartheid, and 3) adequately funded.

The actual establishment was not yet accomplished. Some delegations had anxieties about the "financial impact of the proliferation of Secretariat services," but others attempted to allay those fears. After all, it "would not be a new independent body, but a unit working closely with the Special Committee."[89] It was, in fact, designed to be the full-time "secretariat" for the Special Committee, which was making ever-increasing demands. In October 1966, Chairman Achkar Marof met with the secretary-general to coordinate the establishment of the new unit, which was authorized in a General Assembly resolution that fall.[90] He later reported to the committee that "it is the Special Committee's duty to help ensure that this unit will be able to perform its functions in the most effective way."[91] By January, the Under-Secretary for Political and Security Council Affairs was able to announce the formation of the new unit, with staff recruitment already under way.[92]

Of equal importance with the secretariat unit was the public stance of Secretary-General U Thant, who uncompromisingly opposed South Africa on the apartheid issue. This case is exceptional for the lack of neutrality displayed by U Thant, a rare departure from the previous procedure of secretaries-general.[93] The impact of his stance was to legitimize one side of the argument with the prestige of his office. This was not a drastic step, in view of the apparent sentiment in the General Assembly, but because of the partisan nature of his remarks on a pending issue, it represented an undermining of the ideal of an "impartial international Secretariat." From the point of view of U Thant, the principle of opposition to apartheid was sufficiently accepted as an international norm that it would not be controversial for him to adhere to the cause.

Two important trends were affecting the strength of the African voice in the UN by 1966. The African group was quieter about apartheid, being unable to agree on a solution to the issue. On the other hand, the Special Committee was seizing the initiative, even though it spoke for only one element of the OAU, the more radical states. The solidarity of the Africans was crumbling as some African countries, especially the former High Commission territories and those contiguous to South Africa, took a less absolutist view on dealing with South Africa. Malawi, of course, was the initiator of this new school of thought, a view of southern Africa that caused the formerly unanimous majority view in the OAU to lose strength over the next six years. The manifestations in the OAU were clear: the resolutions became increasingly ritualistic, as it became painful to attempt to debate the issue. Because the measures recommended also evoked less compliance, the effectiveness of sanction and boycott measures gradually diminished.[94] Some noncompliance was the result less of choice than of unusual trade patterns established before independence and difficult to alter. For instance, "at a meeting of the OAU calling for a boycott of South African goods, [President Kenneth] Kaunda [of Zambia] pointed out that every village store in Zambia had goods on its shelves with South Africa labels. . . . On the breakfast tables of Zambia, the cornflake packets were printed in Afrikaans as well as English." The greatest effort was expended on condemning Western nations for continuing their trade with South Africa.[95]

Thus there was great appreciation in the OAU for the concern shown by the General Assembly, beginning with Resolution 2011 (XX). The item of cooperation with the OAU remained on the agenda of the General Assembly in the following two sessions, during which the Assembly thanked the secretary-general for his efforts.[96]

In early 1967, the Commission on Human Rights became more specifically interested in South Africa when, at the urging of the Special Committee, it began consideration of the question of the treatment of prisoners in South Africa.[97] On that subject the commission passed Resolution 2 (XXIII), which indicated the "desire of the Commission of

Human Rights to maintain close collaboration with it [the Special Committee] in achieving their common objective."[98] The commission also appointed a special rapporteur to survey previous UN action on apartheid.[99] There was a clear effort by the commission to cooperate with other bodies interested in apartheid, including specialized agencies; the ILO and UNESCO, for instance, collaborated with the special rapporteur.[100]

The Commission on Human Rights was also willing, however, to pursue a topic on its own for the sake of harassing South Africa. Its investigation of the infringement of trade union rights in southern Africa is characteristic. Allegations of such violations had become quite common by the middle of the decade, and on March 3, 1966, the WFTU sent a letter to the ILO, asking that the charges be investigated, because South Africa had signed a number of ILO conventions guaranteeing certain rights to trade unions. South Africa's membership in the ILO, however, had terminated three days previously, and so the organization saw little purpose in following up that charge. South Africa did still belong to the United Nations; the question was referred to the Commission on Human Rights, which informally established a small working group to investigate the charges. By the beginning of 1967, the 42nd session of ECOSOC, it was clear that there was some substance to the allegations against South Africa, and ECOSOC itself authorized an *ad hoc* Working Group of Experts, employing the same people who were dealing with the problem for the commission, to examine the allegations. A report was delivered to ECOSOC at the 44th session (1968), and since it was obvious that South Africa was not engaging in proper actions, ECOSOC passed a resolution condemning South Africa.[101] The report was then made public by the Office of Public Information one year later under the title *Infringements of Trade Union Rights in Southern Africa* as part of the educational campaign on apartheid.[102]

Many different organizations were studying apartheid by that time. As the report on trade union rights said, "various branches of the United Nations Secretariat, in particular the Apartheid Unit and the Department of Trusteeship and Non-Self-Governing Territories, were of assistance to the Group" as well as the ILO and the OAU.[103] This was in addition to the Working Group itself, ECOSOC, and the Special Committee. The recommendations of the report, of course, dealt with those organizations mentioned above, but there was greater interest than usual in nongovernmental organizations, especially trade unions: "The Group recommends that the Economic and Social Council should appeal to the Great International Trade Unions to continue to offer trade unionists in South Africa the benefit of solidarity funds."[104]

The campaign of the Commission on Human Rights was to grow even stronger in later years, perhaps not surprisingly, since apartheid had been labeled by all organs of the United Nations as the one gross violation of human rights that all states (except South Africa) could readily condemn. The experience of ECOSOC and its subsidiary commissions with the apartheid issue, however, does reinforce the argument of H. G. Nicholas that the Commission on Human Rights had "almost entirely political objectives."[105] This politicization had two effects on ECOSOC's treatment of apartheid. First, it was taken up as a political question, and pursued when politically feasible. It also meant, however, that the commission sought (unsuccessfully) the cooperation of the most politicized organs of the UN family: the Special Committee and the Security Council. This choice of tactics was confrontational in nature, and underscored the ineffectiveness of ECOSOC and its subsidiaries in attacking the apartheid question.[106]

As other organs became increasingly agitated about Namibia, the Special Committee found useful allies for action against South Africa. Indeed, there was a fear on the part of some Special Committee members that the Namibia issue might attain such importance as to obscure the question of apartheid in South Africa itself, as had happened to the question of the Indo-Pakistanis in South Africa.

Enlarging its campaign of international education on the question of apartheid in 1967, the Special Committee experimented with several dramatic tactics in its effort to counter the South African propaganda program. Much of the fireworks was coordinated with the International Year for Human Rights (1968), but other moves were viewed as aspects of a new campaign. The importance of the General Assembly session lessened as the Special Committee obtained an independent life of its own as a year-round activity. The International Day for the Elimination of Racial Discrimination was celebrated on March 21, 1967, the anniversary of Sharpeville, with a special meeting of the Special Committee in the main hall of UN headquarters. All UN delegations were invited to send observers, and most did, with the occurrence becoming an annual event. In a coordinated manner, the Commission on Human Rights held a session on the same day in Geneva. The Special Committee also began traveling, first to the European Conference against Apartheid held in Paris in May 1967, and later to the Kitwe Conference on Racial Discrimination held in Zambia during July and August. The most significant jaunt of the committee members was tied in with the Kitwe Conference, before which they stopped in London, Paris, Dar es Salaam, and other cities to take testimony in the field and demonstrate their existence to a larger audience.[107] Many organizations cooperated by giving testimony, such as ILO, UNESCO, UNHCR, as well as anti-apartheid groups. The technique of holding hearings away from headquarters was to be repeated in later years.

The 1967 report of the Special Committee to the General Assembly, however, had little new to offer in the way of measures against apartheid, mainly suggesting reconsideration by the Security Council, and intensified activity by the Secretariat Unit on Apartheid. In the form of a resolution, the recommendations passed in the General Assembly with little controversy.[108]

The Twenty-Third Session offered the Special Committee an opportunity to examine the effects of its educational campaign against apartheid, since it was the Year for Human Rights. As part of its work, the Special Committee held hearings in London, Stockholm, and Geneva in June, not long after the International Conference on Human Rights, which convened in Teheran in April and May of 1968. That conference did adopt an extraordinarily strongly worded resolution on apartheid, apparently endorsing any means, violent or nonviolent, in the fight against apartheid:

The International Conference on Human Rights, . . .

Solemnly proclaims that: . . .

7. Gross denial of human rights under the repugnant policy of apartheid is a matter of grave concern to the international community. . . . It is therefore imperative for the international community to use every possible means to eradicate this evil. The struggle against apartheid is recognized as legitimate.[109]

Rarely had the absolutist notion of "good" and "evil" been given such a prominent place in the resolutions of an international conference. The only result of the Special Committee's efforts, however, seemed to be a plethora of resolutions in the General Assembly that battered apartheid from all sides, but without cumulative effect. The principal resolution, adopted 85-2-14 as Resolution 2396 (XXIII), merely urged an increased work load on the secretary-general, especially in his unit on apartheid, and the proposal to keep a register of all persons persecuted in South Africa for their opposition to apartheid. The managers of the UN Trust Fund for South Africa were also urged to be more aggressive in their aid to persons persecuted in South Africa.[110] There were, as well, resolutions that dealt with capital punishment, political prisoners, racial discrimination, and related subjects that explicitly mentioned apartheid.[111] South Africa was unmoved.

The shotgun approach of the General Assembly was gaining popularity elsewhere, namely in the ECOSOC and its subsidiaries. By 1968, the Commission on Human Rights was producing numerous resolutions annually that explicitly condemned apartheid.[112] In fact, apartheid and racial discrimination in southern Africa had become the principal object of the commission's attention.

The 1968 report to ECOSOC of the Commission on Human Rights, aside from reflecting the increasing emphasis on southern Africa, indicated an interesting new direction in members' thoughts:

Members of the Commission welcomed the recommendation of the Special Rapporteur concerning the need for greater co-ordination among the United Nations bodies dealing with the problem of apartheid, and urged that a closely co-ordinated plan of action, pursuing clear objectives should be worked out.

Even more strikingly, when discussion turned to the actual organization of coordination, representatives "suggested that the Special Committee on the Policies of Apartheid . . . should be the main center of activity."[113] Little more, however, was done about coordination in 1968, and ECOSOC passed the five resolutions recommended by the commission.[114]

The work of the Special Committee moved into a new phase following the Twenty-Third Session, with the resignation of Achkar Marof, and the advent of the new chairman, Abdulrahim Farah of Somalia, on January 14, 1969. In a sense, the old phase had reached its logical conclusion; the educational campaign was institutionalized in the UN structure, not only in committees of the General Assembly and ECOSOC, but also in the UN Secretariat's Office of Public Information. It was time, then, for the injection of new leadership if the anti-apartheid campaign was to survive the persuasive power of South Africa's "outward-looking" foreign policy and the weakening of the OAU. In Farah, they seemed to have found a leader with that inclination for new policy.

In his first report, Chairman Farah pointed out that the Special Committee had three main lines of action: economic sanctions and embargoes, which might lead to a peaceful solution; dissemination of information (the educational program); and active support for the liberation movements in South Africa.[115] It was clear that the first two emphases had been developed by the previous chairmen, and Farah planned to develop the coordination with the liberation movements. He formally proposed, for example, the establishment of a radio station by the UN to broadcast to South Africa twenty-four hours a day. In the resolutions passed by the General Assembly in late 1969, the imprint of the new chairman was quite obvious. Resolution 2506 B (XXIV) not only repeated the old demands and suggestions, but also requested that member states contribute nonmilitary aid to the South African nationalist movements in cooperation with the OAU and the UN Secretary-General. What made it clear that the tenor of resolutions on apartheid had changed was the decreased majority voting in favor of the resolution: 80–5–23.[116] The new chairman was clearly willing to sacrifice the previous unanimity for a resolution with more force. The General Assembly was willing to go along with the Special Committee, but not quite so enthusiastically.

The Commission on Human Rights also moved into a new phase in early 1969. Among its traditional resolutions on apartheid was a new proposal that provided for yet another organ to deal with apartheid. Described as an ad hoc committee on coordination, the new group was designed to be an adjunct of ECOSOC, with a mandate to facilitate and coordinate the attack on apartheid and racial discrimination in southern Africa.[117] All UN organs concerned with southern Africa were to be the object of study, with a view to implementing drastically improved coordination. The proposal, incidentally, came not from the African group, but from the Latin Americans, especially Chile, one of whose nationals, Hernan Santa Cruz, was serving as special rapporteur on apartheid to the Commission on Human Rights.

When the draft resolution was considered in the Social Committee of ECOSOC, it received a quick and stunning defeat. The strongest opposition came from the unlikely combination of France, Upper Volta, India, and the USSR.[118] This coalition was drawn together by the question of money. All felt that organs dealing with apartheid had proliferated enough and, as Upper Volta delegate Sanon put it, it was "confusing and unnecessary to establish yet another committee to deal with the question of apartheid and racial discrimination in southern Africa."[119] Several delegations argued that even if the committee were created on an ad hoc basis, it would inevitably become permanent by some natural law of bureaucracies.

The solution to the impasse was offered by Britain, which submitted a new resolution to provide for a study by the secretary-general; this study would examine the mandates and current responsibilities of the various organs concerned with southern Africa.[120] At that point, some of the more basic reasons for the dispute in the Social Committee came to the fore. The delegate from Upper Volta, for instance, indicated his concern that the proposed commission might undercut the Special Committee on Apartheid[121]—the recurrent problem of organizational competition that was previously seen in connection with the expert committees of the Security

Council.

Of equal salience was the point of the Jamaican delegate, who spoke in defense of the proposed commission, with special emphasis on what he called the "geographical factor." Even with the benefits of modern communication, geography could make consultation difficult, or at least prohibitively expensive. It was pointed out that :"neither of the two Special Rapporteurs [Ganji and Santa Cruz] concerned with that field [apartheid] was resident in New York, and that made it difficult for them to consult with other bodies."[122] This was a result of the activities of the Commission on Human Rights being centered in Geneva, not in New York, where General Assembly committees habitually convened. The argument did not persuade the other delegates to loosen their pocketbooks, however, and the British motion carried the day.

The plenary session accepted the alterations in the resolution by the Social Committee, and passed Resolution 1414 (XLVI).[123] The death blow to a possible commission on apartheid under ECOSOC came a year later when ECOSOC merely "noted" receipt of the secretary-general's report on coordination.[124] It thus appears that two factors were sufficient to quash this initiative against apartheid from the Latin American group in ECOSOC. One was finances. The other was the existence of several committees in the General Assembly, as repeatedly emphasized by speakers from all blocs; and these committees were considered fully capable of carrying out any functions proposed for this new body at ECOSOC.

The rejection of this committee meant much more, however, especially in the behavior of the African states. Many were disillusioned with the Commission on Human Rights, which could provide nothing more than publicity and rhetoric. In a sense, the incident reflected the political maturity of the African states, many of which were recognizing the current inability of the UN to implement the African program for southern Africa. The force to overthrow the South African regime could clearly come only from within Africa, and the time for spending money for rhetoric was over.

The defeat of the special rapporteur's program for ECOSOC was also a sign of the lessening role for the specialized agencies in the anti-apartheid drive. UN organs were obtaining the voluntary cooperation of just two specialized agencies by 1969: the ILO and UNESCO. Both offered and provided repeated aid in the preparation of UN reports on apartheid, especially in conjunction with ECOSOC. Neither, of course, could affect South Africa directly, since its membership in both organizations had lapsed. The ILO continued to publish annual reports on the labor situation in South Africa, as well as a special volume in March 1969, *The ILO and Apartheid.* UNESCO, too, published occasional pamphlets on apartheid, such as *Four Statements on Apartheid* in late 1969. Their effect on South African racial policies, therefore, was only indirect, and they were important as symbols of solidarity with the UN position on South Africa.

The relationship between the UN and the OAU began changing as well, as Africans realized that the UN could offer nothing but more of what had already been tried. Symbolic ties continued to be forged: U Thant addressed the 1968 OAU meeting in Algiers, expressing his solidarity with the feelings of OAU members towards South Africa:

> Indeed, recent developments point to the danger of violence which, though limited in scope at this stage, might well have grave consequences for the future of that part of the world and for international harmony. The chance of averting this danger depends essentially on the willingness of the great Powers and major trading partners of South Africa to persuade the South African Government to abandon its present course. At the same time, any steps which the members of the OAU may decide to initiate in this direction should assist in preventing a catastrophic aggravation of this situation.[125]

U Thant's idealistic view of combining peaceful change with pressure on the South African government was a position held by the Africans during 1960–65, but abandoned well before the secretary-general came out publicly in their support. By then, the Africans felt they would have to implement a solution unilaterally: some chose dialogue, and some chose violence.

The role of the South African government in slowing down the campaign against apartheid appeared to be only indirect. Certainly many diplomatic initiatives were undertaken by the South Africans to strengthen ties with Western European states and those African states willing to talk to them. By the late 1960s, South Africa had so little remaining presence in international organizations that, virtually by definition, its diplomatic goals had to be pursued through separate bilateral ties.

The period of retrenchment, therefore, was a sobering time for the OAU. It reached the apparent limits of its powers, direct and indirect, to implement sanctions at that time. Equally difficult to budge were the remaining international organizations that kept South Africa as a member. The campaign for ostracism was virtually ended. Even the educational campaign, institutionalized by the UN Secretariat and the Special Committee, offered few challenges and showed few results. Symbolic conflict had run its course; some innovative thinkers turned to violent tactics, understandable in a time of despair. Whether violence would occur depended to a large degree on the strength of the institutional channels of protest established by the OAU, the UN, and other organizations during the stormy decade of the 1960s.

5

A Diplomatic Plateau

The descriptive use of cyclical or linear paths for international history would be misleading in this case, for what had occurred by 1970 was a stalemate—not at the same level of tension as in 1952–59, and with somewhat greater understanding of the stakes in the conflict by both sides. The black Africans had forced South Africa into a new diplomatic posture, but the relative strengths of white and black Africa resulted in a reasonably static situation, a diplomatic plateau of uncertain duration.

The decade of the 1970s witnessed the return of stability to most international organizations. Disruptions by Africans in protest against a South African role in specialized agencies occurred within the framework of constitutional instruments. The confrontational tactics of the previous decade had lost favor with the majority, as South Africa used various diplomatic maneuvers to keep the African states in disarray.

Outside the UN, a remarkable phenomenon was occurring: the greatest pressure was placed on those organizations of which South Africa was no longer a member. The ILO, UNESCO, and the Commonwealth felt the power of the African bloc, as greater demands were expressed for action against the former member. Near the top of the African shopping list were renewed social sanctions to end all contact, direct and indirect, official and unofficial, with South Africa.

A new effort undertaken by the Africans was that of obtaining legitimacy and power for the liberation movements in southern Africa, including South Africa. Particular emphasis was placed on legitimacy, or the recognition of the movements as governments-in-exile. The Africans encouraged transactions (such as humanitarian aid) between the specialized agencies and the liberation movements, on the theory that any form of functional contacts constituted a form of recognition by the international community. In the African mind, there was undoubtedly a parallel to the General Assembly actions regarding Namibia, where a council had been created to govern, with full knowledge that the council did not have the power to obtain entry to Namibia over South Africa's objections. The intergovernmental organizations, in the case of South Africa itself, also recognized that parallel, and demonstrated great reluctance to grant any legitimacy to the liberation movements. That campaign of the Africans will undoubtedly be prolonged.

International organizations, by the 1970s, demonstrated predictable responses to demands for action against apartheid. The issue had been examined so often that there were few surprises for the organizations. The responses were quick, the secretariats knew their powers, and the issue was handled with dispatch. Where severe conflicts had appeared in the previous decade, they were largely ignored in the 1970s, and few efforts were made to prod the World Bank group or the IAEA into action against South Africa. Realism pervaded much of the African camp, and they chose to aim their cannon where the shot might do some damage.

The Security Council, interestingly enough, moved to the periphery of the apartheid dispute for much of the period 1970–74, achieving momentary prominence only when the Africans formally challenged South African membership in the UN in 1974. On all occasions, though, Security Council debates showed little flexibility, and thus the Africans had little faith in promoting change through the council. The wording of resolutions on South Africa was highly predictable. The veto powers of France, Britain, and the United States ensured that South Africa would be labeled a "potential threat to the peace" rather than a "threat," and the remaining paragraphs would repeat those provisions approved during the 1960s relating to the arms embargo and the exhortations to South Africa to change its policies. The Special Committee on Apartheid of the General Assembly could find no new method of prodding the council, and it too, therefore, adopted language to be customarily included in its reports, urging the council to act under Chapter VII of the UN Charter. In the drama from 1970 onwards, then, the Security Council is merely a stage for the expression of particular African grievances against South Africa, and not a source of action.

The issue of social sanctions and education remained alive. Indeed, they were often separated only by the fact that some organizations had forced South Africa out (and thus could apply only educational efforts), and others had not. We shall thus examine them together, and then go on to see the outcome of the efforts to obtain aid for the liberation movements at the UN and to find other legal sanctions that might affect the juridicial basis of South African racial policies.

Social Sanctions and Education

Most remarkable about the period after 1969 was the African discovery that various organizations that had already removed South Africa from their rolls could still be useful in both the educational campaign and indirect social sanctions. The effort to obtain social sanctions also took bizarre turns, as in the question of Britain selling arms to South Africa: frigates would not be used against African nationalists, but the mere fact of selling them to South Africa would imply a degree of respectability to South Africa that the Africans refused to allow. The keystone in the structure of the educational campaign during 1970-74 was the celebration in 1971 of the International Year against Racism and Racial Discrimination. Education, otherwise, continued to be an area in which results could not be measured.

As in the 1960s, the Commonwealth was the center of the first controversy of the new decade.[1] South Africa was, of course, no longer a member, and yet it became the center of a new storm endangering the existence of the Commonwealth.

The question raised by the East African Commonwealth members related to the formal announcement by Britain in early July 1970 that arms sales to South Africa would be resumed by British manufacturers. Protests were sent to Prime Minister Edward Heath by the Canadian and Indian governments; the other states attempted to remain outside the argument. Heath and British Foreign Minister Sir Alec Douglas-Home had clearly underestimated the strength of adverse foreign reaction to the announcement, especially after the British government had taken special precautions to ensure that the ships and planes sold to South Africa would not be designed for use against an internal rebellion or against neighboring states.

There being few means to immediately affect the British view through Commonwealth mechanisms, the Africans turned elsewhere. The presidents of Kenya, Uganda, Tanzania, and Zambia met and consulted, with strong threats of withdrawal from the Commonwealth emanating from three leaders in the event Britain did sell arms to South Africa. A break in diplomatic relations between Britain and three angry African presidents appeared at that point to be the minimum likely consequence of the disagreement. Up to that point, of course, South Africa did nothing. The proposed arms would be useful, but not essential, to the South Africans; on the other hand, the restrengthening of defense ties with Britain (and implicitly, NATO) would be very important to South Africa, but it was not an active partner in the Commonwealth squabble, and said very little.

As a second step, the Africans took their complaint to the UN Security Council. The issue was framed as broadly as possible, including France in the indictment for persistent arms sales to South Africa, in violation of the recommendatory Security Council arms embargo.[2] The constraints on the Afro-Asian group drafting the resolution were obvious, for not only were French and British vetoes certain in case of a strong resolution, but it was thought that such a resolution might even lack the necessary majority of nine in the Security Council.

The resulting resolution in the Security Council was little stronger than what had been passed in 1963–64. It is true that South Africa was no longer characterized as a "disturber" of the peace, but rather as a "potential threat to international peace and security." The Africans saw little to rejoice about in that change, for it was clear that the Security Council could split hairs forever in an effort to avoid the explicit language of Chapter VII of the UN Charter. Thus, without naming states, the council merely went on the record in Resolution 282 (1970) as condemning in general those states that violated the nonmandatory arms embargo of the resolutions in 1963–64.[3] Neither Britain nor France suffered a setback in the council.

The Africans could not persuade the British to back down, however, and the issue seemed headed for a face-to-face confrontation at the Commonwealth heads of state meeting in Singapore in January 1971. The effort to influence Heath's government was shifted to the world press, and as the discussions became more public, the views of the leaders became firm, making compromise all the more difficult. Either the two sides were bluffing, or the January conference would be the last gathering of Commonwealth heads of state.

The African unity on the apartheid issue was rapidly disintegrating during 1970 as well. The meeting of the OAU heads of state in August 1970 was notable for the resolutions not passed. The resolution on apartheid was even more general than usual, merely commending the UN on its organization of the International Year of Action against Racism and Racial Discrimination (1971).[4] What was shattering the OAU was a strong response by several African states to the call of South African Prime Minister Vorster for a dialogue. Vorster had departed from tradition in holding the first news conference by a South African head of government since 1948 to announce that "he was willing to discuss South Africa's policies of racial segregation with leaders of the black nations of Africa." The first talks were scheduled with President Banda of Malawi.[5] Previously, Vorster had maintained a public policy of not discussing "internal problems" with outsiders, but he had decided to expand contacts. Felix Houphouet-Boigny of the Ivory Coast soon responded, agreeing to conversations with South African leaders, and was supported by the leaders of Ghana, Dahomey, Gabon, Lesotho, and Malawi. Houphouet-Boigny's press conference of April 28, 1971, included his statement that "apartheid . . . is a matter within the domestic jurisdiction of South Africa, and it is not by force that it will be eradicated." Madagascar then signed a trade agreement with South Africa, including a loan of about $5 million from South Africa. The potential economic rewards were large for the impoverished black states, but clearly there were political motives involved as well. The French government would have appreciated a little more support from the Francophone African states in its dealings with South Africa,[6] and some Africans simply had little respect for the OAU and African unity.

The South Africans were flexing their diplomatic muscles through the summer and fall of 1970. The prime minister traveled abroad (a highly unusual step in itself) to Malawi, Rhodesia, Portugal, Spain, France, and Switzerland. Rather than merely reacting to external events, South Africa was offering initiatives: associate membership in the European Economic Community, recruitment of capital for the Cabora Bassa hydroelectric project in Mozambique, as well as unnamed defense interests.[7] The Minister of Foreign Affairs, Dr. Hilgard Muller, visited Madagascar to form solid ties, mostly of an economic nature—ties that were to be broken easily in a few years. The South African efforts should not be overestimated, however, for in a sense they represented a reassertion of the natural order, with South Africa playing the role that an economically powerful, industrialized regime in that part of the world would play.

South Africa, as usual, took its knocks in the General Assembly. Action continued to be processed through the UN machinery; the General Assembly accepted the recommendations of the Special Committee on Apartheid. That committee's mandate was expanded for the upcoming International Year against Racism in General Assembly Resolution 2671 (XXV), which also requested the secretary-general to convene a joint meeting of General Assembly committees concerned with southern Africa.[8] The resolution was not innovative, and reflected past concerns, especially in providing for expansion of the Special Committee. The major powers still refused to serve on the committee, and the new recruits were India, Syria, Sudan, Guatemala, and the Ukrainian SSR.[9]

The Special Committee, in any case, was deadlocked in its fight with South Africa. The two sides were producing propaganda of equal strength and therefore changing few minds. Much effort continued to be poured into transient diplomatic maneuvering, as in the Commonwealth dispute over the British arms sales to South Africa. In the General Assembly, the African states pushed through Resolution 2624 (XXV) on October 13, 1970, urging states to implement the arms ban in Security Council Resolution 282 (1970). The resolution did not affect the British. In a gratuitous slap at the South Africans, the credentials of that delegation to the General Assembly were rejected November 13, 1970, on a vote of 60–42–12. This had no effect on South African participation.

Despite the obvious efforts to influence the thinking of the British leaders, little had changed in the constellation of positions before the Commonwealth meeting. Singapore in January 1971 was a time for compromise, and surprisingly enough, nobody decided to withdraw from the Commonwealth in protest. The solution adopted was the creation of a study group to examine the security of the trade routes around the Cape of Good Hope, which had been the ostensible justification for the proposed sale of arms to South Africa. The British were not committed to acceptance of the group's conclusions, and it appeared to be an effort to allow everyone to do as originally intended, but not cause the loss of too much prestige.[10] In effect, the British delayed the sale of arms to South Africa, for a short time, to allow the African members time to either change their minds or use diplomacy to persuade the British government not to sell arms. The study group had not even met, when the British government announced that it would sell seven helicopters to the South Africans; several nations then withdrew from the study group, and it was never convened.[11] The Commonwealth survived, but with even fewer areas of common agreement.

The fall of 1970 was also the time of the initiation of a remarkable UNESCO campaign that was to involve a whole group of organizations not previously included in this study. Indeed, the question of nongovernmental organizations (NGOs) is important primarily to illustrate the derivative power of organizations in the UN family. At the 16th General Conference of UNESCO, in October 1970, a draft resolution was submitted by a group of African and Caribbean countries on the subject of "Peace, Colonialism, and Racialism."[12] The resolution proposed to cover a variety of subjects, including apartheid, and was so sweeping as to provoke opposition from a variety of states, including the USSR and the United States. Under pressure, the principal drafter, Trinidad and Tobago, softened the language, and it eventually passed by a safe margin.[13] It included provisions such as the "break-off of all relations with those international non-governmental organizations . . . [that] cooperate in any way with the Government of the Republic of South Africa in the latter's apartheid policy." The resolution also requested "the Director-General to undertake investigations" of NGOs with consultative status at UNESCO to see that their "branches, sections, affiliates, or constituent parts" in South Africa did not cooperate with South African racial policies. The resolution went on to request the "Director-General to intensify his efforts to counteract the propaganda of the Government of the Republic of South Africa by furnishing the Organization of African Unity and those countries desirous of receiving it with information. . . ." Much of the membership at the General conference was dubious about the UNESCO Secretariat's commitment to the anti-apartheid fight, and considered this resolution to be a method of obtaining more action.

An unusual coalition led the effort for the resolution. The delegation from Trinidad and Tobago took leadership of the African group, and dexterously guided the resolution to enactment. The only concession that the Trinidadians were forced to concede was that further guidance would be obtained from the Executive Board between sessions of the General Conference, rather than having an automatic end of ties with NGOs that had contacts with South Africa.

The director-general then undertook, at the direction of the resolution, a two-year correspondence with the 287 NGOs enjoying relations with UNESCO.[14] The replies from the NGOs came in slowly, and the Executive Board was faced with difficult decisions: i.e., was an organization that had individual members in South Africa who might believe in apartheid subject to penalties? Over the subsequent year, the Executive Board decided that forty-two organizations would be suspended from relations with UNESCO, the penalty prescribed by the General Conference.[15] The decision of the Executive Board at the 88th Session laid out in precise detail the exact steps to be taken by the suspended affiliates if they wished to resume observer status at UNESCO. Some of them did respond, by the time of the 90th meeting of the Executive Board in October 1972, and only ten NGOs remained in the bad graces of UNESCO, six of them for never having responded to the letters from the director-general.[16] The measures, therefore, taken by UNESCO had not resulted in upheavals in the world of NGOs. Rather, there were slight adjustments on the part of about thirty organizations who wished to meet UNESCO standards.[17]

The impact of a policy change by a unit of the UN family thus spread far beyond the intergovernmental organizations themselves. The policing of the international community was not restricted to the usual components of international life, sovereign states. Instead, there was the growing phenomenon of the involvement of NGOs in affairs beyond their immediate specialized concerns.

In other specialized agencies, old battles continued, as the drive to ostracize South Africa continued. ICAO had its troubles in the 1970–71 diplomatic season, as the East Africans attempted to expel South Africa. They proposed such a step in the 18th Council Meeting of ICAO, in November 1970.[18] The rest of the council first voted for a closed meeting (8–6), and then defeated the Tanzanian efforts to have the question placed on the agenda of the 18th ICAO Assembly. Tanzania insisted that ICAO needed to implement UN General Assembly Resolution 2555, but the rest of the council disagreed. The vote to include the item was only 11–5–1, and the motion needed 14, a statutory majority.

The issue that did arise at the 18th session of the ICAO Assembly was the nature of South African participation.[19] The draft resolution proposed withholding information and documents, except what was required by the Convention on Civil Aviation (under articles 48B, 53, and 57B); it also proposed withholding invitations to South Africa for all ICAO meetings. In the Executive Committee, the resolution passed 51–30–13. In the plenary session, however, votes were taken by secret ballot on the motion to penalize both Portugal and South Africa. Portugal managed to stay in by a vote of 40-41-6, and South Africa lost 44-39-4.[20] At the ICAO council meeting immediately thereafter, the council rejected by a vote of 8–9 a bid to disinvite South Africa to a conference on unlawful interference with aircraft. Most seemed to feel that such a retroactive step would be illegal or spiteful or both. The assembly resolution was implemented, however, at the subsequent council meeting in October 1971 by a vote of 13–3–11.[21] South Africa remained a member.

In the Inter-Govermental Maritime Consultative Organization (IMCO), too, South African participation was under
attack. What was curious was that South Africa was not a
member, but the Secretariat sent all material to South Africa
and invited it to conferences dealing with the South Atlantic
and Indian Oceans. At the 7th Assembly, the IMCO decided
to continue that form of collaboration with South Africa, in
a secret ballot by a vote of 27–23–3, on October 15, 1971. In
the council, similar motions to end ties with South Africa
were made in May 1972 by the USSR and Algeria, but were
deferred to the November session. On November 8, the
council rejected a motion to bar South Africa, 4–12–1, with
only the USSR, Poland, India, and Algeria voting affirma-
tively. The issue was thus left open for the November 1973
meeting of the IMCO Assembly.

An interlude of high diplomacy took place in late January
1972 in Addis Ababa where the Security Council held its first
meeting away from headquarters, at the behest of the African
states. The resolution proposed by Guinea, India, Somalia,
Sudan, and Yugoslavia was rather mild,[22] probably as a
result of the Africans' desire for an impressive rather than
substantive meeting. The language used in the resolution
illustrates their wish to avoid provoking serious disagreement; the phrasing regarding South Africa's presence was
"seriously disturbing international peace and security."[23]
The apartheid policy itself was not and had not recently been
the prime concern between the Africans and the council.
Namibia had been the principal topic during 1971, and was
even the subject of a Zambian complaint against South
Africa regarding alleged border crossings at the Caprivi
Strip–Zambezi River junction.[24] The Security Council meeting in Addis Ababa was important to the African cause,
particularly for the wide publicity provided for their point of
view.

A second perspective of the Security Council meeting in
Addis Ababa existed in relation to the ongoing cooperation
between the UN and the OAU.[25] The issue had been temporarily tabled in 1968, and then placed on the agenda of the
General Assembly again in 1969. The African purpose in
raising the issue was no longer simply to obtain observer
status for the OAU at UN Headquarters and meetings. The
OAU and its committee needed functional help from the

UN, and the symbolic legitimacy that only the UN could confer. The goal of African unity was greatly threatened in the late 1960s, as political unity was manifestly absent, and economic development plans were not working miracles. Thus the OAU, and its African members, turned to the UN to obtain sorely needed help in nearly all aspects of the regional organization's activities.

The symbolic efforts made by the UN to help the OAU included holding the Security Council meeting in late January and early February 1972 in Addis Ababa, where OAU Headquarters was located. That move was the result of a campaign by African states to obtain greater attention for southern African problems.[26] The observer status of the OAU was also expanded, including many meetings with broad agendas, such as the UN Commission on International Trade Law, UN seminars on the status of women and family planning, and the Advisory Committee for the Application of Science and Technology to Development.[27]

Functional ties included some technical cooperation, with the UN training interpreters for the OAU and coordinating the release of information on southern Africa, and particularly ties between the ECA and the OAU. Most economic work done under the joint ECA-OAU aegis was in fact performed by the ECA, and fortunately both of them were located in Addis Ababa. With good reason, the General Assembly continues to urge even closer cooperation between UN organs and the OAU.[28]

The work in education and propaganda concluded with a renewal of demands for support and unity from Africans. The meeting of the OAU in June 1972 in Rabat, Morocco, was dramatic in both private discussions and public statements. It was a time of hopefulness, as a planning stage for the tenth anniversary celebration in Addis Ababa in June 1973. The public sense of excitement was heightened by King Hassan's commitment of one million dollars to the OAU Liberation Committee. In the discussions, however, the issues of southern Africa were sources of dissent as well as unity. The administrative secretary-general, replaced at that meeting, stated that "at the OAU there now existed a divergency in the approach to solutions to problems raised by the persistence of colonialism, racial discrimination, and Apartheid in Southern Africa."[29] This was the question of "dialogue," still plaguing the African camp with divisiveness. What he was asking for, in the conclusion of his report, was more money and and "extended mandate" for public relations in the US and at the UN.[30] The OAU Council of Ministers could hardly give him either, though, for they had little money, and too many members were skeptical of what the Secretariat might do with his larger mandate. The meeting was a time of discord on other items, such as French arms sales to South Africa, which split the Francophone states from the Anglophone. But the themes had not changed over nine years. The OAU, as ever, was dependent upon efforts to move other organizations to action.

Aid to the Liberation Movements

The newly prominent effort of the Africans was to obtain both symbolic and concrete aid for the liberation movements in southern Africa. While the groups at work liberating South Africa were extraordinarily weak, they were included as objects of aid, in part because there were many South African refugees to whom aid could be directed.

In the UN family, the organization first involved with the issue, logically enough, was the administrative structure of the UN High Commissioner for Refugees (UNHCR). The UNHCR had, in the course of the 1960s, and at the urging of the General Assembly Special Committee on Apartheid, decided to do more than merely provide subsistence to the refugees. During the period 1964–70, for instance, cooperation between UNESCO and the UNHCR grew in response to the need for education for the refugees in Southern Africa.[31] At all times, however, the help was to be extended by UNESCO, "in response to a request from the Government" of the country in which the refugees were residing. Aid was to be granted "within the context of the national development plans of the countries in which the refugees have taken asylum."[32] This last point was accepted by the African states for some time, until they realized that if they wanted to establish the separate, legitimate existence of the liberation movements as governments, the criteria for aid as set forth above might need to be changed.

The OAU initiated the formal effort to obtain legitimacy

for the liberation movements in southern Africa. One argument in favor of direct aid to the movements was the precedent of aid from particular states. The northern European states, for example, were prominent in such efforts, as can be seen in the approximate totals of the following table:

	1968-69	1969-70	1970-71	1971-72
Sweden	$70,000	$140,000	$360,000	$1,000,000
Norway		140,000	100,000	225,000
Netherlands			70,000	
Denmark			30,000	900,000
Finland			30,000	

There was much more aid, but this aid was legally appropriated and distributed, and therefore of much more diplomatic importance than, say, two tons of guns and ammunition covertly supplied to the liberation movements. The OAU then turned to the specialized agencies for more humanitarian aid.

In UNESCO, the OAU found an organization reasonably receptive to the expansion of aid, especially after the appointment of a full-time UNESCO representative to the OAU in July 1970.[33] From the 84th Executive Board meeting onward, after 1970, UNESCO became committed to aiding the liberation movements, and to examining the question of possible association of the liberation movements with U-NESCO. These goals were reaffirmed by the General Conference in 1972. In UNESCO Resolution 10.1, the General Conference decided "to associate with the Organization's activities, including those of the General Conference, the representatives of the African liberation movements recognized by the Organization of African Unity."[34]

The director-general of UNESCO had originally been of the opinion that representatives of the liberation movements could easily participate in UNESCO conferences in their private capacities, as individuals.[35] Even after the decision of the General Conference mentioned above, the director-general still felt that constitutional problems existed, that certain provisions would have to be altered to put the decision into force.[36] The Executive Board decided in April 1973 to give the liberation movements observer status at UNESCO, when the issue under discussion pertained to the movements. In addition, the board gave the director-general discretion as to other conferences or consultation in which he might invite participation of the liberation movements.[37] With the apparent reluctance of the director-general to become strongly involved in southern Africa, the full participation of the liberation movements had to await specific action by the General Conference.

UNESCO was responsible for the involvement of other organizations, too, and the most prominent was the UN Development Program (UNDP). In 1970–71, UNESCO agreed to a request from the OAU to give educational aid to the refugee populations outside liberated areas, and allocated $40,000 for the purpose.[38] UNESCO was prepared to administer additional funds if they could be obtained from extra-budgetary sources, and so the UNDP was approached. The UNDP suggested a grant figure of $500,000, an amount that would be subtracted from allocations for Tanzania, Zambia, and Guinea, or from the African regional allocation. The Africans objected strongly.[39] The OAU Council of Ministers decided that they wanted assistance explicitly to the liberation movements, and directed Secretary-General Telli to obtain that.[40] Telli's ploy was then to ask UNDP Administrator Rudolph Peterson to create a special UNDP fund for financing OAU projects for refugees and liberated areas in southern Africa; Peterson rejected that idea as being *"a priori* restrictive and contrary to the very spirit of our cooperation,'' which Telli had to accept.[41] The program then went ahead, on the UNDP terms, with $353,000 allocated to the UNESCO program for refugees in Africa. It included textbook printing, literacy work, cultural activities, and employment aid for refugees.[42]

The Africans were thus encountering resistance to their idea of obtaining the rights of governments for the liberation movements. Efforts were also made in the ITU, where the fruits of the African efforts were allocations for the training of refugees in telecommunications employment.[43] In the WHO, too, the OAU requested aid for the liberation movements. The Executive Board objected, until it was pointed out that the UNDP could provide the funding, on the precedent of the UNESCO case. The director-general was then directed to develop the proposals further.[44] Clearly the effort to assist the liberation movements was facilitated by the absence of South Africa and Portugal from those organizations, but the important step, the recognition of the movements as substitute governments, was not taken by any organization, and would not be done for some time in relation to South Africa itself.

Legal Sanctions

The movement for legal sanctions against South Africa received a strong boost from non-African sources as the 1970s began. The area of legal sanctions has been a difficult tool for use against South Africa, in view of the rather primitive modes of international jurisprudence available to the opponents of apartheid. The Convention against Racial Discrimination has already been discussed above, and South Africa, of course, has not adhered to that convention, making it useless as a weapon against apartheid.[45]

In 1970–71, the USSR and Guinea began the construction of a new legal platform from which to indict South Africa for its racial policies. The initial effort was a Draft Convention on the Suppression and Punishment of the Crime of Apartheid.[46] The draft convention asserted first of all that apartheid was a "crime against humanity" (Article 1). In support of this contention, the USSR cited Article 6(c) of the Nuremburg Tribunal Establishment and General Assembly Resolution 2775 (XXVI) of November 29, 1971, in which apartheid was described in the above words. One can question, naturally, the authority of the General Assemlby to establish legal standards of that import, but a draft convention using those words, when ratified and in force, would go a long way toward establishing the new standard. The General Assembly chose to take no action on the Soviet proposal at that time, referring it back to the Commission on Human Rights for further study.[47]

The Commission on Human Rights had a parallel effort underway. A group of experts had been studying the South African racial policies from the point of view of existing international penal law, and came up with two conclusions: there was no basis for prosecution of South Africa under existing law, and yet, at the same time, South Africa was violating the Nuremburg Laws (General Assembly Resolution 95 (I)), the Convention on the Non-Applicability of Statutory Limitation to War Crimes and Crimes against Humanity, and the Declaration on Human Rights.[48] At the 28th Session of the commission, no action was taken, but the commission did request the views of governments, and asked the General Assembly to consider the convention as a priority matter. Some of the Western delegations were concerned about the direction of thought on the draft convention, and attempted to move its consideration from the Third Committee to the Sixth (Legal) Committee, but to no avail. In the 27th Session, it was considered once again, the provisions were refined to provide for enforcement and investigation by a subcommittee of the Commission on Human Rights, but the delegations tabled the question again. They needed further study by their governments.[49]

The efforts to create the convention were delayed by several factors. A legal instrument is a complex document, and the governments having a strong interest (the Africans) had few legal experts to give the question the immediate attention that the USSR wanted. The Africans needed to be careful that they would not become subject to the provisions of the conventions if it were framed so broadly as to include their particular racial problems. A second complication was a counterproposal by Nigeria, Pakistan, and Tanzania that the same purposes could be accomplished by a protocol to the Convention on the Elimination of Racial Discrimination.

Interested states managed to sort out the various complications surrounding legal sanctions at the 28th Session, with the passage of the Draft Convention on the Suppression and Punishment of the Crime of Apartheid.[50] The convention was opened for signature in November 1973, but will not enter into force until ratified by twenty states, and will have little impact on South Africa until ratified by this unique overt practitioner of apartheid.

The importance of the convention was clearly limited, if only because nearly all states recognized that apartheid was already covered by the Convention to Abolish All Forms of Racial Discrimination. Because of that overlap, the Convention against Apartheid was not opposed with any particular vigor. It simply seemed to be a redundancy.[51] How the convention might achieve greater importance in the future is hard to predict.

Final Act: UN Standoff on Expulsion

Events in Southern Africa from 1974 onward led to a dramatic testing of South Africa's position in the UN and a subsequent decision by the interested governments to bypass the UN as a forum for meaningful negotiation. The changes of government in Portugal, the subsequent independence of Mozambique and Angola, and the move by all parties in Rhodesia to negotiate indicated that the southern African situation was again fluid. For the South African government, the historic changes under way led them into a dialogue acknowledging the legitimacy of a white government in South Africa. For most African states, however, the new fluidity in southern Africa meant that they saw an opportunity to place greater pressure, perhaps the final push, on South Africa's apartheid policies. The results of that confrontation indicated to the world how solid the ongoing stalemate in South Africa was.

South Africa's test in the UN came in the Twenty-Ninth Session of the General Assembly, during the fall of 1974. The first vote was straightforward: a decision not to accept the credentials of the South African delegation. Such a move had been routine in recent years; so the decision by the General Assembly on September 30 was potentially meaningless. The only concern on the part of the South Africans was the presence of Algeria's Abdelaziz Bouteflika in the president's chair, a position that gave him the theoretical power to enforce the credentials decision. Bouteflika was in the midst of putting together a "third world" coalition for a grand offensive on economic issues, and was thus willing to accommodate the Africans on the apartheid issue. Bouteflika's decision, however, was delayed as the Africans moved to the Security Council to press for the removal of South Africa from the organization entirely.

In the Security Council, the arguments of the various delegations reflected the experience of fifteen years, as they balanced the power of social sanctions against the power of persuasion (through universal membership in the UN). The Africans demanded with great fervor the removal of a moral cancer from the UN, and cited the virtually unanimous opinion of the General Assembly in their favor. Compromise efforts for a resolution were not successful, and when the African resolution providing for the expulsion of South

Africa was put to a vote on October 30, 1974, it was vetoed by the United States, Britain, and France. Such a united response by the Western states was not expected, and it underlined the profound division in the UN over South Africa: divergent senses of morality, and in terms of political power, numbers versus strength.

The Africans condemned the Western vetoes, but found themselves largely powerless to do anything about them. Some moderate African diplomats did take solace in the fact that the Western powers had once again committed themselves to placing pressure on South Africa, but only on a bilateral basis and without accountability to the UN.

Having achieved no satisfaction in the council, the Africans turned to the General Assembly, and urged Bouteflika to enforce the decision on credentials. He did so, in a decision on November 12, and was upheld in a vote of 91–22.[52] For the first time in UN history, a member state was suspended from participation in the General Assembly session, much as it had happened to South Africa in numerous other plenary bodies of international organizations.

The African-organized majority in the UN had thus reached the limits of its constitutional authority. South Africa was banished from the General Assembly, making the ostracism of that state even more dramatic. South Africa had thus been removed from the most public places of the international diplomatic arena. Social sanctions on a multilateral level were effectively complete.

The UN and other organizations have continued to pass resolutions condemning South Africa's policies. In the fall of 1976, the UN General Assembly passed ten separate resolutions on apartheid, calling for a complete economic boycott, an arms embargo, the exclusion of South Africa from all international events, and so forth. South Africa's response was categorical rejection of the resolutions as irrelevant and unconstructive. South Africa, in any case, has not attended the General Assembly or submitted credentials for its delegates since the Twenty-Ninth Session (1974) described above. It has not met any financial commitments since that date either, since the only penalty for not doing so is the loss of voting rights in the General Assembly. The dispute over apartheid has thus arrived at a remarkably stable condition: freedom for the General Assembly to pass any and all resolutions, and the freedom for South Africa to ignore them. The Africans won the battle for social sanctions in international organizations, and apartheid remains.

6

From the Present
to the Future

The involvement of the international community in the apartheid dispute over a period of more than two decades produced a mixed bag of successes and failures. The time of our emphasis, 1960 to 1976, displayed more prominently than any other period the ups and downs of international interest, attempts at solution, and organizational effectiveness.

In terms of the internal apartheid policy and the condition of the black man in South Africa, little changed. The signs of change that did appear—increased multiracialism in sports, tolerance of ad hoc black labor groupings, and encouragement of semi-independent Bantustans—did little to draw together the relative positions of black and white in South African society. In absolute terms, the South African nonwhite became more prosperous economically, but his grievances remained just as profound.

South Africa, after all, rejected formally all attempts by international organizations to interfere in what it considered a domestic situation. The result was that South Africa ignored all resolutions, requests, ultimata, and inquiries that suggested international jurisdiction over domestic apartheid policies. With regard to the black African independent states, however, South Africa realized that, by their self-generated interest and involvement in the question of apartheid, an international dispute was evolving. South Africa could not ignore the challenge of its neighbors, tending as it did towards violence or at least economic damage, and responded with a strong diplomatic counterattack. We have seen its importance in the last half of the 1960s.

An additional failure of international organizations in this dispute was the unwillingness of sovereign states and groups of states to respond to the UN resolutions on apartheid. If there was hope that the members of international organizations would collectively apply their political and economic leverage to end apartheid, that hope was repeatedly turned to despair. This failure cannot be traced to any one state or group of states. The failure of economic sanctions, for instance, can be related in a substantive fashion to the policies of Britain and the United States, but also symbolically to the inability or reluctance of many African states to sever ties with South Africa. Even the Communist states were less than totally dedicated to the anti-apartheid cause, abstaining on some occasions when voting in favor of the proposed resolution would have been significant.

The responses of states to resolutions of organizations make irrelevant one allegedly important issue: the blame for the slight success of the anti-apartheid drive. The international system, where enforcement is still carried out by sovereign states, is simply not ready to support efforts to end apartheid forcefully.

Where international organizations can be said to have exercised their powers with some success is in controlling the international manifestations of the conflict. This was a separate component of the apartheid dispute, distinguishable from the domestic aspects by the independent African states acting as surrogates for the black South Africans. The international component was more than simply outside intervention in a domestic dispute; because of the difficulty of having an effect *within* South Africa, the African states had to find a new arena *outside* South Africa. In that way, a new international dispute liable to lead to warfare was created, and international organizations attempted to limit that conflict. In the form of the African states versus South Africa, the dispute was brought to international forums, from which black South Africans were generally excluded. African states had to take the lead, since only member states usually had the standing before international organizations to discuss apartheid, and in any case, only independent states had the diplomatic resources to maintain the campaign over a period of time.

Some symptoms of the internationalized dispute were easier to control, especially in the UN. Harbingers of violence between black and white Africa appeared infrequently, because of the inefficiency of the OAU Liberation Committee, and the deterrent power of the UN.[1] As tends to happen with many issues on the agenda of the General Assembly, the apartheid dispute was gradually shunted into a routine that guaranteed the least possible controversy. Many members consider the minimizing of conflict within the organization more important than the fight against apartheid. In view of the many and divergent opinions on how to fight apartheid, many prefer to follow a standard procedure and pass the same delicately worded resolution each year. Other organizations managed to defuse the apartheid issue in its international manifestations more rapidly, i.e., most specialized agencies decided to remove South Africa. Specialized agencies, after all, preferred not to devote time and energy to political problems that were considered best handled by the United Nations.

Efforts to obtain social sanctions against South Africa have resulted in: forced withdrawal from the Commonwealth, the International Labor Organization, the Food and Agriculture Organization, and the World Health Organization; withdrawal from UNESCO; suspension from the Economic Commission for Africa; exclusion from conferences of the ITU, UPU, ICAO, and various specialized conferences, particularly those held by the UN for the African region. Thus, the clear legal fact is that South Africa has not been expelled from any major intergovernmental organizations. As Louis Sohn points out, however, the distinction between expulsion and forced withdrawal is one of little importance.[2] The fact that South Africa did in four cases withdraw under severe pressure indicates some sensitivity to the international disapproval of its apartheid policies. Even more indicative of its sensitivity has been its voluntary withdrawal from UNESCO and many of the UN General Assembly sessions, where South African diplomats became unwilling to endure the perennial verbal battering.

The effect of social sanctions appears to have been very limited in putting an end to apartheid. The South African case certainly confirms conclusions reached with regard to the Spanish exclusion (1945–50) from the UN family and the Soviet expulsion from the League of Nations.[3] The South Africans have not altered their policies, not even conceding the principle of equality for citizens of South Africa. There has thus remained alive the alternative approach of the Western states, that perhaps South Africa can be "educated away" from its present racial policies while remaining within the international community.[4] It might be noted that there was no mention of expulsion in the report of the Security Council Group of Experts in April 1964. The only punishment for noncooperation mentioned was economic sanctions. Social sanctions, in forcing the withdrawal of South Africa from organizations, have clearly been used for symbolic purposes, and in that sense, may have had a salutary effect on the frustrated opponents of apartheid.

There is a range of tactics to be considered between outright expulsion and inaction, even though some observers tend to overestimate the value of those gradualist tactics in the South African case. Examples include suspension of voting rights or services, rejection of credentials, and exclusion from certain conferences or committees. While these tactics might educate other states, South Africa has generally withdrawn from organizations when confronted by resolutions embodying such sanctions. The object of retaining it within the organizations is thus defeated. In some cases, such as the ICAO or the UN, South Africa has merely accepted its exclusion from certain subsidiary bodies as the price of maintaining membership without all the rights and privileges normally attached thereto. For South Africa, the idea of participating in only some of the activities of an organization is not new, for it has done so voluntarily since the early 1950s in the UN. The fact that it is now compelled to do so by majority vote has affected its apartheid policy little, if at all.

Such a conclusion raises an issue much too ambitious to be treated here, namely the extent to which South African society thrives on adversity. Clearly some elements of the population would like to conform to international standards, and their impact on government policy does much to affect the pace of change in South Africa, if not its ultimate direction. For some South Africans, the guiding environment is the world at large, and for others it is the non-

Communist, Western world. For many South Africans, however, the concept of apartheid, or "separateness," is a norm intended not only for South Africa but also for South Africa's relations with the world. The history of Transvaal Afrikaanerdom is infused with a maintenance of a guard against outsiders, whether Bantu, Cape English, or the rest of the world. As in the past, the social sanctions imposed by international organizations could actually feed the will to resist on the part of those South Africans. Such a hypothesis, however, deserves the attention of trained sociologists, sensitive to the degree of preservation of values and norms in the various segments of South African society.

The apartheid dispute illustrates the good faith of nearly all international organizations to attempt the maintenance of a common policy on political issues. Over the test of time, it became clear which organizations would be unwilling to adhere to a tacitly agreed-upon policy, dissenting in a radical or conservative fashion. The African regional organizations, of course, tended to the radical side, while the World Bank group and the IAEA were more conservative. The success in maintaining a harmonious policy between most organizations, however, indicated the degree to which a sense of an international community existed in the UN family, or to which this issue helped to create that sense.[5]

The cooperation between organizations is even more remarkable when one realizes that many of them were in roles for which they were ill-equipped, namely attempting to handle political questions which are generally left to the Security Council. As various organizations took hesitant action toward removing South Africa from their memberships, South Africa refused to adjust its apartheid policies. While South Africa ceases to attend many conferences, it remained a member of most specialized agencies. In maintaining its constitutional rights as a member, South Africa caused the tension over its apartheid policy to remain within the organizations, diverting valuable resources to the handling of the dispute at regional and general conferences. Clearly the African states were as much at fault as South Africa and its defenders, but the dispute was one that disrupted the normal services of several specialized agencies, particularly in the African region. The Security Council, endowed with "primary responsibility" for peace and securi-

ty, chose to take no action other than the creation of committees. Then the educational campaign (conferences, press
releases, seminars, special studies, taking of testimony,
propaganda distribution, expansion of Special Committee
membership, etc.), became operative, utilizing capabilities
the organizations did possess, and thereby providing the ongoing core of the anti-apartheid movement in the governmental international community.

The South Africans, as a result of their uncertain status in
the UN General Assembly, now find themselves in the midst
of another agonizing reappraisal of their proper course of
action in relation to the UN family. At the end of the
Twenty-Ninth Session of the UN General Assembly, the
Vorster government withdrew its permanent representative
to the UN for consultations. Even more important, South
Africa ceases paying financial assessments to the UN, a move
it has also undertaken against the ICAO, for which it
subsequently lost voting rights. In the UN case, the South
Africans appear to be operating more on the precedent of the
Republic of China, which anticipated its eventual removal
from the UN by not paying its dues to the organization.[6]

The current South African need for self-examination is
not simply the product of present circumstances; rather, it
stems from the historically ambivalent attitude of the South
Africans toward the international community. Divided into
Boer and Briton, nationalist and internationalist, white and
non-white, inward-trekking and outward-looking, the
South Africans would, in any case, be in the midst of
emotional and diplomatic dilemmas. The crises in international organizations, however, persistently raise those contradictions and challenge South Africa to seek a solution.

Thus the future is hardly a realm for safe projections. The
anti-apartheid campaign will continue, but with widely
varying tactics and strength, depending upon the diplomatic
leaders among the African and Western states. Random
events in Africa can easily cause dramatic changes in the
apartheid equation, given the weakness of institutionalized
policies in many of the African countries.

Within the arena of international organizations, the anti-
apartheid campaign is largely burned out. It seems clear,
from the experience of organizations from which South
Africa was removed, that follow-up measures against a

nonmember have little effect. And in the UN itself, where South Africa remains a rather inactive member, the issue of South African membership is becoming part of a large issue fought out by the Great Powers. Such a point was made by former United States Ambassador John Scali as he vetoed the effort to expel South Africa in October 1974: "Expulsion would set a shattering precedent which could gravely damage the UN structure. It would bring into question one of the most fundamental concepts on which our charter is based— the concept of a forum in which ideas and ideals are voiced and revoiced along with conflicting views."[7] The problem of the South African "precedent" has escalated since that time, as analogous campaigns for expulsion have been undertaken against other unpopular states such as Israel.

In the specialized agencies, the "mop-up operation" against South Africa continues, as seen in recent years. The UPU, for instance, again excluded South Africa from its meetings (based on the precedents of 1964 and 1969) at the Seventeenth Congress in May 1974. South Africa lost its voting powers at the ICAO, as a result of refusing to pay its financial contribution in full during 1972–74. Likewise, at the World Meteorological Organization meeting in April 1975 South Africa was suspended from membership, amid speculation about its permanent status. These instances simply illustrate the quandary of the specialized agencies, which are organizations with functional interests, in which the majority of the voting power is held by states uncommitted to universality of membership. Such a trend, however, is unlikely to carry over into the agencies where the Western states have a significant control over the decision making apparatus: the World Bank group and the IAEA. The only major development that would allow for action against South Africa in the World Bank group would be the complete demonetization of gold. An analogous transformation of the role of nuclear weapons in the international system cannot be envisioned, that might allow for a reduction of South Africa's important role in the IAEA.

Support for South Africa from the developed states is becoming predicated increasingly upon the widely cited "interdependence" of the modern world. The growth of economic transactions, and particularly the importance of South African mineral resources to the developed states, virtually ensures that the United States and Western Europe will not be diminishing their support for a peaceful resolution of the apartheid dispute. The economic and military establishments of the developed states, for instance, find that some limited support of the South African regime is a logical corollary of their growing dependence upon South African uranium supplies.[8] The South Africans are doing all they can, in the exploration and development of scarce minerals, to ensure that the links between Western industrial health and South African stability are maintained. Such links do help to determine the stance of the developed states in international organizations.

South Africa does not rest content with the political clout obtained through contacts with the West, however, as can be seen clearly in the unremitting efforts of the Vorster government to establish a "dialogue" with the African states. The resistance to such moves encountered by the South Africans appears to be less on the bilateral level, as can be seen in Vorster's secret trip to the Ivory Coast and Liberia in early 1975, and more with the effort to change official policies of the OAU that have been in effect for more than ten years. The cultivation of ties with various African states, symbolized most dramatically by loans to the Central African Republic and the Malagasy Republic, has not yet converted a majority of the OAU members to an endorsement of "dialogue" with the South African government. Whatever the various shifts of official African opinion, however, ranging from the strongly anti–South African resolutions adopted in Dar es Salaam in April 1975 to the moderate view of the OAU Summit in Kampala in August 1975, the South African government continues to commit itself to consultation with amenable African governments whenever possible. Such consultation, however, will have an impact on universal organizations only when the OAU has undergone a major shift in its South African policy.

Thus, in considering the future of the apartheid dispute, one must consider a whole group of variables. Many governments have roles in the conflict, with none of them, other than South Africa, having a clearly decisive role in the future of the dispute. The mere fact that it will be groups of states that determine the future of the conflict, however, ensures an important role for international organizations, at least as indicators of changing positions by governments. The contours of the dispute since 1960 indicate that the directions of the conflict cannot be predicted; but it is certain that apartheid will remain an issue of contention, and that international organizations will continue to be arenas for the battles to take place.

A Note on Sources

Henry Adams once cynically remarked, with some accuracy, that "practical politics consists in ignoring the facts." While much of the international debate over southern Africa does appear to ignore the "facts," this study has attempted to include both facts and politics, in order to bridge the gap between present political forces and an objective understanding of the situation that might eventually yield a resolution of the dispute.

This study, fortunately, focuses on the international transactions that affect the political outcome in South Africa. Thus, much is a matter of public record, primarily of the international organizations that have concerned themselves with the apartheid dispute. Access to such documentation by scholars is generally not difficult, given the existence of depository libraries in most regions where the UN keeps full collections of official documents. Somewhat more difficult to obtain are the records of the specialized agencies, available at their headquarters and, to some degree of comprehensiveness, at major American university library collections.

The documentation of the African organizations is not coherently collected and available at any one spot. Copies of documents from the 1960s issued by the Organization of African Unity and the Conference of Independent African States can be found in the hands of many American scholars interested in African political affairs.

The notes, therefore, frequently do not cite a publisher or a location for the documents. Most of the documents are mimeographed, but utilize standard documentation classifications in order to facilitate further study by scholars interested in pursuing this topic further. The most commonly used notation includes: SCOR (Security Council Official Records), GAOR (General Assembly Official Records), ESCOR (Economic and Social Council Official Records)—

all issued by the UN. Working documents are identified by their UN identifications: A/, referring to General Assembly documents; S/, referring to Security Council documents; and E/, referring to Economic and Social Council documents.

In the case of the specialized agencies, the documents are identified by the originating agencies. Occasionally the suffix -OR is added to an organization, such as the WHO, in order to indicate that the organization itself uses such forms of classification for its own Official Records.

In the African organizations, the Organization of African Unity uses only two classifications: HG/, referring to documents that relate to the meetings of Heads of Government; and CM/, referring to documentation for the Council of Ministers of the OAU.

Other forms of material used in this study, such as books, articles, and newspapers, have been identified in a fashion that should be readily familiar to the reader seeking further information. Needless to say, a study such as this could not explicitly draw upon all published materials relating to South Africa; the most useful are included in the notes.

Notes

Chapter 1

1. The essential work on this subject is Leo Kuper, *An African Bourgeoisie: Race, Class, and Politics in South Africa* (New Haven: Yale University Press, 1965); relatively dispassionate analyses are given in Leo Marquard, *The Peoples and Politics of South Africa* (London: Oxford University Press, 1969) and in Edgar H. Brookes, ed., *Apartheid: A Documentary Study of Modern South Africa* (London: Routledge & Kegan Paul, 1968); the most recent analysis of economic trends and contradictions is by Heribert Adam, *Modernizing Racial Domination: South Africa's Political Dynamics* (Berkeley: University of California Press, 1971), in which he suggests that South Africa may not be, as many assume, "the most outdated relic of a dying colonialism," but rather "one of the most advanced and effective patterns of rational, oligarchic domination" (p. 16).

2. See L. M. Thompson, *The Unification of South Africa, 1902-10* (London: Clarendon Press, 1960).

3. See Gilbert W. D. Dold and C. P. Joubert, *The Union of South Africa: The Development of Its Laws and Constitution* (London: Stevens and Sons, 1955), pp. 37-101.

4. In 1956, the Parliament expanded the Supreme Court to eleven members, thereby ensuring decisions in favor of the government, after the Senate Act of 1955 and the Appellate Division Quorum Act of 1955. See Albie Sachs, *Justice in South Africa* (Berkeley: University of California Press, 1973), pp. 144-45.

5. See Anthony S. Mathews, *Law, Order and Liberty in South Africa* (Capetown: Juta and Co., 1971).

6. See S. M. Seymour, *Bantu Law in South Africa* (Capetown: Juta and Co., 1970); and Patrick Duncan, *Sotho Laws*

and Customs (Capetown: Oxford University Press, 1960).

7. Mary Benson, *South Africa: The Struggle for a Birth-right* (New York: Minerva Press, 1969), p. 249.

8. South African Institute for Race Relations, *A Survey of Race Relations in South Africa, 1971* (Johannesburg: SAIRR, 1971), p. 83 (cited hereafter as SAIRR, *Survey 1971*).

9. See *Maltreatment and Torture of Prisoners in South Africa* (UN Doc. ST/PSCA/SER. A/13, UN Sales No. E 73. 11. k.1) (New York: United Nations, 1973); and International Commission of Jurists, *Erosion of the Rule of Law in South Africa* (The Hague: International Commission of Jurists, August 1968).

10. SAIRR, *Survey 1971*, p. 72.

11. Ibid.

12. See H. R. Hahlo, *The South African Law of Husband and Wife*, 2d ed. (Capetown: Juta and Co., 1963); and H. J. Simons, *African Women: Their Legal Status in South Africa* (London: C. Hurst and Co., 1968), especially pp. 261-288.

13. Some of the later acts were the Native Labor Regulation Act of 1911, Native Administration Act of 1927, Native Service Contract Act of 1932, Natives (Urban Areas) Consolidated Act of 1945, and Natives (Urban Areas) Act of 1923, amended in 1930.

14. SAIRR, *Survey 1971*, p. 142.

15. SAIRR, *Survey 1971*, p. 142.

16. In Sachs v. Donges and Donges v. Dadoo, both cases described in *South African Law Reports* 2, pp. 265 and 321.

17. See T. H. Van Reeven, *Land: Its Ownership and Occupation in South Africa* (Capetown: Juta and Co., 1962).

18. SAIRR, *Survey 1971*, p. 155.

19. SAIRR, *Survey 1971*, p. 156.

20. For the early labor history of South Africa, see H. J. Simons and R. E. Simons, *Class and Colour in South Africa, 1850–1950* (Baltimore: Penguin Books, 1969). See also M. Schaeffer, *Regulation of Employment and Industrial Conciliation in South Africa* (Capetown: Juta and Co., 1957); and C. Norman-Scoble, *Law of Master and Servant in South Africa* (Durban: Butterworth and Co., 1956).

21. See SAIRR, *Survey 1971*, pp. 183 and 217.

22. SAIRR, *Survey 1971*, pp. 228-229.

23. SAIRR, *Survey 1971*, p. 278.
24. Computed from figures in SAIRR, *Survey 1971*, p. 289.
25. Martin Legassick, *The National Union of South African Students: Ethnic Cleavage and Ethnic Integration in the Universities* (Occasional Paper No. 4) (Los Angeles: UCLA African Studies Center, 1967).
26. Many monographs on the non-whites have been published, the most useful being: Mary Benson, *South Africa: The Struggle for a Birthright* (New York: Minerva Press, 1969); H. J. Simons and R. E. Simons, *Class and Colour in South Africa, 1850–1950* (London: Penguin Books, 1969); and UNESCO, *Apartheid: Its Effects on Education, Science, Culture and Information* (Paris: UNESCO, 1967); the best work on the subject, however, is the annual survey by the South African Institute for Race Relations, *A Survey of Race Relations in South Africa* (Johannesburg, annual).
27. The history of intra-white tensions is described most vividly in the biography by W. K. Hancock, *Smuts* (Cambridge: Cambridge University Press, 1962, 1967) and in Margaret Ballinger, *From Union to Apartheid* (Capetown: Juta and Co., 1969). The present implications of the tensions are explored in Brian Bunting, *The Rise of the South African Reich* (London: Penguin Books, 1964); and Colin Legum, "Colour and Power in the South African Situation," *Daedalus*, spring 1967, pp. 483-95.
28. The most eloquent testimony to the failure is in the record of the treason trials, available on microfilm at the Hoover Institution, Stanford University. The best guide to the records is by Thomas Karis, *The Treason Trial in South Africa: A Guide to the Microfilm Record of the Trial* (Stanford, Calif.: Hoover Institution Press, 1965).
29. See, e.g., Julius Stone, "Reflections on Apartheid after the South West African Cases," *Washington Law Review* 42 (June 1967): 1069-82.
30. Its foreign policy has been studied relatively little, the notable works being by Amry Vandenbosch, *South Africa and the World* (Frankfort: University of Kentucky Press, 1970); Edwin S. Munger, *Notes on the Formation of South African Foreign Policy* (Pasadena: The Castle Press, 1965); Gail-Maryse Cockram, *Vorster's Foreign Policy* (Preto-

ria: Academica, 1970); and Gerrit Olivier, "South African Foreign Policy," in Denis Worrall, ed., *South Africa: Government and Politics* (Pretoria: Van Schaik, 1971). Of most direct relevance to apartheid and foreign policy are Philip Mason, "South Africa and the World—Some Maxims and Axioms," *Foreign Affairs* 43 (October 1964): 150-164; Peter Calvocoressi, *South Africa and World Opinion* (Capetown: Oxford University Press, 1961); and the sections on foreign relations in the annual survey of the SAIRR, *A Survey of Race Relations in South Africa.*

31. See, e.g., Douglas Brown, *Against the World* (London: Collins, 1966), who opposes sanctions against South Africa; and William R. Frye, *In Whitest Africa: The Dynamics of Apartheid* (Englewood Cliffs, N.J.: Prentice-Hall, 1968), who argues against violence of any kind.

32. Colin Legum, correspondent for the *Observer* and prolific writer, is perhaps the closest follower of the South African scene, as in the book he wrote with Margaret Legum, *South Africa: Crisis for the West* (New York: Praeger Publishers, 1964).

33. See the particularly valuable article by Catherine Hoskyns, "The African States and the United Nations, 1959-64," *International Affairs* 40 (July 1964): 466-80; see also Dennis Austin, "White Power," *Journal of Commonwealth Political Studies* 6 (July 1968): 95-106; and his earlier book, *Britain and South Africa* (London: Oxford University Press, 1966), in which he describes the role of the Africans in the UN (especially pp. 97-107).

34. The Africans have even formed organizations expressly to counter the perceived threat from the south, e.g., the Conference of East and Central African States created in 1967 to "form an effective front against the racist regimes in Southern Africa," which has since developed primarily economic interests. See B. W. T. Mutharike, *Toward Multinational Economic Cooperation in Africa* (New York: Praeger Publishers, 1972), pp. 307-10.

35. Human rights as a concept can be elusive; Africans tend to limit it to the struggle against racial discrimination, as pointed out by Ali Mazrui, "The United Nations and Some African Political Attitudes," in Robert W. Gregg and Michael Barkun, eds., *The United Nations System and Its Functions* (New York: D. Van Nostrand Co., 1968), pp. 47-

51. More conventional views are reflected in Hersch Lauterpacht, *International Law and Human Rights* (New York: Praeger Publishers, 1950); Even Luard, ed., *International Protection of Human Rights* (New York: Praeger Publishers, 1967), especially pp. 249-85; Manouechehr Ganji, *International Protection of Human Rights* (New York: Harcourt, Brace & World, 1962); Ernst Haas, *Human Rights and International Law* (Stanford: Stanford University Press, 1970); and Richard B. Bilder, "Rethinking International Human Rights: A Current Assessment," *Wisconsin Law Review* 1 (1969): 171-217.

36. See Dennis Austin, *Britain and South Africa* (London: Oxford University Press, 1966); and William Hance, ed., *Southern Africa and the U.S.* (New York: Columbia University Press, 1968).

37. GAOR, 1st Session, *Resolutions* (A/64/Add. 1), p. 10.

38. General Assembly Resolution 265 (III), May 14, 1949, in GAOR, 3rd Session, Part II, *Resolutions* (A/900), p. 6.

39. General Assembly Resolution 395 (IV) of December 2, 1950, in GAOR, 5th Session, *Resolutions,* Supplement No. 20 (A/1775), p. 24.

40. J. E. S. Fawcett, *The Inter Se Doctrine of Commonwealth Relations* (London: Athlone Press, 1958), pp. 36-37.

41. Agenda Item 66 of the 7th Session, placed on the agenda by a letter from 13 states (A/2183), September 12, 1952. The result of the deliberations was General Assembly Resolution 616, December 5, 1952, in GAOR, 7th Session, *Resolutions,* Supplement No. 20 (A/2361), p. 8.

42. For full voting figures, see David Kay, *The New Nations in the United Nations, 1960–1967* (New York: Columbia University Press, 1970), pp. 200-205.

43. See H. G. Nicholas, *The United Nations as a Political Institution,* 4th ed. (London: Oxford University Press, 1971), p. 116.

44. General Assembly Resolution 616A (VII) of December 5, 1962, in GAOR, 7th Session, *Resolutions,* Supplement No. 20 (A/2361), p. 8.

45. GAOR, 8th Session, *Report of the Commission on the Racial Situation in South Africa,* Supplement No. 16 (A/2505).

46. In a letter to the secretary-general, dated July 8, 1953, paraphrased in GAOR, *Report of the Ad Hoc Political*

Committee (A/2610), December 7, 1953.

47. In favor were Australia, Belgium, Colombia, France, Greece, South Africa, and Britain. Abstaining were Argentina, Canada, Netherlands, New Zealand, Peru, Turkey, and Venezuela (Ibid., p. 4).

48. A/AC.72/L.14, November 24, 1953.

49. Adopted 38-11-11; GAOR, 8th Session, PV. 465 (December 8, 1953), p. 437.

50. GAOR, 9th Session, Supplement No. 16 (A/2719), and GAOR, 10th Session, Supplement No. 14 (A/2953).

51. A/AC.76/1.20, December 6, 1954; A/AC. 80/L.1, November 3, 1955.

52. GA Resolution 820 (IX), December 14, 1954, in GAOR, 9th Session, *Resolutions,* Supplement No. 21 (A/2890), p. 9.

53. GAOR, 10th Session, *Ad Hoc Political Committee,* Summary Records of Meetings, September 21 to December 9, 1955, 12th Meeting, November 9, 1955 (A/AC.80/SR.12), paragraph 52 at p. 46.

54. GAOR, 10th Session, *Plenary Meetings,* 551st Meeting, December 6, 1955, p. 404.

55. See G. H. Jansen, *Afro-Asia and Non-Alignment* (London: Faber, 1966), especially pp. 182-249, 271-77; J. B. D. Miller, *The Politics of the Third World* (London: Oxford University Press, 1966), especially pp. 1-90.

56. George McTurnan Kahin, *The Asian-African Conference, Bandung, Indonesia, April 1955* (Ithaca, New York: Cornell University Press, 1955), p. 3.

57. Ibid., p. 6.

58. Many delegates reportedly rejected the presence of whites at the conference as potentially inhibiting. See Richard Wright, *The Color Curtain: A Report on the Bandung Conference* (Cleveland: World Publishing Co., 1956), pp. 83-84.

59. Final Communiqué of the Bandung Conference, reproduced in Kahin, *The Asian-African Conference,* p. 81.

60. Ibid., p. 33.

61. Conference of Independent African States (CIAS), *Confidential Report* (Accra: CIAS, April 15-23, 1958), pp. 680 and 706; one South African did attend the conference as an interpreter, a fact that upset many of the delegates concerned with security precautions (pp. 763, 766-67).

62. On the First Afro-Asian People's Solidarity Conference, held in Cairo in December, 1957, see G. H. Jansen, *Afro-Asia and Non-Alignment* (London: Faber, 1966), pp. 255-28; J. D. B. Miller, *The Politics of the Third World* (Capetown: Oxford University Press, 1967), pp. 32-33; *The First Afro-Asian Peoples' Solidarity Conference* (Cairo: Permanent Secretariat of the AAPSO, 1958).

63. Conference of Independent African States (CIAS), *Confidential Report* (Accra: CIAS, April 15-23 1958); see references to Bandung (p. 382), Cairo (p. 381), UN action (pp. 386, 393, 399-401, etc).

64. Ibid., p. 400; the Africans were successful in 1963.

65. Ibid., Resolution IV, pp. 102-103, 107.

66. Ibid., Resolution XI, p. 117.

67. There was, in addition, the opposition of the UAR to the existence of a headquarters in Africa, for complex reasons explained by W. Scott Thompson, *Ghana's Foreign Policy, 1957-1966* (Princeton, N.J.: Princeton University Press, 1969), p. 38.

68. Resolution 1016 (XI) of January 30, 1957; GAOR, 11th Session, Supplement No. 17, p. 6 (A/3572).

69. A/3722, November 7, 1957, p. 1. Report of the SPC.

70. A/4147. Submitted by Burma, Ceylon, Cuba, Malaya, Ghana, Haiti, India, Indonesia, Iran, Iceland, United Arab Republic, Uruguay, and Venezuela.

71. United Nations Conference on International Organizations (UNCIO), Commission II, General Assembly, Vol. 8, Doc. 924, 11/12, June 12, 1945, p. 79.

72. A/PV. 803, September 22, 1959, p. 109.

73. A/SPC/SR. 140-148.

74. South Africa, as a general rule, did not attend meetings of the Special Political Committee or plenary meetings of the General Assembly when apartheid or South West Africa was under discussion. The South African delegation also appears to have boycotted sessions fairly consistently when the discussion transgressed its interpretation of Article 2(7).

75. A/PV. 811, September 28, 1959, pp. 227-33.

76. A/SPC/SR. 140, October 30, 1959, p. 68.

77. Ibid., p. 69.

78. This is not an interpretation of the legal significance of Articles 55 and 56, but rather a moral or political analysis.

As Hans Kelsen points out, "Legally, Article 56 is meaning-less and redundant," going on to describe it as "one of the most obscure provisions of the Charter" (*The Law of the United Nations* [New York: Praeger Publishers, 1950], pp. 99-101).

79. A/SPC/SR. 141, November 1, 1949, p. 72.

80. Ibid.

81. A/SPC/SR. 142, November 3, 1959, p. 75.

82. Ibid.

83. Ibid.

84. A/SPC/SR. 145, November 6, 1959, p. 92.

85. Draft Resolution A/SPC/L.37, introduced November 3, 1959, at the 142nd Meeting of the Special Political Com-mittee: GAOR, 14th Session, Special Political Committee, *Summary Records of Meetings,* September 15-December 9 1959, p. 75.

86. A/4271. Report of the SPC, November 12, 1959, pp. 4-5.

87. A/PV. 838, November 17, 1959. Rule 68: "Discussion of a report of a Main Committee in a plenary meeting of the General Assembly shall take place if at least one-third of the Members present and voting at the Plenary meeting consider such a discussion to be necessary."

88. Ibid. Opposed were Portugal, France, and Britain; abstaining were Belgium, Canada, the Dominican Repub-lic, Finland, Luxembourg, and the Netherlands. Italy ab-stained initially, but later asked that its vote be recorded as in favor of the resolution.

89. Leland Goodrich and Anne P. Simons, *The United Nations and the Maintenance of International Peace and Security* (Washington, D.C.: Brookings Institution, 1955), pp. 192-95. For the origins of expert commissions of inquiry, at the Hague Conference of 1899, see Alfred Zimmern, *The League of Nations and the Rule of Law, 1918-1935* (London: Macmillan, 1936), p. 114.

Chapter 2

1. See chapter three for the formation of the Organization of African Unity in May 1963.

2. See the excellent discussion by Margaret Doxey, "Inter-

national Sanctions: A Framework for Analysis with Special Reference to the UN and Southern Africa," *International Organization* 26 (summer 1972): 527-550.

3. See Ali Mazrui, "The United Nations and Some Political Attitudes," *International Organization* 18 (summer 1964): 507-508.

4. S/4279, March 25, 1960.

5. S/4299, March 31, 1960, and SCOR, 856th Meeting, p. 9.

6. Security Council Resolution 134 (1960) of April 1, 1960. SCOR: 15th Year, *Resolutions and Decisions of the Security Council 1960,* p. 1. The model for this paragraph was the resolution passed by the General Assembly in 1958 at the time of the tension in Lebanon and Jordan (GA Resolution 1237 [ES-III] of August 21, 1958, in GAOR, 3rd Emergency Special Session, Supplement No. 1 [A/3905], *Resolutions,* p. 1).

7. SCOR, 855th Meeting, April 1, 1960, p. 9.

8. SCOR, 856th Meeting, April 1, 1960, p. 10.

9. Security Council Resolution 134 (1960).

10. The diplomacy of the late Dag Hammarskjöld, a subject of controversy, has been more than adequately described in Richard I. Miller, *Dag Hammarskjöld and Crisis Diplomacy* (New York: Oceana, 1961); and in Mark W. Zacher, *Dag Hammarskjöld's United Nations* (New York: Columbia University Press, 1971). Also see his own writings in Wilder Foote, ed., *Dag Hammarskjöld—Servant of Peace* (New York: Harper & Row, 1962).

11. *Interim Report by the Secretary-General under the resolution adopted by the Security Council on 1 April 1960,* (S/4305), April 19, 1960, in SCOR, 15th Year, *Supplement for April, May and June 1960,* pp. 2-3.

12. Ibid.

13. *Second Interim Report of the Secretary-General under the resolution adopted by the Security Council on 1 April 1960,* October 11, 1960 (S/4551), in SCOR, 15th Year, *Supplement for October, November, and December 1960,* pp.3-4.

14. The 1st CIAS, held in Monrovia, Liberia, in August 1959, had dealt primarily with the Algerian Civil War. It was at the 2nd CIAS, incidentally, that the African leaders decided to submit the dispute over Namibia (South West Africa) to the International Court of Justice, with the names

of Ethiopia and Liberia as plaintiffs. The ICJ has not to date been directly involved in the apartheid dispute.

15. *Second Conference of Independent African States, Addis Ababa, 14-26 June 1960* (Addis Ababa: Government of Ethiopia, 1960), p. 32. See also pp. 39, 47, and 52.

16. Ibid., p. 56.

17. Ibid., p. 60. He specified the Economic Commission for Africa and the African Development Bank.

18. Ibid., p. 81.

19. Ibid., pp. 104-105, also reproduced in GAOR, 15th Session (Part II), *Special Political Committee, Summary Records of Meetings, 15 March–21 April 1961*, 233rd Meeting, March 27, 1961, p. 32.

20. Only the UAR had diplomatic relations with South Africa.

21. Ibid., p. 102.

22. See Immanuel Wallerstein, *The Politics of Unity* (New York: Random House, 1967), pp. 41-42; and W. Scott Thompson, *Ghana's Foreign Policy 1957-1966* (Princeton, N.J.: Princeton University Press, 1969), pp. 92-93.

23. *Keesing's Contemporary Archives* (London: Keesing's Publications, 1960), p. 17555: and Wallerstein, *The Politics of Unity*, pp. 38-39.

24. See Thompson, *Ghana's Foreign Policy*, pp. 91-92.

25. John H. Spencer, "Africa at the UN: Some Observations," *International Organization* 16 (spring 1962): 384.

26. Mirlande Hippolyte, *Les Etats de Groupe de Brazzaville aux Nations Unies* (Paris: Armand Colin, 1970), pp. 76-77.

27. *Counter-Attack* 9, no. 1 (February 1961): 6.

28. *Memorandum to Mr. Dag Hammarskjold* (South African Indian Congress, January 1961), p. 26.

29. S/4635, January 23, 1961. Hammarskjöld's motives for using "quiet diplomacy" are best explained by Brian Urquhart, *Hammarskjöld* (New York: Alfred A. Knopf, 1972), pp. 494-499.

30. See I. William Zartman, *International Relations in the New Africa* (Englewood Cliffs, N.J.: Prentice-Hall, 1966), pp. 26-34.

31. Quoted in Thomas Hovet, *Africa in the United Nations* (Evanston, Ill.: Northwestern University Press, 1963), p. 56.

32. Zartman, *International Relations in the New Africa*, p. 29; Thompson, *Ghana's Foreign Policy*, pp. 157, 201-202, 216-220. By late 1962, the group was moribund.

33. See Albert Tevoedjre, *Pan-Africanism in Action: An Account of the UAM* (Cambridge, Mass.: Harvard Center for International Affairs, 1965), passim.

34. From the Tananarive meeting, September 1961, in Hovet, *Africa in the United Nations*, p. 52.

35. Hippolyte, *Les Etats de Groupe de Brazzaville aux Nations Unies*, pp. 74-78. Interestingly enough, the UAM group at the UN rarely discussed the apartheid issue because the policy had already been set by the UAM. The ambassadors of UAM members to the UN merely carried out that policy (p. 83).

36. "Exclusion" is a nebulous term to describe what was, in fact, a very hazy political process. Margaret Ball says that "what occurred was expulsion in everything but name, and in taking the line which they did, Commonwealth members opened the door to new departures in respect to group determination of political legitimacy which they one day might well come to regret" (*The "Open" Commonwealth* [Durham, N.C.: Duke University Press, 1971], p. 21).

37. For an excellent summary of the changing Commonwealth, as well as the particular difficulties with South Africa, see J. D. B. Miller, *Survey of Commonwealth Affairs: Problems of Expansion and Attrition, 1953-1969* (London: Oxford University Press for the Royal Institute of International Affairs, 1974), pp. 101-166.

38. Willard Range, *Jawaharlal Nehru's World View* (Athens: University of Georgia Press, 1961), pp. 111-112; and Michael Brecher, *Nehru: A Political Biography* (London: Oxford University Press, 1959), pp. 414-418. Not only did Nehru accept the ground rules, but also South Africa did not want the issue discussed in the Commonwealth, a decision it may have regretted later when the UN gave the issue such attention in less congenial surroundings. See J. E. S. Fawcett, *The British Commonwealth in International Law* (London: Stevens and Sons, 1963), pp. 207-208.

39. See Richard H. Leach, "The Secretariat," *International Journal* (Canadian Institute of International Affairs) 26 (spring 1971): 374-400.

40. J. D. B. Miller, "Politicians, Officials and Prophets,"

International Journal (Canadian Institute of International Affairs) 26 (spring 1971): 369.

41. See Trevor R. Reese, "The Conference System," *International Journal* (Canadian Institute of International Affairs) 26 (spring 1971): 369.

42. Thompson, *Ghana's Foreign Policy,* p. 97.

43. The Afrikaaner–British South African tensions inherent in the referendum are discussed by Amry Vandenbosch, *South Africa and the World* (Frankfort: University of Kentucky Press, 1970), chapter thirteen.

44. Alan H. Jeeves, "The Problem of South Africa," *International Journal* (Canadian Institute of International Affairs) 26 (spring 1971): 422.

45. See Sir Robert Menzies, *Afternoon Light* (Sydney: Cassell, 1967), pp. 186-229. Menzies's view of domestic matters remained constant, as in his "insistence [in 1964] that the release of political prisoners in Rhodesia was a matter purely for the British and Rhodesian governments— although the charge that he was, in effect, condoning the imprisonment of political opponents was neatly turned by the observation that, in fact, he was one of the few persons at the table who did not treat his political opponents in this way" (Reese, "The Conference System," p. 370).

46. See Verwoerd's statement in the South African House of Assembly on March 23, 1961, in Nicholas Mansergh, *Documents and Speeches on Commonwealth Affairs, 1952-1962* (London: Royal Institute of International Affairs, 1963), p. 389.

47. March 24, 1961. Quoted in Mansergh, *Documents and Speeches,* p. 390.

48. Jeeves, "The Problem of South Africa," p. 422.

49. Apartheid was discussed, and condemned, at meetings of the Commonwealth Prime Ministers in 1964, 1965, 1966, and 1969, although the gatherings could never agree on the form of sanctions to be applied to South Africa. See Margaret Ball, *The "Open" Commonwealth,* pp. 127-128.

50. John Holmes, "The Impact on the Commonwealth of the Emergence of Africa," *International Organization* 16 (spring 1962): 298. Fawcett, in *The British Commonwealth in International Law,* indicates that the family feeling had died some years previously; in fact, "the exclusion of South Africa became necessary to preserve any pattern at all" (p.

226). In addition, "the principle [of *inter se*] was decisively rejected by Commonwealth members" in handling the dispute (p. 207). Clearly the Commonwealth had subordinated one of its fundamental rules to an ethical norm, non-discrimination.

51. Miller, "Politicians, Officials, and Prophets," p. 332.

52. Ibid.

53. This point was noted by the Labour opposition in the British Parliament following the decision of South Africa to withdraw from the Commonwealth. See remarks by Gaitskell (pp. 455-457) and Callaghan (pp. 516-520) for the Labour leadership in *Great Britain, Parliamentary Debates*, Commons, 5th Series, Vol. 637 (March 22, 1961), columns 442-532.

54. Nearly all agree that the Afro-Asian bloc lost most of its unity on political issues with the advent of radical African demands. See, e.g., Samaan Boutros Farajallah, *Le Groupe Afro-Asiatique dans le cadre des Nations Unies* (Geneva: Droz, 1963), pp. 438-439.

55. GAOR, 15th Session (Part II), *Special Political Committee*, Summary Records of Meetings March 15–April 21, 1961, 233rd Meeting, March 27, 1961, p. 29.

56. See, for example, the Libyan delegate's speech in ibid., p. 31.

57. Draft resolution A/SPC/L.60 of April 4, 1961, in GAOR, 15th Session, *Annexes*, Agenda Item 72, pp. 6-7.

58. Draft resolution A/SPC/L.59, of April 3, 1961, in GAOR, 15th Session, *Annexes*, Agenda Item 72, p. 2.

59. Report of the Special Political Committee, April 12, 1961 (A/4728), in GAOR, 15th Session, *Annexes*, Agenda Item 72, p. 3-7.

60. See Wallerstein, *The Politics of Unity*, pp. 35-36.

61. GAOR, 15th Session (Part II). *Plenary Meetings*, 981st Meeting, April 13, 1961, pp. 273-275.

62. The most thorough description of the South-West Africa issue is in the nine-volume record of the ICJ pleadings, *South West Africa Cases* (1966). Some helpful material is in Faye Carroll, *South West Africa and the United Nations* (Frankfort: University of Kentucky Press, 1967); and Allard K. Lowenstein, *Brutal Mandate* (New York: Macmillan, 1962). See particularly John Dugard, ed., *The South West Africa/Namibia Dispute* (Berkeley: University of Califor-

nia Press, 1973).

63. See GAOR, 16th Session, *Fourth Committee Trustee-ship,* Volume I, 1220th, 1224-1231st Meetings, of November 22, 27-30, 1961, pp. 397-478.

64. GAOR, 16th Session, *Special Political Committee,* 269th Meeting, October 25, 1961, p. 46.

65. International Labor Organization (ILO), *First African Regional Conference, Lagos, December 1961: Record of Proceedings* (Geneva: International Labour Organization, 1961), p. V.

66. Resolution I of 29 June 1961, in International Labour Office, *Official Bulletin* 44, no. 1 (1961): 16-17. The vote on Resolution I was 163-0 (89 abstentions).

67. The Governing Body decision is in International Labour Office, *Minutes of the 150th Session of the Governing Body,* Geneva, November 21-24, 1961, pp. 15-16. South Africa sent no reply.

68. International Labour Office, *Report of the Director-General,* Report I, 47th Session, Geneva, 1963, p. 141.

69. GAOR, 16th Session, *Annexes,* Agenda Item 76, pp. 3-4. In the Special Political Committee at this time there was also a nonproductive discussion of expulsion of South Africa, a tactic first proposed by the 3rd All-African People's Conference in March 1961, according to R. Barros, *African States and the United Nations versus Apartheid* (New York: Carleton Press, 1967). p. 56.

70. Report of the Special Political Committee (A/4968), in GAOR, 16th Session, *Annexes,* Agenda Item 76, p. 8.

71. Draft Amendments by Ethiopia, Pakistan, and the USSR (A/SPC/L. 73-75), in GAOR, 16th Session, *Annexes,* Agenda Item 76, pp. 5-7.

72. Draft Resolutions A/SPC/L.71 and A/SPC/L.72, in GAOR, 16th Session, *Annexes,* Agenda Item 76, pp. 3-4.

73. GAOR, 16th Session, *Plenary Meetings,* 1067th Meeting, November 28, 1961, p. 884.

74. By a vote of 48-31-22; GAOR, 16th Session, *Plenary Meetings,* November 28, 1961, 1067th Meeting, pp. 887-888.

75. Paragraph 4: 52-30-18; Paragraph 6: 50-33-17; Paragraph 7: 47-32-21.

76. Resolution 1663 (XVI) of November 38, 1961, in GAOR, 16th Session, *Resolutions,* Supplement No. 17 (A/5100), pp. 10-11; Guinea protested against the mildness

of the resolution by abstaining.

77. The vote to adjourn was 51-31-4, in GAOR, 16th Session, *Plenary Meetings*, 1033rd Meeting, October 11, 1961, p. 398.

78. GAOR, 16th Session, *Plenary Meetings*, 1034th Meeting, October 11, 1961. The vote was 51-31-4.

79. Communication received by the secretary-general from the permanent representative of the Union of South Africa, December 12, 1958 (E/CN. 14/9).

80. *Economic and Social Consequences of Racial Discriminatory Practices*, January 6, 1962 (E/CN.14/132 and Corr. 1).

81. Communication from the Republic of South Africa to the ECA, February 18, 1962 (E/CN. 14/L.82).

82. Economic Commission for Africa Resolution 44 (IV), in ECSOR, 44th Session, *Resolutions*, Supplement No. 10, p. 41.

83. ECSOR, Resumed 34th Session, 1239th Meeting, December 19, 1962, p. 17 (E/SR. 1239).

84. Resolution 1761 (XVII) of November 6, 1962, in GAOR, 17th Session, *Resolutions*, Supplement No. 17 (A/5217), p. 9. The provision concerning aircraft sparked controversy with the ICAO at a later date.

85. The Africans realized shortly thereafter that most of South Africa's major trading partners planned to do nothing to implement the above provisions. Strangely enough, the Africans were apparently unconcerned about this turn of events, at least according to Arthur Schlesinger, Jr.: "Our refusal to support sanctions in 1962 was readily accepted by the Africans. . ." *(A Thousand Days* [Boston: Houghton-Mifflin Co., 1965], p. 580).

86. Operative paragraph five, of Resolution 1761 (XVII), see note 85, above.

87. Ibid., p. 10, paragraph 8.

88. It was also a hollow threat from the African point of view, as Rosalyn Higgins points out, for "if South Africa were expelled from the UN, there would be even less chance of securing her compliance with required race-relations behavior," in Stephen M. Schwebel, ed., *The Effectiveness of International Decisions* (Leiden: Sijthoff, 1961), p. 57.

89. General Assembly Resolution 1761 (XVII) of November 6, 1962, in GAOR, 17th Session, *Resolutions*, Sup-

plement No. 17 (A/5217). There was only one unsuccessful attempt at amendment in Plenary, by Trinidad and Tobago.

90. A/AC. 115/L.8 and L.2., June 5, 1963 and July 19, 1963.

91. ECA Resolution 68 (v) of February 23, 1963, in ES-COR, 36th Session,*Resolutions*, Supplement No. 10, p. 40.

92. ECA Resolution 84 (V), of March 1, 1963, in ibid., p. 46.

93. Communication from the Ambassador of South Africa, E/3820, July 19, 1963, immediately following a report of South Africans being excluded from an ECA conference (*New York Times,* July 16, 1963, p. 5).

94. Draft resolutions by United Kingdom (E/L.1024) and Argentina–United States (E/L.1025) submitted July 23, 1963, in response to South African draft (E/L.1019) of July 22, 1963.

95. ESCOR, 36th Session, 1292nd Meeting, July 23, 1963, p. 221.

96. ESCOR, 36th Session, 1293rd Meeting, July 24, 1963, p. 224.

97. E/L. 1019, July 22, 1963.

98. ESCOR, 36th Session, 1294th Meeting, July 24, 1963, p. 232.

99. ESCOR, 36th Session, Supplement No. 1, *Resolutions*, p. 4.

100. South Africa recognized this, and was thus confident of its ability to survive the anti-apartheid drive in the General Assembly. See D. C. Watt, *A Survey of International Affairs 1962* (London: Royal Institute of International Affairs, 1970), pp. 497-498.

Chapter 3

1. While the campaign against South Africa proved this point, an even more dramatic failure involved the Rhodesian Unilateral Declaration of Independence, and relations with Britain.

2. Conference of Independent African States, *Proceedings,* Volume I, Comm. II/Proposal/4, May 20, 1963.

3. I. William Zartman, *International Relations in the New Africa* (Englewood Cliffs, N.J.: Prentice-Hall, 1966),

p. 34.

4. Organization of African Unity, Resolution B of May 26, 1963, in *Proceedings* of the Summit Conference of Independent African States, Volume I, Section I (Addis Ababa: Government of Ethiopia, May 1963), unpaged.

5. S/5348, letter from 32 states, July 11, 1963.

6. SCOR, 1050th Meeting, July 31, 1963, p. 4.

7. *Interim Report* of the Special Committee on the Policies of Apartheid of the Government of the Republic of South Africa, May 9, 1963 (S/5310); *Second Interim Report* of the Special Committee on the Policies of Apartheid of the Government of the Republic of South Africa, July 17, 1963 (S/5353).

8. SCOR, 1052nd Meeting, August 2, 1963, pp. 10-11. For the ILO, see below, p. 123.

9. OAU, Dakar Foreign Ministers' Meeting, August 10, 1963, *Procès-Verbal*, p. 7.

10. Ibid., pp. 21-22.

11. SCOR, 1052nd Meeting, August 2, 1963, p. 16.

12. Draft resolution S/5384 in SCOR, 1054th Meeting, August 6, 1963, pp. 15-16.

13. Ibid.

14. SCOR, 1056th Meeting, August 7, 1963, pp. 4-5.

15. Organizations of African Unity, Dakar Foreign Ministers' Meeting, August 10, 1963, *Procès-Verbal*, p. 14. See also p. 26.

16. Vernon McKay, "Cooperation for Order in Africa," *Current History* 50 (March 1966): 131.

17. Organization of African Unity, Dakar Foreign Ministers' Meeting, August 10, 1963, *Procès-Verbal*, p. 10.

18. Ibid., p. 17.

19. Ibid., p. 16.

20. Ibid., p. 18.

21. Ibid., p. 22.

22. Ibid., p. 25.

23. Mirlande Hippolyte, *Les Etats de Groupe de Brazzaville aux Nations Unies* (Paris: Armand Colin, 1970), p. 91.

24. Ibid., pp. 92-94.

25. Apartheid was mentioned virtually every day of the General Debate (GAOR/PV. 1208-1231, 1233-1239), as well as in seventeen sessions of the Special Political Committee (GAOR/SPC/SR. 379-396), and in numerous meetings of

the Special Committee on Apartheid.

26. General Assembly Resolution 1881 (XVIII) of October 11, 1963, in GAOR, 18th Session, *Resolutions,* Supplement No. 15 (A/5515), p. 19.

27. GAOR, 18th Session, 1238th Meeting, October 11, 1963, p. 13.

28.   Richard Falk and others see these overwhelming majorities as much more significant, indeed, as an important stage in the formation of international law. See his argument in *The Status of Law in International Society* (Princeton, N.J.: Princeton University Press, 1970), pp. 126-173. P. Pierson-Mathy, in "L'Action des Nations Unies contre l'Apartheid," *Revue Belge de Droit International* 6 (1970): 227-228, identifies GA Resolution 1881 and SC Resolution S/182 of December 4, 1963, as turning points. The repetition of resolutions on apartheid passed annually has come to have juridicial value, as reflected in the dissenting opinions of the 1966 South West Africa judgment (ICJ Reports, *South West Africa Cases, Second Phase* [1966], pp. 248-442). Judge Tanaka stated (p. 294) that the "method of generation of customary international law is in the stage of transformation from being an individualistic process to being a collectivistic process." Judge Jessup (pp. 430-432, 441) considered the effect of annual resolutions to be, if not law, at least creation of "standards."

29. See *New York Times,* August 9, 1963, p. 24, and August 12, 1963, p. 7.

30. *New York Times,* October 9, 1963, p. 7.

31. GAOR, 18th Session, 1283rd Meeting, December 16, 1963, p. 3.

32. General Assembly Resolution 1978A (XVIII), December 16, 1963, in GAOR, 18th Session *Resolutions,* Supplement No. 15 (A/5515), p. 20, adopted by a vote of 100-2-1.

33. General Assembly Resolution 1978B (XVIII), December 16, 1963, in GAOR, 18th Session , *Resolutions,* Supplement No. 15 (A/55515), p. 20, adopted by a vote of 99-2.

34. For Ambassador Stevenson's apprehensions see *New York Times,* June 26, 1963, p. 3, and July 11, 1963, p. 1.

35. Third AAOSO Conference in Moshi, Tanganyika, *New York Times,* February 12, 1963, p. 1.

36. See Zdenek Cervenka, *The Organization of African*

Unity and Its Charter (New York: Praeger Publishers, 1969), pp. 17-19.

37. S/5497 and Add. 1, 2; September 16, 1963.

38. Special Committee on Apartheid, 30th Meeting, April 7, 1964 (A/AC.115/SR.30), p. 9.

39. This problem had been foreseen at the San Francisco conference, where the question had arisen: "Should the General Assembly be able to require the Security Council to investigate situations which might seem to the Assembly likely to endanger world peace?" Supported only by Belgium, the question was given a negative vote by the conference, because it "would open the door to conflict between the Assembly and the Security Council." UNCIO, Volume IX, Commission II, General Assembly, Doc. 392 (London and New York: UN Information Organizations, 1946), pp. 50-53.

40. A/AC.115/Sr.31, April 21, 1964, p. 12. OPEC, in fact, decided not to take a group stand at that time. Iran was the main supplier for South Africa. Each country was to make an individual decision. See letter from OPEC, in A/AC. 115/SR.33, August 26, 1964, pp. 4-5.

41. A/AC.115/SR.33, August 26, 1964, p. 4.

42. SCOR/PV. 1075, December 2, 1963, p. 7.

43. Security Council Resolution 182 (1963) of December 4, 1963, in SCOR, 18th Year, *Resolutions and Decisions of the Security Council,* pp. 8-10.

44. Ibid., p. 9.

45. Organization of African Unity, (*Official Records*) *Council of Ministers, Lagos Conference February 24-29, 1964, Procès-Verbal,* p. 156.

46. SCOR/PV. 1077, December 3, 1963, p. 10.

47. Ibid., p. 7.

48. SCOR/PV. 1078, December 4, 1963, p. 3.

49. Ibid., p. 4.

50. Security Council Resolution 182 (1963) of December 4, 1963, in SCOR, 18th Year, *Resolutions and Decisions of the Security Council,* pp. 8-10.

51. SCOR/PV. 1077, December 3, 1963, p. 6.

52. See Anthony Alcock, *History of the International Labor Organization* (New York: Octagon Books, 1971), p. 321.

53. International Labor Organization (ILO), *Record of*

Proceedings, International Labour Conference, 47th Session (Geneva: ILO, 1963), pp. 135-141.

54. Ibid., p. 144.

55. Ibid., p. 145. It was essential that some business be accomplished in order to provide the ILO with operating funds.

56. Alcock, *History of the International Labor Organization*, pp. 323-324, gives this interpretation of events on the basis of interviews with the director-general.

57. ILO, *Record of Proceedings, International Labour Conference, 47th Session* (Geneva: ILO, 1963), p. 167. Alcock, in *History of the International Labor Organization*, suggests that the African group had no leaders, making it difficult for the director-general's office to communicate with it. In this atmosphere, too, "more extreme counsels were likely to prevail" (p. 324).

58. ILO, *Record of Proceedings*, pp. 169-170.

59. Ibid., p. 173.

60. G. B. 156/6/5 (mimeo); presented to the International Labour Conference as *Proposed Declaration Concerning the Policy of "Apartheid" of the Republic of South Africa, 48th Session*, (Geneva: ILO, 1964), Report A.

61. International Labour Office, *Minutes of the 156th Session of the Governing Body* (Geneva: ILO, June 28 and 29, 1963), Appendix VII, p. 42.

62. International Labour Office, *Minutes of the 156th Session of the Governing Body* (Geneva: ILO, June 1963), p. 13.

63. See, e.g., Mr. Zaman's speech (India), ibid., p. 14.

64. Ibid., pp. 17-18.

65. Ibid., p. 19.

66. Resolution I passed 38-4-3, and Resolution II 42-0-3, from A/AC.115/L.12, p. 2.

67. ILO, *Minutes of the 157th Session of the Governing Body* (Geneva: ILO, November 12-15, 1963), p. 14.

68. Ibid., p. 24.

69. Ibid. See also *New York Times*, November 16, 1963, p. 8.

70. Resolution WHA 6.47 (May 1953) in World Health Organization (WHO), *Handbook of Resolutions and Decisions of the World Health Assembly and the Executive Board*, 9th ed. (Geneva: WHO, December 1967), p. 284.

71. See AFR/RC12/14 in WHOOR 127, 16th World Health Assembly, Annex 14, p. 180.

72. Decision of the WHO Executive Board, EB31.R20, in WHO, *Handbook,* p. 272.

73. Resolution WHA 16.43, in WHO, *Handbook,* p. 274.

74. WHOOR 238, 16th World Health Assembly, Committee on Administration, Finance and Legal Matters, p. 381.

75. WHO, *13th Session of Regional Committee for Africa* (Geneva: WHO, September 23, 1963). See also WHOOR 135, 17th World Health Assembly, Part II, p. 443.

76. Reported in a letter from the permanent representative of South Africa to the United Nations to the president of the Security Council, July 31, 1963 (S/5381), in SCOR, 18th Year, 1050th Meeting, July 31, 1963, pp. 2-4.

77. *New York Times,* July 5, 1963, pp. 2 and 18.

78. E/CONF. 47/L.11, August 28, 1963; this was the original African resolution amended by Italy and Yugoslavia, in E/CONF. 47/L.6-8.

79. As reported to the ILO, *Minutes of the 157th Session of the Governing Body* (Geneva: ILO, 12-15 November 1963), p. 75.

80. *New York Times,* September 7, 1963, p. 6. Nongovernmental organizations affected included the International Air Transport Association, the object of African walkouts in October. See Rosalyn Higgins, "South Africa's Standing in International Organizations," *The World Today* 19 (December 1963): 510-511.

81. FAO, Report of the 12th Session of the Conference, November 16-December 5, 1963 (Rome: FAO, 1964), p. 154.

82. Ibid., p. 81.

83. Resolution 38/63, in ibid., pp. 83-84.

84. See Reports XI and XII of the International Labour Conference, 48th Session (Geneva: ILO, 1964).

85. ILO, *Minutes of the 158th Session of the Governing Body* (Geneva: ILO, February 13-17, 1964), p. 17.

86. Approval of these moves came at the subsequent conference: see ILO, *Record of Proceedings,* International Labour Conference, 48th Session (Geneva: ILO, 1964), pp. 484-506.

87. ILO, *Minutes of the 159th Session of the Governing Body* (Geneva: ILO, June 11-13, 1964), pp. 146-147. Under Article 1(5) of the ILO Constitution, South Africa continued

to be bound to conventions of the ILO it had signed, and had a continuing obligation to send reports, even after cessation of membership in 1966.

88. World Health Organization Resolution WHA 17.50, in WHOOR 135, World Health Assembly, 17th Session, Part I, p. 23. Article 7 of the WHO Constitution reads: "If a member fails to meet its financial obligations to the Organization or in other exceptional circumstances, the Health Assembly may, on such conditions as it thinks proper, suspend the voting privileges and services to which a Member is entitled. The Health Assembly shall have the authority to restore such voting privileges and services." The only instance of "other exceptional circumstances" in the preparatory work mentioned a state that might "prepare for or wage biological warfare" (Ibid., Part II, p. 196).

89. Quoted in ibid., Part II, p. 446.

90. Ibid., Part II, p. 201, March 19, 1964.

91. Services to South Africa did continue for some time, in the form of training grants of $16,500 per year. See WHOOR 138, *Proposed Regular Programme and Budget Estimates for the Financial Year 1 January–31 December 1966*, p. 117, and subsequent proposed programs for scheduled grants.

92. See WHOOR 114, 18th World Health Assembly, Geneva, May 4-21, 1965, Part I, Annex 14, pp. 144-145 for replies. The suggested amendment read: "(b) If a member ignores the humanitarian principles and objectives laid down in the Constitution, by deliberately practising a policy of racial discrimination, the Health Assembly may suspend it or exclude it from the World Health Organization." Ibid., Part II, p. 471.

93. In a letter to the director-general of WHO, dated May 15, 1964. Ibid., Part I, Annex 14, p. 142. Article II, paragraph 5, of the UNESCO Constitution reads: "Members of the Organization which are expelled from the United Nations Organization shall automatically cease to be members of this Organization."

94. As of 1971, the amendment had been ratified by only 44 states, and had not yet entered into force.

95. World Health Organization Resolution WHA 19.31, in World Health Assembly, 19th Session, Part I, p. 13. South Africa refused to pay its assessed contribution beginning in 1966, and in consequence lost all services. See exchange of

letters in WHOOR 157, *Executive Board,* Annex 7, pp. 45-46.

96. See the 20th WHA, May 8-26, 1967, Part II, pp. 432, 437.

97. See C. Wilfred Jenks, "Some Constitutional Problems of International Organizations," *British Yearbook of International Law* 22 (1945): 11 and 25; in the case of the IAEA, under Article XVII.E, when a state ceases to be a member, "a State cannot denounce its contractual obligations to the Agency with respect to projects—e.g., it cannot escape any safeguard controls it agreed to on receiving assistance from the Agency." Paul C. Szasz, *The Law and Practices of the International Atomic Energy Agency* (Vienna: IAEA, 1970), p. 102. The degree of South Africa's obligation to the IAEA in regard to specific projects is not available in public documents.

98. Adding to the OAU dilemma was the position of the UAR and Tanganyika, who argued unsuccessfully in the OAU that denuclearization had to be achieved through the IAEA or the UN: unilateral renunciation of nuclear weapons would be opening Africa to a "danger from outside Africa." Their position was, in effect, supported by African tactics at the IAEA. See OAU Council of Ministers, Lagos Conference, February 24-29, 1964, pp. 330-335. Attempts to denuclearize the African continent were also occurring in the UN, where the history of unsuccessful efforts seemed to be plagued by a testy relationship with the OAU. All resolutions urged the OAU to undertake studies and initiate the process of drawing up a denuclearization treaty. Progress was clearly impossible because of disagreements among African states. See United Nations, *The United Nations and Disarmament, 1945-1970* (UN Sales No. 70.ix.1), (New York: United Nations, 1970), pp. 159-160.

99. Declaration on the Incompatibility of the Policies of Apartheid of the Government of South Africa with the Membership of the IAEA, September 30, 1963 (GC(VII)266), in IAEA, 7th General Conference, Agenda Item 10, mimeo.

100. Official Records of the International Atomic Energy Agency, 8th General Conference, 84th Plenary Meeting, September 15, 1965 (GC(VIII)OR.84), p. 2.

101. Letter dated February 17, 1964, A/AC.115/L.49, p. 5.

102. M. A. K. Menon, "Universal Postal Union," *International Conciliation,* no. 552 (March 1965), p. 56.

103. H. G. Schermers, "Some Constitutional Notes on the Fifteenth Congress of the Universal Postal Union," *International and Comparative Law Quarterly* 14 (1965): 632-637; "International Organizations: Summary of Activities," *International Organization* 20 (1966): 834; and *Keesing's Contemporary Archives* (London: Keesing's Publications, June 13-20, 1964), p. 20126. South Africa did adhere to the new convention, but at the 1969 Tokyo Congress, it was once again denied the right to attend the general conference: U-PU Resolution C2 "Expulsion of the South African Delegation from the XVIth Congress," in *United Nations Juridicial Yearbook 1969* (UN Sales No. E. 71. V. 4), p. 118. At the 17th Congress of the UPU in Lausanne, in May 1974, the South Africans were once again excluded from the congress and all other UPU meetings, this time without opposition *(Le Monde Diplomatique,* July 1974, p. 40).

104. OAU, [Official Records] Council of Ministers. *Procès-Verbal,* Lagos Conference, February 24-29, 1964, p. 153.

105. Ibid., p. 152.

106. Ibid., p. 153.

107. Ibid., p. 157.

108. Speech of the Guinean delegate, in ibid., pp. 63-64.

109. Organization of African Unity (Council of Ministers) Resolution 13 (II); text available in United Nations Document A/AC.115/E.58, March 18, 1964.

110. P. Pierson-Mathy implies a change, in describing "L'action de plus en plus coordonnée menée par les états africains au sein des Nations Unies, *particulièrement après la formation* de l'O.A.U." [emphasis added] in her article, "L'Action des Nations Unies contre L'Apartheid," *Revue Belge de Droit International* 6 (1970): 220. Rosalyn Higgins suggests direct causation by the OAU meetings of later events: "The result of these plans [of the OAU meeting] are now becoming visible in a series of events which have taken place in various international organizations" (In "South Africa's Standing in International Organizations," *The World Today* 19 [December 1963]: 507).

111. "After the meeting [Addis Ababa], friendly African leaders like Houphouet-Boigny and Nyerere warned us that in the case of South Africa we could no longer rest on purely verbal condemnation of apartheid" (Arthur Schlesinger, Jr.,

A Thousand Days [Boston: Houghton-Mifflin Co., 1965], 581.

112. See R. Likert, "The Principle of Supportive Relationships," in D. S. Pugh, ed., *Organization Theory* (Baltimore: Penguin Books, 1971), pp. 297-304, for a sociological view of this behavior.

113. A/5692, paragraph 20, p. 3 in GAOR, 19th Session, Annex No. 12.

114. A/5707, p. 1, in ibid.

115. SCOR/PV.1027, June 8, 1964, p. 11.

116. See UN Press Release GA/AP/18 of March 9, 1964, or A/5825, paragraphs 38-40, p. 53, in GAOR, 19th Session, Annex No. 12.

117. Annex to the report by the secretary-general in pursuance of the resolution adopted by the Security Council at its 1078th meeting on December 4, 1963 (S/5471), April 20, 1974 (S/5658), paragraph 121.

118. SCOR, Draft Resolution S/5732, June 8, 1964.

119. SCOR/PV.1028, June 9, 1964, p. 7.

120. SCOR/PV.1027, June 8, 1964, p. 3.

121. See Reports of the Special Committee on the Policies of Apartheid of the Government of the Republic of South Africa, March 23, 1964 (S/5621) and May 25, 1964 (S/5717); also issued as A/5692 and A/5707, in GAOR, 19th Session, *Annexes*, Annex No. 12, pp. 1-46.

122. As reported at length by Mr. Grimes, Liberian delegate to the Security Council, in SCOR, 1127th Meeting, June 8, 1964, pp. 15-16. A full report is given in A/5707 (S/5717), Annex 2. The report of the delegation of the Special Committee on Apartheid that attended the conference is A/AC.115/L.67, reprinted in GAOR, 19th Session, *Annexes*, Annex No. 12, pp. 35-46. See also Ronald Segal, ed., *Sanctions Against South Africa* (Baltimore: Penguin Books, 1964), for the background and texts of papers presented at the conference.

123. SCOR/PV.1132, June 15, 1964, p. 5.

124. SCOR/PV.1133, June 16, 1964, pp. 2-4.

125. SCOR/PV.1135, June 18, 1964, p. 3.

126. In a vote of 8-0-3; SCOR/PV.1135, June 18, 1964, p. 4.

127. See footnote 21 above, and *OAU*, Council of Ministers (III)(I), SR. 3, July 15, 1964, p. 3.

128. *OAU*, CM (III) (I), SR.4, July 15, 1964, passim.

129. *OAU*, CM (III)(I), SR.3, July 15, 1964, p. 7.

130. *OAU*, AHG/RES. 6(I); text in A/AC.115/ L.83, pp. 3-4.

131. *OAU*, CM/RES.48 (IV); text in A/AC.115/L.127, April 26, 1965. There was no resolution on apartheid at the 5th Extraordinary Session of the Council of Ministers, June 10-13, 1965, Lagos.

Chapter 4

1. Mirlande Hippolyte pinpoints September 1965 as the time when the French-speaking states of Africa began having a "tour d'horizon" at weekly meetings (*Les Etats de Groupe de Brazzaville aux Nations Unies* [Paris: Armand Colin, 1970], p. 97).

2. Herman Tavares de Sa, *The Play Within the Play* (New York: Alfred A. Knopf, 1966), p. 124.

3. Conor Cruise O'Brien, *The United Nations: Sacred Drama* (New York: Simon & Schuster, 1968), pp. 48-49.

4. For a contemporary South African critique of its "passive" foreign policy, see G. G. Lawrie, "South Africa's World Position," *Journal of Modern African Studies* 2, no. 1 (1964): 41-54.

5. See Richard Hall, *The High Price of Principles: Kaunda and the White South* (New York: Africana, 1970), pp. 143 and 232. The same conclusions were reached by Ali Mazrui, *On Heroes and Uhuru-Worship* (London: Longmans, 1967), p. 237; and Rosalyn Higgins, in Stephen M. Schwebel, ed., *The Effectiveness of International Decisions* (Leiden: Sijthoff, 1971), p. 45.

6. For the OAU response, see reports of the OAU Heads of State meeting in Rabat, June 1972, where pledges to the Liberation Committee were doubled (*Keesing's Contemporary Archives* [London: Keesing's Publications, July 15-22, 1972], p. 25372).

7. For the text of the Cairo resolution, see A/AC.115/L.91, October 20, 1964.

8. Letter dated June 4, 1963 (A/5850), in GAOR, 19th Session, *Annexes*, Annex No. 12, p. 167.

9. Ibid. As of 1971, the UNHCR maintained the only UN outpost in South Africa.

10. Reports A/5692, A/5707, and A/5825 were noted at the 1330th Plenary Meeting on February 18, 1965.

11. Statement made by Mr. Achkar Marof, chairman of the Special Committee, at the 66th Meeting, July 27, 1965 (A/AC.115/L.146), p. 2.

12. Report of the Special Committee on the Policies of Apartheid of the Government of the Republic of South Africa, August 16, 1965 (A/5957).

13. Ibid., paragraph 182, in GAOR, 20th Session, *Annexes,* Agenda Item 36, p. 39; recalling recommendation of November 30, 1964, that membership be expanded, in Report of the Special Committee on the Policies of Apartheid of the Government of the Republic of South Africa (A/5825), in GAOR, 195th Session, *Annexes,* Annex No. 12, paragraph 638, p. 110.

14. Report of the Special Committee on the Policies of Apartheid of the Republic of South Africa (A/5957), paragraph 42, in GAOR, 20th Session, *Annexes,* Agenda Item 36, p. 26.

15. For discussion in the Special Committee on April 18, 1965, see A/AC.115/SR.61.

16. At its meeting in Ottawa, September 14, 1965, the IPU condemned apartheid in Resolution VII, "The Problem of Apartheid in the Light of the Universal Declaration of Human Rights and the United Nations Charter," in Union Interparlementaire (UI), *Compte Rendu de la LIVe Conférence Interparlementaire* (Geneva: IU,1966), pp. 1204-1205, adopted by a vote of 565-10, with 99 abstentions (see p. 1013).

17. Contained in A/5957, as Appendix 1. Originally issued in *Bulletin of the International Commission of Jurists* (Geneva), no. 22 (April 1965).

18. Letter dated December 1, 1965, from the chairman of the Special Political Committee to the permanent representative of the Republic of South Africa, and reply dated December 3, 1965 (A/SPC/107).

19. See Report of the Credentials Committee, December 14, 1963 (A/5676/Rev. 1) in GAOR, 18th Session, *Annexes,* Agenda Item 3, p. 2, when Algeria, Liberia, and the USSR made formal reservations to the credentials of the South African delegates.

20. Resolution 2113 (XX) of December 21, 1965; in GAOR, 20th Session, *Resolutions,* Supplement No. 14

(A/6014), p. 4.

21. For useful commentaries, see Nathan Lerner, *The U.N. Convention on the Elimination of All Forms of Racial Discrimination: A Commentary* (Leiden: Sijthoff, 1970); and Egon Schwelb, "The International Convention on the Elimination of All Forms of Racial Discrimination," *International and Comparative Law Quarterly* 5 (October 1966): 996-1068.

22. General Assembly Resolution 2106A (XX) of December 21, 1965, in GAOR, 20th Session, *Resolutions,* Supplement No. 14 (A/6014), p. 47.

23. Leo Gross, "The Development of International Law Through the United Nations," in James Barros, ed., *The United Nations: Past, Present and Future* (New York: Free Press, 1972), pp. 197-198; and John H. D. Fried, "How Efficient is International Law?" in Karl W. Deutsch and Stanley Hoffman, eds., *The Relevance of International Law* (Cambridge, Mass.: Schenkman Press, 1968), p. 109.

24. GAOR, 27th Session, *Report of the Committee on the Elimination of Racial Discrimination,* Supplement No. 18 (A/8718), p. 1.

25. General Assembly Resolutions 1780 and 1781 (XVII) of December 7, 1962, in GAOR, 17th Session, *Resolutions,* Supplement No. 17 (A/5217), p. 32.

26. For a description of this process, see Egon Schwelb, "The International Convention," pp. 998-1000.

27. The Discrimination (Employment and Occupation) Convention of 1958, adopted by the ILO General Conference June 25, 1958, in *UN Yearbook on Human Rights 1958* (New York: United Nations, 1958), p. 307 (entered into force June 15, 1960); The Convention against Discrimination in Education of 1960, adopted by the UNESCO General Conference on December 4, 1960, in *UN Yearbook on Human Rights 1961* (New York: United Nations, 1961), p. 437 (entered into force May 22, 1962).

28. Report of the Expert Committee established in pursuance of Security Council Resolution 191 (1964), March 2, 1965 (S/6210), in SCOR, 20th Year, Special Supplement No. 2, pp. 167-169.

29. Ibid., p. 5.

30. Ibid., p. 301.

31. Letter dated July 28, 1965, from 32 African states,

S/6584.

32. Report of the secretary-general on the establishment of a United Nations programme for the education and training abroad of South Africans, November 9, 1965 (S/6891), in SCOR, 20th Year, *Supplement for October, November and December 1965*, pp. 345-353.

33. Letter dated November 22, 1965, from four African states (S/6964), in ibid., p. 398.

34. General Assembly Resolution 1761 (XVII) of November 6, 1962, in GAOR, 17th Session, *Resolutions,* Supplement No. 17 (S/5217), pp. 9-10; and Resolution 2107 (XX) of December 21, 1965, in GAOR 20th Session, *Resolutions,* Supplement No. 14 (A/6014), pp. 61-63.

35. Letter from ICAO secretary-general of March 30, 1965, p. 66, UN D.A/6294, reprinted in *International Legal Materials* 5 (1966): 486-487.

36. Memorandum SG 400/66 of April 5, 1966 (mimeo).

37. See the debate in ICAO, *Council 58th Session*, Montreal, April 26, June 6-29, 1966, Minutes of the 7th Meeting, June 17, 1966, pp. 99-110 (Doc. 8596-C/964).

38. See Teresa Hayter, *Aid as Imperialism* (Baltimore: Penguin Books, 1971), for an analytical, if sometimes polemical, study of the IBRD's role in social and political problems.

39. Communications from the specialized agencies of the United Nations, February 28, 1964 (A/AC.115/L.49), p. 3.

40. Report of the Special Committee on the Policies of Apartheid of the Government of the Republic of South Africa, paragraph 611 (A/5825 and Add. 1), in GAOR, 19th Session, *Annexes*, Annex No. 12, p. 108.

41. Cited in GAOR, 21st Session, 4th Committee, PV. 1645 (November 28, 1966), p. 318.

42. Regarding consultation with the International Bank for Reconstruction and Development, see report of the sècretary-general, September 15, 1967 (A/6825).

43. Resolution 2307 (XXII), December 13, 1967; see also Resolution 2426 (XXIII) of December 18, 1968, in which the GA recommended withdrawal of all outstanding loans to South Africa. The IBRD responded that it could not legally "act in contravention of formal loan agreements" (*International Legal Materials* 8 (1969): 4444.

44. GAOR, 22nd Session, 4th Committee, SR. 1726-1730.

45. UN Doc. A/349 (September 2, 1947); text in *Interna-

tional Organization 2 (1948): 198-201.

46. See Samuel A. Bleicher, "UN vs. IBRD: A Dilemma of Functionalism," *International Organization* 24 (1970): 70.

47. An additional problem, not raised by the Africans, was the role of the IMF and its policy on gold as a reserve currency. When this issue was open for negotiation in early 1970, South Africa apparently gained essentially all that it wanted. See Rodney J. Morrison, "Apartheid and International Monetary Reform," *Review of Politics* 32 (July 1970): 338-346.

48. Among the writings in ICAO is Thomas Buergenthal's excellent chapter on membership problems in *Law-Making in the International Civil Aviation Organization* (Syracuse: Syracuse University Press, 1969), especially pp. 35-54.

49. Text in UN, *Agreements between the UN and the Specialized Agencies* (ST/SG/14), pp. 34-35.

50. Neither provision was applied to Spain, which voluntarily withdrew until the "renovation" of its international reputation in 1950, through General Assembly Resolution 386 (V) of November 4, 1950, in GAOR, 5th Session, *Resolutions,* Supplement No. 20 (A/1775), pp. 16-17.

51. Articles 62 and 88 of the convention.

52. Report of the Special Committee on the Policies of Apartheid of the Government of the Republic of South Africa (A/5825), November 30, 1964, paragraph 496, in GAOR, 19th Session, *Annexes,* Annex No. 12, p. 98. The official report of the conference did not include the UAR statement: ICAO, *Report of the Fourth Africa–Indian Ocean Regional Air Navigation Meeting* (Doc. 8477, AFI/IV) Rome, November 23-December 18, 1964.

53. "Statements by Delegates to the Assembly of the International Civil Aviation Organization," *ICAO Bulletin* 20, nos. 8-9 (1965): 26.

54. ICAO Assembly, 15th Session, Doc. 8516 (A15-P/5), p. 142. For a concise explanation of the voting, see *Yearbook of Air and Space Law 1965* (Montreal: McGill University Press, 1967), pp. 196-198.

55. Resolution ICAO Doc. 8528 (A15-P/3), text in *Yearbook of Air and Space Law 1965*, p. 198.

56. See ICAO Assembly, Report of the Executive Commit-

tee, 15th Session, Doc. 8522 (A15-Ex/43), pp. 26-31 (1965).

57. No measures were taken by the UN in relation to South African membership in ICAO. At the July 1971 meeting of the General Conference, South Africa was excluded from regional and local conferences of ICAO by ICAO Resolution (A18-4); the text is in GAOR, 26th Session, *Report of the Special Committee on Apartheid* (A/8422/Rev. 1), Supplement No. 22, p. 52.

58. The conference was held in Geneva because no African state would give the South African delegates visas. The African regional conferences of the World Health Organization were also held in Geneva from 1962 to 1964 for the same reason.

59. "La conférence africaine se réunit mais ne peut poursuivre ses travaux," *Journal des Télécommunications* 31, no. 11 (November 1964): 296. Immanuel Wallerstein, in *Politics of Unity* (New York: Random House, 1967), p. 70, states that the conference adjourned when the Western delegates walked out; in fact, the Africans walked out first, the Western delegates walked out to protest the African move, and then the Secretariat quit.

60. ITU, Plenipotentiary Conference, Montreux, 1965, Summary Record of the 15th Meeting of Committee 4 (Organization of the Union), October 13, 1965, Doc. No. 301, p. 5.

61. The debates and votes are described in ITU, Plenipotentiary Conference, Doc. 148-E (pp. 16-17), Doc. 155-E (p. 10), Doc. 156, Doc. 158 (p. 8), from September 15, 1965, to September 21, 1965. The text of the Egyptian resolution, ITU Resolution No. 45, is also in *United Nations Juridical Yearbook 1965* (UN Sales No. E.67.V.e), p. 143. The same conference, in ITU Resolution No. 44, ended South African participation in African regional conferences or meetings of the ITU. In 1967, South Africa acceded to the ITU Convention of 1965 on its own behalf and that of Namibia, which had just been taken from South Africa by GA Resolution 2145 (XX) of October 27, 1966. Protests resulted in ITU Administrative Council Resolution No. 619, which stated that South Africa could no longer represent Namibia in the ITU. The text of the resolution (from ITU Docs. 3643, 3689, and 3712/CA22-May 1967) is in *United Nations Juridical Yearbook 1967* (UN Sales No. E.69.V.2), p. 267. At the 1973

Plenipotentiary Conference of the ITU (in Málaga-Torremolinos, Spain) South Africa did not send a delegation, but was nevertheless excluded by a vote of the conference. (I am grateful to Professor Harold K. Jacobson for some of the above details.)

62. See E/CONF.46/CRED/SR.2, as Algeria, Liberia, and the Ukrainian SSR opposed approval of the South African credentials.

63. E/CONF.46/SR.24, 8 April 1964. See formal letters of protest by Communist bloc nations in UNCTAD, *Proceedings,* Geneva March 23-June 16, 1964, Volume VIII (New York: 1964), pp. 67-68.

64. UNCTAD, Second Session, New Delhi (TD/SR.37), pp. 3-4.

65. UNCTAD, Second Session, New Delhi (TD/SR.78), pp. 475-471; text in Volume 1, Reports and Annexes, p. 57.

66. For the text of A/C.2/L.1030 on December 2, 1968, see *International Legal Materials* 8 (1969): 213-219.

67. GAOR, 23rd Session, PV.1741, December 13, 1968, pp. 1-20. See also Peter R. Baehr's well-written *The Role of a National Delegation in the General Assembly* (New York: Carnegie Endowment, 1970), which explains much of the politics behind this vote (expecially pp. 61-65).

68. On the move to suspend South Africa from UNCTAD, the negative votes were: Australia, Austria, Belgium, Bolivia, Botswana, Brazil, Canada, Costa Rica, Denmark, El Salvador, Finland, France, Greece, Honduras, Iceland, Ireland, Italy, Japan, Lesotho, Luxembourg, Malawi, Netherlands, New Zealand, Nicaragua, Norway, Panama, Paraguay, Portugal, South Africa, Swaziland, United Kingdom, United States, and Uruguay. Abstaining were nine Communist states, Argentina, Botswana, Central African Republic, China, Colombia, Cyprus, Dominican Republic, Guatemala, Iran, Laos, Malaysia, Maldive Islands, Malta, Mauritius, Morocco, Nepal, Peru, Singapore, and Turkey. On the procedural vote, often a better indicator of viewpoint, the positive votes (favoring South Africa) included Botswana, Central African Republic, Lesotho, Malawi, Mauritius, South Africa, and Swaziland (ibid).

69. See also Richard E. Lapchick, *The Politics of Race and International Sport: The Case of South Africa* (New York: Greenwood Press, 1975).

70. Report of the Special Committee on the Policies of Apartheid of the Government of the Republic of South Africa (A/5825), in GAOR, 19th Session, *Annexes*, Annex No. 12, p. 83.

71. A poll taken at the time among white South Africans indicated that they were overwhelmingly in favor of permitting foreign non-whites to participate in South African events; yet they were just as overwhelmingly opposed to full integration of South African domestic sports. See Heribert Adam, *Modernizing Racial Domination: South Africa's Political Dynamics* (Berkeley: University of California Press, 1971), pp. 87-89.

72. See Dennis Brutus, "Year of the Olympics," in Colin Legum, ed., *Africa Contemporary Record 1968-1969* (London: Africa Research, 1969), pp. 59-63.

73. See detailed description later in this chapter.

74. See the detailed study by Vernon McKay, "South African Propaganda: Methods and Media," *Africa Report* 11 (February 1966): pp. 41-46.

75. Report of the secretary-general, December 16, 1965 (A/6174), in GAOR, 20th Session, *Annexes*, Agenda Item 108, pp. 2-5.

76. Report of the secretary-general, September 6, 1966 (A/6408), in GAOR, 21st Session, *Annexes*, Agenda Item 22, p. 1. For details of the OAU's functional problems, see Richard E. Bissell and W. Scott Thompson, "Development of the African Subsystem," *Polity* 5 (spring 1973): 335-361.

77. UN Document A/AC.115/SR.69, May 11, 1966.

78. See A/6143, Report of the 3rd Committee, December 8, 1965, pp. 18-19; and E/4055, Communication of ECOSOC to the Special Committee on Apartheid.

79. Expansion of the committee was provided for in General Assembly Resolution 205A (XX); the texts of the refusals of 15 states are in A/6226/Add. 2.

80. Report of the Special Committee on the Policies of Apartheid of the Government of the Republic of South Africa, June 19, 1966 (A/6356, also issued as S/7387), in GAOR, 21st Session *Annexes*, Agenda Item 34, p. 3.

81. Ibid. See also the *Statement* made by Mr. Achkar Marof, chairman of the Special Committee, on April 7, 1966 (A/AC.115/L/170, April 8, 1966).

82. See chapter five for the eventual expansion of the

Special Committee in 1970.

83. For an insider's highly critical view of the Committee of 24, see Seymour M. Finger, "A New Approach to Colonial Problems at the United Nations," *International Organization* 26 (winter 1972): 143-153.

84. See ECOSOC Resolutions 1102 (XL) of March 4, 1966, 1146 (SLI) of August 2, 1966, and 1164 (XLI) of August 5, 1966.

85. Report of the Special Committee on the Policies of Apartheid of the Government of the Republic of South Africa, June 19, 1966 (A/6356), in GAOR, 21st Session, *Annexes*, Agenda Item 34, p. 15. The General Assembly was having increasing trouble obtaining compliance by specialized agencies with its resolutions on southern Africa. Following passage of Resolutions 2105 (XX) and 2107 (XX) on Portuguese Africa and Namibia, the ITU, UPU, and IBRD gave noncommittal responses, and the FAO refused to end assistance to those areas until the UNDP made a decision, which would bind the FAO. See *Note* by the Secretariat on requests to international institutions, including the specialized agencies, August 19, 1966 A/AC.109/194).

86. A/AC.115/SR.82, p. 3.

87. General Assembly resolution 2202 (XXI), December 16, 1966, in GAOR, 21st Session, *Resolutions,* Supplement No. 16, pp. 20-21 (A/6316).

88. As reported in the Special Committee on Apartheid on September 14, 1966 (A/AC.115/SR.80), p. 10. The conference was cosponsored by the Special Committee on Apartheid, the Brazilian government, and ECOSOC.

89. Ibid.

90. General Assembly Resolution 2144 (XXI), October 26, 1966, in GAOR, 21st Session, *Resolutions,* Supplement No. 16 (A/6316), pp. 46-68.

91. *Statement* made by Mr. Achkar Marof on January 5, 1967 (January 9, 1967 [A/AC.115/L.190]).

92. The new unit was busy, and became a vital arm of the committee, commencing with its May 1967 report on foreign investments in South Africa. That report was the basis of resolutions in 1967 and 1968. A second report, on repressive legislation in South Africa, was issued in 1969 for public consumption, as part of the educational campaign.

93. See Arthur W. Rovine, *The First Fifty Years, The*

Secretary-General in World Politics, 1920-1970 (Leiden: Sijthoff, 1970), pp. 416-420.

94. Richard Hall, *The High Price of Principles*, p. 91. For a full analysis of Zambia's problem, which was more severe than that of any other black African state north of the Zambezi, see the useful collection of articles in *Zambia and the World* (Lusaka: University of Zambia, 1970), mimeo. Rosalyn Higgins asserts that Britain and the UN, under Article 50, were the potential keys to alleviating Zambia's problem, in Stephen M. Schwebel, ed., *The Effectiveness of International Decision* (Leiden: Sijthoff, 1961), pp. 45-46.

95. See, for example, the resolution adopted at the 6th Assembly of Heads of State, Algiers, September 1968, in *Keesing's Contemporary Archives* (London: Keesing's Publications, October 26-November 2, 1968), p. 22991.

96. General Assembly Resolution 2193 (XXI) of December 15, 1966, in GAOR, 21st Session, *Resolutions,* Supplement No. 16 (A/6316), p. 6. The question, however, was dropped from the agenda in 1968, and then revived in 1969, as described below, p. 123.

97. See E/CN.4/935, a letter from the Special Committee on Apartheid to the Commission on Human Rights concerning prison conditions. The Commission also examined the report of the Brasília Conference (ST/TAO/HR/27).

98. March 6, 1967, in ESOCR, 42nd Session, Supplement No. 6, Commission on Human Rights, E/4322 (E/ND.4/ 940), pp. 76-78.

99. See his report: Office of Public Information, *Apartheid and Racial Discrimination in Southern Africa* (OPE/397-06279), April 1970.

100. International Labour Conference, 52nd Session, Geneva, 1968, *Fourth Special Report of the DG on the Application of the Declaration Concerning the Policy of "Apartheid" in the Republic of South Africa,* p. 30.

101. Resolution 1302 (XLIV) May 28, 1968, in ESCOR, 44th Session, May 6-31, 1968, *Resolutions,* Supplement No. 1, pp. 11-12.

102. Report of the Ad Hoc Working Group of Experts Established under Resolution 2 (XXIII) of the Commission on Human Rights, February 15, 1968 (E/4459), published as OPI/365 (Publication feature no. 9, June 1969).

103. United Nations Office of Public Information (UN-

OPI). *Infringements of Trade Union Rights in Southern Africa* (1969), pp. 6-8.

104. Ibid., p. 39.

105. H. G. Nicholas, *The United Nations as a Political Institution,* 4th ed., (London: Oxford University Press, 1971), p. 139.

106. The founders at San Francisco may have intended this; in 1945, "the Committee considered an amendment designed to strengthen the position of the Economic and Social Council by specifying that questions raised by the Specialized Agencies should be brought to the attention of the General Assembly through the Council." It was rejected. See the Report of the rapporteur of Committee II/3, approved by Commission II, June 11, 1945, in UNCIO, Volume 8, Commission II, General Assembly, Doc. 924, II/12, June 12, 1945, pp. 4-6.

107. Report of the sub-committee established in pursuance of paragraph 8(a) of General Assembly Resolution 2202 (XXI), September 26, 1967 (A/AC.115/L.206), with testimony taken July 4-21, 1967.

108. Report of the Special Committee on the Policies of Apartheid of the Government of the Republic of South Africa, October 18, 1967 (A/6864), in GAOR, 22nd Session, *Annexes,* Agenda Item 35, p. 1; General Assembly Resolution 2307 (XXII), passed 89-2-12 on December 13, 1967, in GAOR, 22nd Session, *Resolutions,* Volume I, Supplement No. 16 (A/6716), pp. 19-20.

109. Final Act of the International Conference on Human Rights, Teheran, April 22–May 13, 1968 (A/CONF.32/41), published in September 1968 (UN Sales No. E.68.XIV.2).

110. General Assembly Resolution 2397 (XXIII), December 2, 1968, adopted 102-2-0, in GAOR, 23rd Session, *Resolutions,* Supplement No. 18 (A/7218), p. 21.

111. See General Assembly Resolutions 2394, 2403, 2426, 2438, 2440, 2446, 2448, and 2465 (XXIII), all of which restated opposition to apartheid in different ways, in GAOR, 23rd Session, *Resolutions,* Supplement No. 18 (A/2718), pp. 42, 3, 61, 47, 48, 51, 52, and 4, respectively.

112. At the 24th Session of the commission, in March 1968, apartheid was named in Resolutions 2, 3, 4, 5, 14, and 15 (SSIV, in ESCOR, 44th Session, Commission on Human Rights, *Report on the Twenty-Fourth Session* (E/4475),

Supplement No. 4, pp. 145, 146, 149, 150, 160, and. 161, respectively.

113. ESCOR, 44th Session, Commission on Human Rights, *Report on the 24th Session*, February 5–March 12, 1968 (E/4475 [E/CN.4/972], p. 24).

114. ECOSOC Resolutions 1330, 1331, 1332, 1333, 1335 (XLIV), May 31, 1968, in ESCOR, 44th Session, *Resolutions*, Supplement No. 1 (E/4548), pp. 15-19.

115. GAOR, 24th Session, *Report of the Special Committee on Apartheid*, Supplement No. 25 (A/7625/Rev.1), October 13, 1969, pp. 31-37.

116. The negative votes were Australia, Portugal, Britain, United States, and South Africa. Abstaining were most of the Western European members of NATO (GAOR, 24th Session, Plenary Meetings, 1816th Meeting, November 21, 1969).

117. Draft Resolution I, in ESCOR, 46th Session, Commission on Human Rights, *Report on the 25th Session*, February 17–March 21, 1969. E/4621 (E/CN4/1007), pp. 202-203.

118. See E/AC.7/SR.619, p. 151; /SR.620, p. 161;/SR.-621, pp. 169-170.

119. E/AC.7/SR.620, p. 161.

120. E/AC.7/L.557, passed unanimously in the 624th meeting, and directed to the plenary session of ECOSOC.

121. E/AC.7/SR.621, pp. 173-174.

122. E/AC.7/SR.619, p. 153.

123. 6 June 1969. ESCOR, 46th Session, *Resolutions* (E/4715), p. 14.

124. E/4817, 6 May 1970. Report of the secretary-general. The Social Committee never discussed the report (E/AC.7/SR.645, p. 226), and the plenary session of ECOSOC did likewise; ESCOR, Resumed 48th Session, *Resolutions*, Supp. 1A (E/4832/Add. 1), p. 15.

125. Quoted in Colin Legum, ed., *Africa Contemporary Record, 1968-1969* (London: Africa Research, Ltd., 1969), p. 328.

Chapter 5

1. The entire episode is elaborately described in J. D. B.

Miller, *Survey of Commonwealth Affairs: Problems of Expansion and Attrition, 1953-1969* (London: Oxford University Press for the Royal Institute of International Affairs, 1974), pp. 163-165.

2. For Resolution 181 (1963), 182 (1963), and 191 (1964), see Miller, *Survey of Commonwealth Affairs,* pp. 105, 119, and 154.

3. SCOR, 25th Year, *Resolutions and Decisions of the Security Council 1970,* p. 12.

4. Text in a letter to the Security Council dated October 9, 1970, S/9962, in SCOR, 25th Year, *Supplement for October, November, December 1970,* pp. 24-26.

5. *New York Times,* March 31, 1971, p. 13.

6. *Economist,* November 21, 1970, p. 27.

7. *Economist,* June 13, 1970, p. 47.

8. General Assembly Resolution 2671 (XXV), December 8, 1970; first meeting held May 3-4, 1971.

9. *UN Monthly Chronicle* 8 (January 1971): 45.

10. *Economist,* January 23, 1971, p. 23.

11. Miller, *Survey of Commonwealth Affairs,* p. 165.

12. UNESCO Document 16 C/DR/Plen 4, October 22, 1970.

13. UNESCO Document 16 C/Resolution 8, November 7, 1970.

14. See his report in UNESCO Document 17 C/12, *Report by the Director-General,* September 21, 1972.

15. UNESCO Documents 87 EX/Decision 5.4, 88 EX/20, 88 EX/Decision 6.5, and 89 EX/31.

16. UNESCO Document 90 EX/Decision 7.2.

17. By early 1973, one more organization, the European Broadcasting Union, had petitioned for reinstatement by announcing the resignation of the South African Broadcasting Corporation from the Union's membership. UNESCO Documents 92 EX/42 and 92 EX/Decision 5.8.3.

18. ICAO Document C-WP/5250, Attachment B, November 26, 1970.

19. ICAO Assembly, 18th Session, Vienna, June 15–July 7, 1971, Agenda Item 39.

20. ICAO Resolution A18/4, mimeo.

21. On the basis of ICAO Document C-WP/5427, September 3, 1971.

22. S/10609, in SCOR, 27th Year, *Supplement for Janu-*

ary, February, March 1972, p. 85.

23. Security Council Resolution 311 (1972).

24. See SC Resolution 300 (1971) of October 12, 1971, in SCOR, 26th Year, *Resolutions and Decisions of the Security Council 1971,* p. 9.

25. See chapter four.

26. Formally recommended in GA Resolution 2863 (XXVI) of December 20, 1971, and decided by the Security Council in Resolution 308 (1972).

27. For further details, see UN Documents A/8386 (September 21, 1971), and A/8859 (October 27, 1972).

28. As can be seen in GA Resolution 2962 (XXVII) of December 22, 1972.

29. OAU Document CM/444, *Report of the Administrative Secretary-General on the Activities of the African Group at the United Nations,* Council of Ministers, 19th Session, p. 1.

30. Ibid., p. 8.

31. See UNESCO Resolution 6.41 of the 13th General Conference (1964), Resolution 1.36 of the 14th General Conference (1966), Resolution 1.171 of the 15th General Conference (1968), and Resolution 1.113 of the 16th General Conference (1970).

32. UNESCO Resolution 1.113, 16th General Conference (1970).

33. UNESCO Document SCH/WS/289, April 2, 1973, p. 3.

34. Adopted at the 17th General Conference (1972), in UNESCO Document 92 EX/26, April 16, 1973.

35. UNESCO Document 89 EX/29.

36. UNESCO Document 92 EX/26, April 16, 1973, p. 2.

37. UNESCO Document 92 EX/Decision 5.5, April 1973.

38. UNESCO Document 87/Resolution 4.2.5.

39. OAU Document CM/431, *Report of the Administrative Secretary-General on the Draft Agreement between the UNDP and the OAU,* February 1972.

40. OAU Resolution CM/Res. 263 (XVIII), February 19, 1972.

41. OAU Document CM/461, *Progress Report of the Administrative Secretary-General on the Draft Agreement of Co-operation between OAU and UNDP,* Annex 1, June 5, 1972, p. 2.

42. UNESCO Document SCH/WS/289, April 2, 1973, p. 6.

43. ITU Documents No. 4304-E (CA27-46) of March 27, 1972, and No. 708-Doc. 4409, which was approved at the 27th Administrative Council meeting of May 1972.

44. WHO Document EB 49/20, Add. 1, January 3, 1972.

45. See chapter four.

46. UN Document A/C.3/L.1871, October 29, 1971.

47. GA Resolution 2786 (XXVI), December 6, 1971.

48. UN Document E/CN.4/1075, February 15, 1972, in ESCOR, 46th Session,*Report of the ad hoc working group of experts under Commission Resolution 8 (XXVII)*, E/4816, p. 72.

49. See replies received in A/8768 and Addendum, September 14, 1972 et al., and GA Resolution 2922 (XXVII) of November 21, 1972.

50. GA Resolution 3068 (XXVIII), November 30, 1973.

51. See note 45, above.

52. *New York Times,* November 13, 1974, p. 1.

Chapter 6

1. See chapter three for the Africans' awareness that they could arm the South African blacks only to a limited degree without losing sympathy for their cause. The harbingers of violence included the fortifying of the Caprivi Strip, the use of several units of South African police in Rhodesia, and the training of African National Congress members from South Africa in the United Arab Republic, Algeria, and Morocco.

2. Louis B. Sohn, "Expulsion or Forced Withdrawal from an International Organization," *Harvard Law Review* 77 (June 1964): 1416.

3. Ibid., p. 1424. See also Leo Gross, "Was the Soviet Union Expelled from the League of Nations?" *American Journal of International Law* 39 (1945): 35-44.

4. See George Kennan, "Hazardous Courses in Southern Africa," *Foreign Affairs* 49 (January 1971): 218-236; and George Ball, *The Discipline of Power* (Boston: Little, Brown and Co., 1968), pp. 252-259.

5. What is needed to treat this point thoroughly is a study of international secretariats, along the lines of K. W. Deutsch

et al., *Political Community in the North Atlantic Area* (Princeton, N.J.: Princeton University Press, 1957, or Daniel Lerner and Morton Gordon, *Euratlantica* (Cambridge, Mass.: M.I.T. Press, 1969).

6. See Richard E. Bissell, "A Note on the Chinese View of UN Financing," *American Journal of International Law* 69 (July 1975): 628-633.

7. "U.S. Votes Against Expulsion of South Africa from the U.N.," *Department of State Bulletin* 71, no. 1849 (December 2, 1974): 777.

8. See Roger Murray, "Europe Looks South to Pretoria for Uranium Needs," *African Development* 9 (February 1975): 50.

Books Written under the Auspices of the Center of International Studies, Princeton University

Gabriel A. Almond, *The Appeals of Communism* (Princeton University Press, 1954).

William W. Kaufmann, ed., *Military Policy and National Security* (Princeton University Press, 1956).

Klaus Knorr, *The War Potential of Nations* (Princeton University Press, 1956).

Lucien W. Pye, *Guerrilla Communism in Malaya* (Princeton University Press, 1956).

Charles De Visscher, *Theory and Reality in Public International Law*, translated by P. E. Corbett (Princeton University Press, 1957; rev. ed. 1968).

Bernard C. Cohen, *The Political Process and Foreign Policy: The Making of the Japanese Peace Settlement* (Princeton University Press, 1957).

Myron Weiner, *Party Politics in India: The Development of a Multi-Party System* (Princeton University Press, 1957).

Percy E. Corbett, *Law in Diplomacy* (Princeton University Press, 1959).

Rolf Sannwald and Jacques Stohler, *Economic Integration: Theoretical Assumptions and Consequences of European Unification*, translated by Herman Karreman (Princeton University Press, 1959).

Klaus Knorr, ed., *NATO and American Security* (Princeton University Press, 1959).

Gabriel A. Almond and James S. Coleman, eds., *The Politics of the Developing Areas* (Princeton University Press, 1960).

Herman Kahn, *On Thermonuclear War* (Princeton University Press, 1960).

Sidney Verba, *Small Groups and Political Behavior: A Study of Leadership* (Princeton University Press, 1961).

Robert J. C. Butow, *Tojo and the Coming of the War* (Princeton University Press, 1961).

Glenn H. Snyder, *Deterrence and Defense: Toward a Theory of National Security* (Princeton University Press, 1961).

Klaus Knorr and Sidney Verba, eds., *The International System: Theoretical Essays* (Princeton University Press, 1961).

Peter Paret and John W. Shy, *Guerrillas in the 1960s* (Praeger, 1962).

George Modelski, *A Theory of Foreign Policy* (Praeger, 1962).

Klaus Knorr and Thornton Read, eds., *Limited Strategic War* (Praeger, 1963).

Frederick S. Dunn, *Peace-Making and the Settlement with Japan* (Princeton University Press, 1963).

Arthur L. Burns and Nina Heathcote, *Peace-Keeping by United Nations Forces* (Praeger, 1963).

Richard A. Falk, *Law, Morality, and War in the Contemporary World* (Praeger, 1963).

James N. Rosenau, *National Leadership and Foreign Policy: A Case Study in the Mobilization of Public Support* (Princeton University Press, 1963).

Gabriel A. Almond and Sidney Verba, *The Civic Culture: Political Attitudes and Democracy in Five Nations* (Princeton University Press, 1963).

Bernard C. Cohen, *The Press and Foreign Policy* (Princeton University Press, 1963).

Richard L. Sklar, *Nigerian Political Parties: Power in an Emergent African Nation* (Princeton University Press, 1963).

Peter Paret, *French Revolutionary Warfare from Indochina to Algeria: The Analysis of a Political and Military Doctrine* (Praeger, 1964).

Harry Eckstein, ed., *Internal War: Problems and Approaches* (Free Press, 1964).

Cyril E. Black and Thomas P. Thornton, eds., *Communism and Revolution: The Strategic Uses of Political Violence* (Princeton University Press, 1964).

Miriam Camps, *Britain and the European Community 1955-1963* (Princeton University Press, 1964).

Thomas P. Thornton, ed., *The Third World in Soviet*

Perspective: Studies by Soviet Writers on the Develop-ing Areas (Princeton University Press, 1964).

James N. Rosenau, ed., *International Aspects of Civil Strife* (Princeton University Press, 1964).

Sidney I. Ploss, *Conflict and Decision-Making in Soviet Russia: A Case Study of Agricultural Policy, 1953-1963* (Princeton University Press, 1965).

Richard A. Falk and Richard J. Barnet, eds., *Security in Disarmament* (Princeton University Press, 1965).

Karl von Vorys, *Political Development in Pakistan* (Princeton University Press, 1965).

Harold and Margaret Sprout, *The Ecological Perspective on Human Affairs, With Special Reference to Interna-tional Politics* (Princeton University Press, 1965).

Klaus Knorr, *On the Uses of Military Power in the Nuclear Age* (Princeton University Press, 1966).

Harry Eckstein, *Division and Cohesion in Democracy: A Study of Norway* (Princeton University Press, 1966).

Cyril E. Black, *The Dynamics of Modernization: A Study in Comparative History* (Harper and Row, 1966).

Peter Kunstadter, ed., *Southeast Asian Tribes, Minorities, and Nations* (Princeton University Press, 1967).

E. Victor Wolfenstein, *The Revolutionary Personality: Lenin, Trotsky, Gandhi* (Princeton University Press, 1967).

Leon Gordenker, *The UN Secretary-General and the Main-tenance of Peace* (Columbia University Press, 1967).

Oran R. Young, *The Intermediaries: Third Parties in Inter-national Crises* (Princeton University Press, 1967).

James N. Rosenau, ed., *Domestic Sources of Foreign Policy* (Free Press, 1967).

Richard F. Hamilton, *Affluence and the French Worker in the Fourth Republic* (Princeton University Press, 1967).

Linda B. Miller, *World Order and Local Disorder: The United Nations and Internal Conflicts* (Princeton University Press, 1967).

Henry Bienen, *Tanzania: Party Transformation and Eco-nomic Development* (Princeton University Press, 1967).

Wolfram F. Hanrieder, *West German Foreign Policy, 1949-1963: International Pressures and Domestic Response*

(Stanford University Press, 1967).

Richard H. Ullman, *Britain and the Russian Civil War: November 1918-February 1920* (Princeton University Press, 1968).

Robert Gilpin, *France in the Age of the Scientific State* (Princeton University Press, 1968).

William B. Bader, *The United States and the Spread of Nuclear Weapons* (Pegasus, 1968).

Richard A. Falk, *Legal Order in a Violent World* (Princeton University Press, 1968).

Cyril E. Black, Richard A. Falk, Klaus Knorr, and Oran R. Young, *Neutralization and World Politics* (Princeton University Press, 1968).

Oran R. Young, *The Politics of Force: Bargaining During International Crises* (Princeton University Press, 1969).

Klaus Knorr and James N. Rosenau, eds., *Contending Approaches to International Politics* (Princeton University Press, 1969).

James N. Rosenau, ed., *Linkage Politics: Essays on the Convergence of National and International Systems* (Free Press, 1969).

John T. McAlister, Jr., *Viet Nam: The Origins of Revolution* (Knopf, 1969).

Jean Edward Smith, *Germany Beyond the Wall: People, Politics and Prosperity* (Little, Brown, and Co., 1969).

James Barros, *Betrayal from Within: Joseph Avenol, Secretary-General of the League of Nations, 1933-1940* (Yale University Press, 1969).

Charles Hermann, *Crises in Foreign Policy: A Simulation Analysis* (Bobbs-Merrill, 1969).

Robert C. Tucker, *The Marxian Revolutionary Idea: Essays on Marxist Thought and Its Impact on Radical Movements* (W. W. Norton, 1969).

Harvey Waterman, *Political Change in Contemporary France: The Politics of an Industrial Democracy* (Charles E. Merrill, 1969).

Cyril E. Black and Richard A. Falk, eds., *The Future of the International Legal Order. Vol. I: Trends and Patterns* (Princeton University Press, 1969).

Ted Robert Gurr, *Why Men Rebel* (Princeton University Press, 1969).

C. Sylvester Whitaker, *The Politics of Tradition: Continuity and Change in Northern Nigeria 1946-1966* (Princeton University Press, 1970).

Richard A. Falk, *The Status of Law in International Society* (Princeton University Press, 1970).

Klaus Knorr, *Military Power and Potential* (D. C. Heath, 1970).

Cyril E. Black and Richard A. Falk, eds., *The Future of the International Legal Order. Vol. II: Wealth and Resources* (Princeton University Press, 1970).

Leon Gordenker, ed., *The United Nations in International Politics* (Princeton University Press, 1971).

Cyril E. Black and Richard A. Falk, eds., *The Future of the International Legal Order. Vol. III: Conflict Management* (Princeton University Press, 1971).

Francine R. Frankel, *India's Green Revolution: Political Costs of Economic Growth* (Princeton University Press, 1971).

Harold and Margaret Sprout, *Toward a Politics of the Planet Earth* (Van Nostrand Reinhold, 1971).

Cyril E. Black and Richard A. Falk, eds., *The Future of the International Legal Order. Vol. IV: The Structure of the International Environment* (Princeton University Press, 1972).

Gerald Garvey, *Energy, Ecology, Economy* (W. W. Norton, 1972).

Richard Ullman, *The Anglo-Soviet Accord* (Princeton University Press, 1973).

Klaus Knorr, *Power and Wealth: The Political Economy of International Power* (Basic Books, 1973).

Anton Bebler, *Military Rule in Africa: Dahomey, Ghana, Sierra Leone, and Mali* (Praeger Publishers, 1973).

Robert C. Tucker, *Stalin as Revolutionary 1879-1929: A Study in History and Personality* (W.W. Norton, 1973).

Edward L. Morse, *Foreign Policy and Interdependence in Gaullist France* (Princeton University Press, 1973).

Henry Bienen, *Kenya: The Politics of Participation and Control* (Princeton University Press, 1974).

Gregory J. Massell, *The Surrogate Proletariat: Moslem Women and Revolutionary Strategies in Soviet Central Asia, 1919-1929* (Princeton University Press, 1974).

James N. Rosenau, *Citizenship Between Elections: An*

Inquiry Into the Mobilizable American (Free Press, 1974).

Ervin Laszio, *A Strategy for the Future: The Systems Approach to World Order* (Braziller, 1974).

John R. Vincent, *Nonintervention and International Order* (Princeton University Press, 1974).

Jan H. Kalicki, *The Pattern of Sino-American Crises: Political-Military Interactions in the 1950s* (Cambridge University Press, 1975).

Klaus Knorr, *The Power of Nations: The Political Economy of International Relations* (Princeton University Press, 1975).

James P. Sewell, *UNESCO and World Politics: Engaging in International Relations* (Princeton University Press, 1975).

Richard A. Falk, *A Global Approach to National Policy* (Harvard University Press, 1975).

Harry Eckstein and Ted Robert Gurr, *Patterns of Authority: A Structural Basis for Political Inquiry* (John Wiley & Sons, 1975).

Cyril E. Black, Marius B. Jansen, Herbert S. Levine, Marion J. Levy, Jr., Henry Rosovsky, Gilbert Rozman, Henry D. Smith, II, and S. Frederick Starr, *The Modernization of Japan and Russia* (Free Press, 1975).

Leon Gordenker, *International Aid and National Decisions: Development Programs in Malawi, Tanzania, and Zambia* (Princeton University Press, 1976).

Carl Von Clausewitz, *On War*, edited and translated by Michael Howard and Peter Paret (Princeton University Press, 1976).

Richard E. Bissell, *Apartheid and International Organizations* (Westview Press, 1977).

Index